A Place on the Corner

Studies of Urban Society

Other books in this series

Michael Crozier, *The World of the Office Worker*

Albert Hunter, *Symbolic Communities*

William Kornblum, *Blue Collar Community*

Robert McKenzie and Allan Silver, *Angels in Marble*

David Popenoe, *The Suburban Environment*

Gerald D. Suttles, *The Social Construction of Communities*

Gerald D. Suttles, *The Social Order of the Slum*

Mayer N. Zald, *Organizational Change*

Elijah Anderson

A Place on the Corner

The University of Chicago Press
Chicago and London

ELIJAH ANDERSON is assistant professor of
sociology and education at the University
of Pennsylvania.

The University of Chicago Press, Chicago 60637
The University of Chicago Press, Ltd., London

© 1976, 1978 by The University of Chicago
All rights reserved. Published 1978
Printed in the United States of America

82 81 80   5432

Library of Congress Cataloging in Publication Data

Anderson, Elijah.
A place on the corner.

(Studies of urban society)
Bibliography: p.
Includes index.
1. Small groups—Case studies. 2. Social
status—Case studies. 3. Participant observa-
tion—Case studies. 4. Chicago—Social conditions.
I. Title.
HM133.A55   301.44′0977311   78–1879
ISBN 0–226–01953–5

To my mother, Carrie-Bell

Contents

Preface   ix

Chapter One
The Setting   1

Chapter Two
The Elaboration of Primary Ties
and Personal Identities   31

Chapter Three
The Regulars   55

Chapter Four
The Wineheads   93

Chapter Five
The Hoodlums   129

Chapter Six
Social Order and Sociability   179

Chapter Seven
Conclusion   207

Notes   217

Bibliography   227

Index   235

Preface

Between 1970 and 1973 I engaged in participant observation at "Jelly's" bar and liquor store on the South Side of Chicago and gathered materials for this study. During this period I hung out with black working and nonworking men who spent a good deal of their time in the bar or "on the corner." At all times of the day and night and throughout the seasons of the year, I socialized with the people—drinking with them, talking and listening to them, and trying to come to terms with their social world. They carried on their business and talked about life, and they taught me much. In what follows I attempt to convey some of what I have learned.

My main purpose here is to sort out and focus on those items that make up the local status system at Jelly's and on the ghetto streets generally. In what follows, I address these basic questions: What are the rules and principles under which these men operate? What social hierarchies are present here? How are they expressed in social interaction? How do the various statuses here intersect or conflict or support one another? How, and along what lines, do people here remind others and demonstrate to others that they deserve to be deferred to? What does it take to "be somebody" here?

I would like to acknowledge the help and support of various institutions, teachers, colleagues, students, and friends who were generous with needed support and advice on this project. I would like to express my gratitude for the intellectually stimulating and supportive environment for field studies at the Sociology Department of Northwestern University and at the Center for Social Organization Studies at the University of

Chicago. For financial support I am grateful for a National Institute of Mental Health research fellowship (1F01 MH49967–01), a Ford Foundation fellowship, a grant from the James Michener Fund while I was on the faculty of Swarthmore College, and a Summer Faculty Award from the University of Pennsylvania.

Although many people contributed to my research efforts, space will not allow me to thank them all personally here. But in particular I would like to acknowledge the following for their support and helpful comments on this work: Bernard Beck, the Reverend Fletcher Bryant, Morris Janowitz, Jack Katz, Charles Moskos, Arthur Paris, Karen Peterson, Jennie Keith-Ross, Robert Washington, and William J. Wilson. I thank my colleagues at the University of Pennsylvania who read and commented on portions of the manuscript: Erving Goffman, Dell Hymes, William Labov, and Philip Rieff. Thanks are due to Doris Sklaroff for her competent typing of successive drafts of the manuscript. I would like to extend special thanks to Victor Lidz, who has followed and supported this research project from the very beginning when I was a graduate student at the University of Chicago; I am grateful for his various readings of the manuscript, his encouragement, and his helpful advice. Also, I want to thank Harold Bershady for helpful editorial comments. I would like to thank my friend Renée C. Fox for her moral support and encouragement toward the end of the work. I would like to take this opportunity to thank Frank Westie, Walt Risler, and Irving Zeitlin, all of whom were my undergraduate teachers, for encouraging me to pursue advanced work in sociology.

I owe much in my own ways of sociological thinking to the inspiration of my teachers Howard S. Becker and Gerald D. Suttles; from them I learned the sociological method and the technique of participant observation. Both provided intellectual support and advice at crucial junctures during the research. I am very grateful to my wife, Nancy, who knows this book with me. And last, but certainly not least, I am greatly indebted to the cats down at Jelly's, whose privacy must be protected through anonymity.

1 The Setting

Urban taverns and bars, like barbershops, carry-outs, and other such establishments, with their adjacent street corners and alleys, serve as important gathering places for people of the "urban villages" and ghetto areas of the city.[1] Often they are special hangouts for the urban poor and working-class people, serving somewhat as more formal social clubs or domestic circles do for the middle and upper classes. The urban poor and working-class people are likely to experience their local taverns as much more than commercial businesses.[2] They provide settings for sociability and places where neighborhood residents can gain a sense of self-worth. Here people can gather freely, bargaining with their limited resources, their symbols of status, and their personal sense of who and what they are against the resources of their peers and against what their peers see them *really* to be. Here they can sense themselves to be among equals, with an equal chance to be somebody, even to be occasional winners in the competition for social esteem.[3] This is their place. They set the social standards. And when they feel those standards are threatened, they can defend them. Other settings, especially those identified with the wider society, with its strange, impersonal standards and evaluations, are not nearly as important for gaining a sense of personal self-worth as are the settings attended by friends and other neighborhood people.

"Jelly's," the subject of this study, is a bar and liquor store located in a run-down building on the South Side of Chicago. Situated at a corner of a main thoroughfare, Jelly's is a hangout for working and nonworking, neighborhood and nonneighborhood black people, mostly men. They gather at Jelly's at all times of the day and night, and some even sleep on the streets or in the nearby park.

A few doors away from Jelly's is a laundromat; down the street are a dry cleaner, a grocery store, and, farther on, a poolroom. As cars and buses pass, their passengers sometimes gawk at the people of Jelly's. From the safety of their cars, often with rolled-up windows and locked doors, passersby can see wineheads staggering along, a man in tattered clothing "nodding out," leaning on Jelly's front window, and a motley, tough-looking group of men gathered on the corner, sometimes with a rare white man among them. Those on foot hurry past, not wanting to be accosted by the people of Jelly's.

Periodically, the humdrum routine is punctuated with some excitement. An elderly black woman bursts out of Jelly's, clutching her jug of wine and her pocketbook as she hurries along, minding her own business. The group on the sidewalk comes to life as one of the men grabs at her purse and yells, "Gimme some o' what you got there, woman!" "I'll geh ya' this fist upside yo' head!" she responds, shaking her fist and confidently moving on about her business. Children play nearby and among the men. They rip and run up and down the street and occasionally stop a man, apparently unmindful of how he looks, to say, "Got a quarter, mister?" The man bends over, puts his hands on his knees, negating any "tough" look he might have had, and begins to kid with the children, teaching them about being "good li'l kids" and giving up a quarter or whatever he can spare. Later that same evening the same man may show his tough side by drawing a switchblade and placing the edge against another man's throat, desperately "threatening" his victim. Blue-and-white police cars cruise by, each with two policemen, one black and one white. The police glance over and slow down, but they seldom stop and do anything. Ordinarily they casually move on, leaving the street-corner men to settle their own differences.

After being around Jelly's neighborhood for a while and getting to know its people, the outside observer can begin to see that there is order to this social world. For example, the wineheads turn out to be harmless, for they generally do the things people expect them to do: they drink on the street, beg passersby for change, and sometimes stumble up and down the street cursing at others. One also begins to understand that what looks like a fight to the death usually doesn't come near a fatal end. Often such a "fight" turns out to be a full-dress game in which only "best friends" or "cousins" can participate—but at times even they can't play this game without its ending in a real fight. After a while one gets to know that old black woman leaving Jelly's with the "taste" as Mis' Lu, "a nice ol' lady who been 'round here fo' years," and "studs 'round dese here streets'll cut yo' throat 'bout messin' with her. She hope raise half the cats 'round here." Secure in her knowledge of how she is regarded, she walks the streets unafraid, "back-talking" to anyone "messin' " with her.

On these streets near Jelly's, one can't help noticing the sidewalks and gutters littered with tin cans, old newspapers, paper sacks, and whatever. The city does not pay as much attention to this area as many residents would like, but somehow it doesn't really seem to matter to anyone. People go about their business. One storefront has been boarded up for months and wineheads sometimes sleep there. The inset doorway is a perfect place to lie in wait for an unsuspecting holdup or rape victim. Most people who use this general area have come to accept their deteriorated physical world as it is. They simply make the best of it. Many have become so resigned that they would find it extraordinary if someone took an active interest in trying to do something about it—even something as minor as fixing up and painting. This is Jelly's neighborhood.

But once inside Jelly's, people don't have to be concerned with the conditions outside. They become involved as soon as they meet others on the corner, or as soon as they walk through Jelly's door. Somebody is waiting at least to acknowledge their presence, if not to greet them warmly. They come here "to see what's happenin' "—to keep up on the *important* news. They meet their "runnin' buddies" here, and sometimes they commune with others. Inside, or outside on the corner, they joke, argue, fight, and laugh, as issues quickly rise and fall. In this milieu it is time-out and time away from things outside. It is time-in for sharing one's joys, hopes, dreams, troubles, fears, and past triumphs, which are all here and now to be taken up repeatedly with peers whose thoughts about them really matter.

As this short description indicates, there is more to social life in and around Jelly's than might be suggested by a cursory inspection, informed by the stereotypes and prejudices of those not involved. Life here cannot be understood as simple "social disorganization."[4] Nor can one reach a full understanding by viewing social relations here simply as "effortless sociability."[5] When one gets close to the life of Jelly's and develops the necessary meaningful relations with its people, he can begin to understand the social order of this world. People make him aware of the general prescriptions and proscriptions of behavior by somehow fitting him in, including him as they attempt to sort out and come to terms with their minute-to-minute, ordinary everyday social events. Individuals are thus seen acting collectively, interpreting and defining one another; they make distinctions between and among those with whom they share this social space. They are seen fitting themselves in with one another's expectations and collective lines of action, each one informed by a sense of what actions are allowed and not allowed to different kinds of people in varying sets of circumstances.

The Barroom

Jelly's bar and liquor store has two front entrances, one leading to the barroom and the other to the liquor store. Each room has its own distinctive social character. The barroom is a public place; outfitted with bar stools, a marble-topped counter, and mirrors on the wall, it invites almost anyone to come in and promises he will not be bothered as long as he minds his own business. In this sense it is a neutral social area. Yet people who gather on this side of Jelly's tend to be cautiously reserved when approaching others, mainly because on this side they just don't know one another. In contrast, the liquor store is more of a place for peers to hang out and outwardly appears to have a more easygoing, spontaneous ambience.

An open doorway separates the two rooms, and some people gravitate from side to side, the regular clientele usually settling in the liquor store. The social space of the barroom is shared by regular customers and visitors. Sometimes these visitors are people who have been seen around Jelly's but who have yet to commit themselves to the setting. Sometimes they are total strangers. At times there will be as many as twenty visitors present, compared with eight or nine regular customers. Regular customers are interspersed among the visitors, but though the space is shared, they seldom come to know one another well. The visitors tend to arrive, get their drinks, sit at the bar for a while, then leave. The regular clientele, on the other hand, do their best to ignore the visitors; they treat them as interlopers. And there exists a certain amount of distrust and suspicion between the two groups.

Owing to this suspicion and distrust, the barroom is characterized by a somewhat cautious and reserved atmosphere. When strangers accidentally touch or bump one another, the person in the wrong quickly says " 'scuse me." On occasions when the " 'scuse me" is not forthcoming and further agression seems likely, other precautionary measures may be taken. One night during the early stages of my fieldwork, when I was talking with John, a visitor I had just met, a stranger to both of us seemed drunk and unruly. He tried to enter our conversation. Putting his hand on John's shoulder, he asked, "What ya'll drinkin'? Lemme' drink wit you!" John tried to ignore the man, but he persisted. Abruptly and firmly John said, "Al'right, now. Man, I don't know you, now! I don't know you." Taking this comment as the warning it was, the stranger cut short his advances. Immediately he sobered and walked away without saying another word. John then looked away from him, rolling his eyes toward the ceiling, and we continued our conversation.

On this side strangers can demand some degree of deference, for people here are usually uncertain of just what the next person has in mind, of what he is capable of doing, and of what actions might provoke him to do it. On the barroom side, people often don't know *who* they're sitting or standing next to. In the right circumstances the next person might show himself to be "the police" or "the baddest cat in Chi." Or he could be waiting to follow somebody home and rip him off. In the words of the regular clientele, unknown people on this side generally "bear watching."

One consequence of the suspicion and distrust on this side is that social relationships between visitors and the regular customers tend to be guarded. Often people engaged in a conversation at the bar will screen what they say so as not to reveal their telephone numbers or addresses to anyone unless he has been proved trustworthy. Before talking to a stranger, a person often will try to "read" him carefully to get some sense of what kind of person he is, to know how far he is to be trusted. For this people pay close attention to a variety of symbols the person displays, using them to interpret and define him so they will know better how to treat him. They listen to the person's language or, as the men say, his "total conversation" and examine it for clues to his residence, associates, and line of work. They check out the way he is dressed. They watch him interact with others, with an eye and ear to "who they are" and how they treat him. They may even ask someone else, either secretly or publicly, about his trustworthiness. When talking, many tend to check themselves if the wrong people are listening too closely. When people give their names they sometimes use "handles" like Wooly or Bird or Homey, names that permit interaction without allowing others to trace them to their homes or to other settings they feel protective about. Before giving personal trust, they feel a great need to place the next person.

Another consequence of this distrust is the emergence on the barroom side of a civility based not so much on the moral dictates of the wider society as on the immediate potentially violent consequences of uncivil acts. People have been known to pull guns and knives on this side of Jelly's—and to use them. One man was shot to death, ostensibly for stepping on another's carefully spit-shined "fifty-dollar Stacy-Adams" shoes and not saying excuse me. Once a short, slight man was pushed around by a bigger man. The little man is said to have gone home to get his "roscoe" (pistol), returned, and made the larger man crawl on his knees and swear never to do him wrong again. Cases like these, kept in the lore of Jelly's, remind people of what can result from unmindful interaction, and help keep people discreet and civil with one another. People often just don't know the capabilities of others on this side—what they will do and why.

The strange visitors of the barroom side are usually in the process of making their rounds to various drinking places on the South Side. They pass through Jelly's on their way to someplace else and have a relatively small social stake there. Most of them know few of the regular customers, and they usually do not know Jelly at all; those who do know him often know only that he is the owner of the place. Generally speaking, the regular customers see the visitors as outsiders in search of "action"—"on the hustle," as "trying to get over," or as "trying to get into something." Thus they tend to keep them at some distance and try to seek and maintain advantage during encounters. To the regular customers, the visitors, by and large, remain unknown. This makes for a certain amount of apprehension on the part of both groups and works to maintain distrust between them.

Although most of the visitors respect this definition of affairs, a visitor sometimes ventures into the liquor-store area and begins to hang. He is usually not encouraged to linger. When such a person enters, others usually stop talking or at least quiet down until he leaves. Their eyes follow him, reminding him that he is an intruder. Among the regular clientele he is regarded as an outsider, as one of "Jelly's customers," or even as "just a customer." Sensing that the liquor-store area is either beneath him or apart from him, or that it is too dangerous, the visitor usually finishes his business and returns to the barroom or goes on to another joint. Normally the visitors come to the bar, spend some time, then leave, remaining somewhat unknown to Jelly's regular clientele.

Getting In

My first few weeks at Jelly's were spent on the barroom side among the visitors and others. This side, for the reasons shown above, was the place most accessible to new people, where strangers could congregate. It was also a place where I could be relatively unobtrusive, yet somewhat sociable. It was here that the process of getting to know Jelly's began, where increasingly I gained some license to exist and talk openly with people. Initially this meant getting to know the people and becoming somewhat involved in their relationships with one another; becoming familiar with the common, everyday understandings people shared and took for granted, the social rules and expectations they held for one another.

One of my earliest encounters was with a young man named Clarence, a visitor just passing through Jelly's. The following conversation with him illustrates both the potential for intimacy and the transience characterizing a great many relations among visitors on the barroom side.

At one point, a thirty-one-year-old man named Clarence asked me what I did for a living. I told him I was a student at the University of Chicago. He looked very surprised, but suspicious.

"When you get out of there, they got to treat you like a white man," he said. He was smiling gently, and he was sincere. He seemed both suspicious and a bit proud of my being at the university.

"How do you like it?" he asked cautiously.

"I like it all right," I said.

"You quite a ways from there, aren't you," he said in a half-stating, half-questioning way.

"Yeah, but I got a car," I said. "I come over here once in a while to get a drink and relax."

"Yeah, you got to get away from all them honkies after a while. I know how it is," he said. "Where you stay?"

"Near Fifty-third and Harper," I answered.

"I know that area pretty good—used to hang out over there back in the fifties," he said. Clarence then mentioned some joints we both knew. From that point on we had easy conversation, laughing and talking, watching the people come and go.

Clarence offered to buy me a beer. I accepted and we kept talking. The jukebox blared and people continued to enter and leave, shouting, laughing, meeting friends. Rose, the barmaid, seemed to be enjoying her work, as she laughed and talked between serving up drinks.

"What do you do, Clarence?" I asked.

"I do odd jobs," he said. "I go from house to house to get work. I've worked up a nice little business for myself. I paint, wash walls, and do handyman work. It's a pretty good thing. Sometimes I make as much as $200 a room." While saying this, he seemed defensive.

"Are you married?" I asked.

"Yeah, I got a little boy. I been married twice, and now this marriage is on the rocks. My wife done told me she don't have no sexual feelings for me no more. She sleep in one bedroom, I sleep in the other. What kind of a marriage is that, huh? Hell, I ain't had that woman for four months. And she tell me there ain't nobody else—she just don't dig me no more. That's rough, boy. That's rough. Look like history tryin' to repeat itself. But I ain't gon' let what happened to me before happen again."

"What happened before?" I asked.

"Well, I was married once before and had a little boy. You know, my wife told me right in front of my momma that she didn't love me and never did. Said she just married me to get away from her foster parents legally. See, when I met her, she was just a young girl and I felt sorry for her. She didn't have no family, nobody 'cept her foster folks. So I figured I'd let her into my family. See, I got a mother and father and four brothers and two sisters living here in Chicago. Thought she'd be happy with them. And she was. I think she really loved them with all her heart. But then one day, she decided to split to California. And what make it so bad is that she took my baby boy with her. You know what, Eli? That really hurt me to my heart. Man, sometimes I'd lay 'wake all night and cry for my little boy. When my vacation time came, I went out looking for her in LA for a whole week, but I didn't have no luck. Before I went I tried to get in touch with her foster parents, but both of them had up and died, so there ain't no hope. I even tried to track her down through public aid. Thought maybe she'd got on ADC out there, but no luck, man."

"I am sick about that, just sick. That boy was my spittin' image, Eli, and now he's just out there. He needs me to show him what's happening', you know, to raise him, know what I mean? Well, I done lost one baby, but I ain't gon' lose this one. If it wasn't for this here baby, I'd leave tomorrow. But I care too much for my little boy. It's your generation you got to think about, Eli. It's your generation and you can't let that go by."

As I finished each beer, Clarence would call to Rose and order another Schlitz for me and a gin and tonic for himself. I offered to buy some of the rounds, but he would not let me. For more than two hours we lounged around the barroom of Jelly's, watching the people come and go, gravitating from the barroom to the liquor store and back. The people seemed to be thoroughly enjoying themselves.

"You know, Eli, sometimes I regret I didn't finish high school and go to college. See, I didn't get no education. You got a good chance, you gettin' yourself educated and all, you gon' make something out o' yourself. Hell, get all you can, while you can. Don't be like me. Hell, I wish I could be in your place, goin' to school and all. But I tell you something else. You know, too much education is a bad thing. You can mess around and become a cranium. You ain't no cranium, are you? I hear some of them people at that university are really nutty—out there in left field somewhere. I hope you don't turn out like that. Get all you can, while you can, but don't turn into no cranium."

After a while our conversation drifted and dragged from topic to topic, and later I decided to go home. I thanked him for the drinks and told him that when I saw him again I would treat him. He told me not to worry about it; that he had really enjoyed talking. We parted and he went his way and I went mine.

The talk between Clarence and me, and the long and involved talks I had with so many other visitors, was more likely to have happened on the barroom side than in the liquor store. As Simmel indicates,[6] it seems easier to divulge personal information to strangers than to close peers, particularly information deemed "harmful." It is easier here in part because most of the visitors don't see one another again as buddies and thus may not have an immediate interest in status competition. In a social and emotional sense, their passing relationships can be very open to certain kinds of personal information.

I never saw Clarence again at Jelly's. During my first weeks on the barroom side, I became involved in many such conversations. Usually I never saw the person again or, if I did, the relationship would not pick up where it had left off. Seeming somewhat atomized on this side, most people did not seem to expect more than an agreeable and open ear from their counterparts. The visitors I had encountered on occasion came around once in a while, but when they did show up they were often somewhat detached and aloof from the center of things at Jelly's. For example, after asking around about Clarence, I found that Rose, the barmaid, was the only person who "knew" him, and that she knew him only by sight. Having seen him around only once or twice, she found it hard to place Clarence when I asked her about him. This is indicated by the following field note, which also gives a feel for the barroom.

At three o'clock in the afternoon I walked into the bar. I counted twenty-four people. Some were sitting at the bar, others were standing around or walking to or from a seat, the restroom, the jukebox, or the liquor-store area that is adjacent to the bar and connected by an open doorway. Four women were present, all dressed in attire fitting for a black church service (e.g., two-piece suits, earrings, lipstick, makeup, and wigs). The men wore flannel shirts, work clothes, army fatigues, sports clothes, and suits. One man, about sixty-five years old, wore an old, baggy blue suit with no tie. Generally it seemed that the women had given more attention to their appearance than had the men. The patrons ranged in age from about twenty-two to about sixty-five.

As I entered the barroom some of the people sitting at the bar turned and looked my way, then returned to their drinks and conversations. Others just followed me with their eyes. I recognized one man I had met on a previous visit, but he didn't recognize me; he was too high.

I took a seat at the bar. I sat next to a heavyset, short brown-skinned woman who looked about forty-five years old. She was dressed in a two-piece black wool suit; she wore dark red lipstick, a red wig, and a pair of large gold earrings. She was seated to my right; the seat on my left was vacant.

As I sat down, Rose acknowledged my presence.

"How you doin', baby?" she inquired.

"Okay, how are you?" I responded.

"Oh, I guess I'll do. What you gon' have?" she said.

"I'll have a Bud and a bag of chips," I said. As she returned with my order, I asked her if she had seen Clarence, a young man I had met on a previous visit. She couldn't place Clarence. This surprised me because the first time I met him, he and Rose were interacting as if they were old friends. At that point I asked if she had seen Bob, another fellow I had met at the bar.

"No," she answered, "Bob ain't been in here today."

"What about Sonny?" I went on.

"Yeah, he was in here not too long ago," she said. I gave her the money for the beer and chips, and she left to wait on someone else. I opened my bag of chips and began to nibble them and drink my beer. Twice, as she passed me, Rose helped herself to my potato chips.

The Liquor Store

After I had been in the field at Jelly's for about four weeks I met Herman, a forty-five-year-old janitor. He wore a baggy army fatigue jacket, blue gabardine slacks, and black "keen-toed" shoes. On his head was a beige "high-boy" hat with a black band. Herman was a small brown-skinned man, about five feet eight inches tall and weighing about 145 pounds. At our first meeting I had been sitting at the bar for about twenty minutes, carrying on a conversation with Rose. Herman took the seat next to me and joined in the conversation. In this first encounter, Herman and I talked in much the same way as I had talked with other visitors to the barroom. At this point in the study, of course, I had not yet begun to make careful distinctions among the different types of people at Jelly's; the very notion of visitor, for instance, came to me only later. Herman was witty and seemed very easygoing, yet at times he spoke in a slow drawl. He impressed me as a person experienced on the ghetto streets, for his conversation was spiced with well-placed references to such experiences. Because of my previous encounters in the barroom, which on the whole had not been outstandingly productive, I at first took Herman as just another person I probably would not see again. But, as

I was to find out, Herman was not just another visitor, but a member of the regular clientele of Jelly's.

In the course of our initial encounter Herman and I talked briefly but became very involved. Among other things, he mentioned that he had seen me around before, though I had not noticed him. During this conversation, his questions centered on the issue of what I was doing there. Although he never stated this directly, he did ask some leading questions. Not broaching it at first, he led up to it in a subtle conversation of gestures and words. Interested in "who I was," Herman asked me, "What do you do, Eli?" He wanted to know how I spent my time and whether I was gainfully employed. As I was to discover, around Jelly's whether someone works for a living is an important clue to his definition. For most people this helps to determine whether he is to be trusted within the setting, and to what degree.

In response to Herman's inquiries about my occupation, I said, "I'm a graduate student over at the University of Chicago."

"That's nice," said Herman, seeming a little surprised. "How long you been over there?" As I answered his questions, he seemed to take this as a kind of license to ask more and more about me. And I took his inquiries as cues that I could do the same. Taking this license, I asked him more about himself. During this exchange of information I noticed a marked change in Herman's demeanor toward me. He became more relaxed and sure of me. He gestured more as he spoke, punctuating his words with hits and jabs to my shoulder. He was a very friendly and affable man. At times I reciprocated by punctuating my own words with smiles and friendly exclamations. On the ghetto streets and in ghetto bars friendly students are not to be feared and suspected but are generally expected to be "square" and bookish. With all the information he had about me, including my willingness to give it, he could place me as "safe" within his own scheme of standards and values.

My openness encouraged Herman to be open with me. As a result, there was now some basis for trust in our relationship. In telling me more about himself, Herman said he was a janitor but quickly added,

"I'm a man among men," implying that, contrary to what some might expect of a janitor, he held himself in high esteem. Then he told me about his work and about how early he had to get up in the morning. After more of this familiarizing talk, we parted company on good terms. We had spent more than two hours laughing and talking together. I had held this kind of information exchange with others before, and I didn't expect anything unusual to come from this particular meeting. But it was encounters like this that made me conscious that who I was and how I fit into the cognitive picture of Jelly's did preoccupy some of its more persistent members. When I went to Jelly's the next day, I met Herman again. As I entered the barroom I greeted Rose and others as I usually did. I took a seat at the bar and from my stool watched the activities of the men in the liquor-store room.

In that room people were engaged in spontaneous fun—laughing, yelling, playing with one another, and being generally at ease. To me that room seemed very exciting, but it was clear that I would have been out of place there for it seemed to be only for peer-group members. I sensed that there I would have been reminded of my outsider status again and again. While in the barroom, among the visitors and a few of the peer-group members who gravitated over now and then, I felt *in place*. Looking into the liquor-store room, I saw Herman. Catching his attention, I beckoned to him, and he came over to me in the barroom. We shook hands and greeted each other, then held a friendly conversation over a couple of beers. But soon he returned to the liquor-store area, where more of his buddies seemed to be. That Herman had buddies, and so many of them, was one of the important distinctions between him and many of the visitors I had previously met at Jelly's.

In contrast to the visitors on the barroom side of Jelly's, the regular customers on the liquor-store side tend to be spontaneous, loud, and relatively sure of themselves during interactions. Herman and the others acted very much at home there—and they were. Herman was a very sociable person and seemed to be in and out of everyone's affairs. I could see that very little went on at Jelly's without his knowledge. Recognizing this turned out to have important consequences for my entrée to the social world of Jelly's, for it was clear that not many new people stayed around without his soon getting to know them. It became apparent that Jelly's was very much Herman's place; it was his turf, a place where he felt protected from the wrong kind of outsiders.

Apparently he saw me as the right kind of outsider, because when I saw him again in a few days, Herman invited me to share his turf. Again, I was sitting in the barroom, while Herman was laughing and talking with a group of men in the liquor-store room. When I saw them through the open doorway that divided the two areas, I was about to leave. I decided to go through the liquor store to greet Herman, but also to get a closer view of the activity of that room.

As I approached the men I heard Herman say, "Hey, here come my friend, Eli!" Then he said to Sleepy, one of the other men, "He al'right. Hey, this the stud I been tellin' you about. This cat gettin' his doctor's degree." At this point Herman shook my hand and greeted me. I returned the greeting. The others of the group seemed cautious and somewhat incredulous about accepting the "me" presented by Herman. Yet they were polite and approving and remained silent while he and I went through the greeting action. The men just watched, checking us out and talking among themselves. Shortly, Herman began introducing me to the others.

"Hey, Eli. Meet Jake, T. J., and this here's Sleepy." The men then acknowledged me, nodding and saying their hellos. I exchanged greetings with them.

Herman, beer in hand, boasted to the men about a Christmas party he was going to attend where he worked. While he bragged, the others looked on and listened. Much of the conversation and interaction within small groups like this one involves people's attempts to present themselves as important—as "somebody" according to some standard the group values. This situation was dominated by one of these presentations, and it was Herman's show. Herman bragged on about the party. To make it especially meaningful he accentuated the occasion, describing it as something extravagant and special. Herman talked of the "foxy chicks" he would be kissing under the mistletoe and of the "intelligent folks" he would be "conversin'"

with. Jake responded by saying, "Aw, that nigger's crazy." Other responses were similar, but Herman persisted.

At one point in his presentation Herman invited me to the Christmas party.

"Hey, Eli. You wanna come to a Christmas party tomorrow?"
asked Herman.

"What's this?" I answered, surprised at the invitation.

"The place I work gon' have a Christmas party tomorrow. Gon'
be some real fine foxes there, some good whiskey, too," said Herman.

"Sure, I'll come. What time?"

"Meet me at 2:30 at _____, OK?"

"I'll be there," I said.

The men of the group continued to check us out. Herman was
treating me as a friend, as an insider, as though my status in the
group were somehow already assured. Certainly Herman would not
invite just anyone to a party at work. Other group members wouldn't
have expected this and in fact would have been surprised if he had
asked one of them. After this demonstration by Herman, I could feel
the others in the group warm up to me; they looked at me more
directly and seemed to laugh more easily.

I began to feel comfortable enough to stand around in the group
and listen to the banter, but not to participate in it, my reticence
reflecting my sense of my visitor status. But I did laugh and talk with
the fellows, trying to get to know people I had often wondered about
during the past four or five weeks. These were people I had seen
around but had never before attempted to "be with."

For the next fifteen or twenty minutes Herman busied himself
boasting about his various exploits, while other members of the group
tried to show inconsistencies between Herman's accounts and the
facts they knew. In the language of Jelly's, they tried to "shoot him
down." Some of the men even took sides, attempting to counter each
other's disputes over the validity of Herman's account of his role-to-
be at the Christmas party. This style of banter is rather normal among
peers on the liquor-store side of Jelly's. It moves from topic to topic
as issues rise and fall, become important or trivial. After a while, I
told Herman and my new friends I had to be getting home.

For me the evening had been remarkable. It was the first time I had been introduced to anyone well connected within the social setting of Jelly's; the first time I had actually been sponsored by someone with an important social stake there. And no less significant, it was my first social venture on the liquor-store side of Jelly's—a real achievement. I had become involved with peer-group members, people for whom others at Jelly's really mattered. The whole experience marked the real beginning of my entrée: It was the time from which I began to gain a feeling of place at Jelly's. Moreover, it pointed up to me the importance of this setting as one in which social selves were cast, debated, negotiated, and then defended—in a word, socially constructed.

When Herman introduced me to his friends I was in effect being sponsored, and in many ways this made my status passage into the peer group relatively easy.[7] For those present, his introduction expressed who I was to be at Jelly's—mainly Herman's "decent" friend. I say decent because Herman used this word when he introduced me around. Through this association, others were encouraged to invest a certain degree of trust in me and to become friendly toward me. To be sure, this was a slow process, but from then on those present, and many who had not been there, acted as though I had some license to be around.

When Herman sponsored me and invited me to the party, I assumed some usefulness for and responsibility toward him. As I was to learn, one thing I could give Herman was verification of his role at the party—and of the identity that went along with it.

Going for Cousins

When I arrived at his place of work on the day of the party, Herman showed me around the buildings he kept clean as janitor. He led me from room to room, from hallway to hallway, and from floor to floor, taking great pride in their immaculate look. As he showed me around, he said in an aside that he would have to introduce me to others as his "cousin," since he could not let "just anybody" in there. I agreed to be his "cousin," which was still a dubious status in the minds of those we were to encounter at the party, if not in Herman's own mind. But this was Herman's show. He was the director.

Before introducing me around Herman quietly asked me my mother's name. I told him. Then he told me his mother's name, and assured me all the while that this was "just in case somebody don't believe us." In exchanging our mothers' names, though, Herman and I demonstrated a certain degree of trust. Such confidential information is not generally disclosed to just anyone without reservation. For if one were to let such information out to the "wrong" person, he would become open to the possibility of being "scored on" in a game of personal attribution.[8] Such games can at times become very sharp, and participants who have any attribute that may be taken as a failing can have their feelings badly hurt. Many of the men around Jelly's, owing to their ages and their special relationships to the wider society, have "checkered" pasts. They will sometimes shy away from such games, not only by showing reticence when they are being played, but also by closely guarding their intimate secrets. Among the men who know one another's secrets and are friendly enough to play these games, volatile and dangerous exchanges can develop.

Another important point suggested by Herman's careful preparation of our story is that those at Jelly's who attempt a venturesome self-presentation have learned that they must expect to be seriously challenged. Hence they feel pressured to "have their shit together"— that is, to have a convincing and ready account of who they are. In the peer group at Jelly's this means that a person who expects to have his version of his identity taken seriously must have a "strong rap" (an impressive verbal account of himself) prepared, with good illustrations, details, and evidence. But, also very important, the person must have supporters in the setting who will act in agreement with the meanings he wants to attribute to his self-presentation. Rules for this presentation conform to a literal standard—the "show me" variety.

In the peer group, people "shoot down" and "blow away" each other's accounts frequently and with relative ease.[9] One important reason for this is that status here is a competitive proposition. But also, group members believe that their peers lack a secure control of those items that serve as props and resources for commanding high social rank. In their minds everyone in the setting is likely to be judged "a nobody," especially when group members invoke the standards of the wider society. In this competitive context, "to be somebody" one must display convincing proof, which is usually put up front before someone else actually calls for it. All of this indicated to me that identity as somebody is not just achieved and consolidated once and for all, but rather must be constantly renewed during social interaction. In attempting to deal with this situation, people frequently would preface their personal accounts with such self-props as "Please believe me . . ." or "I ain't gon' tell you no lie . . ." or "No shit. . . ." Peer group members often expected others to be lying about themselves and these others expected to have their accounts challenged.

In the world outside Jelly's—for example, at his place of work— Herman employs his own notions of what it takes to be believed, to be taken seriously, and to protect himself from being "shot down" or "blown away." These notions, grounded in Herman's experience on the streets around Jelly's, are the background to his careful preparation of our "story" for the people at the Christmas party.

At the party, Herman introduced me as his cousin who "goes to the University of Chicago, gettin' his Ph.D." He even told one black secretary that I was the cousin he had long been telling her about. Herman was the only janitor at the party; the others present were professionals and office workers. He and I were the only representatives from any setting at all like Jelly's. Yet with Herman's direction we moved easily among these people. With each introduction he beamed with pride over his " 'cousin,' who's gettin' his Ph.D."

When the affair was over and we were leaving, Herman said to me, "I'm a man among men," declaring his own sense of accomplishment and self-esteem. Obviously, he felt that the whole show had been a great success. As we walked to my car, he repeated, "Yeah, I feel like a man among men. Eli, I knew you was a decent stud when I first met you. Now, you don't owe me nothing, you didn't have to come, but you came. You my best friend, hear?" Herman was elated at the success of his show and at how he had impressed the people "at work." As we were driving back to Jelly's Herman told me why

he had chosen me to come to the party, rather than any of his buddies
at Jelly's. "I wouldn't trust none o' them studs comin' all up on my
job. Them cats don't know how to act 'round decent folks and intelligent folks. And sometimes I ain't so sure 'bout myself, 'specially if I
get a little high on. Might get up there and start actin' a damn fool.
Ha-ha." But Herman was sure about me. He was convinced that I
knew how to act around "decent folks and intelligent folks." After
all, I had "all that education." But equally important, I could come
back and report to all the fellows at Jelly's, especially "ol' fat-assed
Jelly" himself, about how we had partied with "decent folks at the
Christmas party." He reminded me to do just that as he got out of
my car.

When I did return to Jelly's, I told the fellows of the peer group
how Herman and I had partied. With this verification of his story
and, in a sense, of the identity he wanted them to know, I became
all the more closely linked with him around Jelly's. All of this made
a big hit there, and Herman's rank, at least when the outside world
was the issue, became a little less precarious.

Group members seemed to accept my verification of Herman's
adventures at work. Now when he spoke about "partying" people
listened and were not as disparaging as they had been the day he
invited me to the party. For the time being, at least to his face, the
men seemed to have called a moratorium on attempting to "shoot
him down" on this issue. And on more than one occasion Herman
felt confident enough to try to impress others by recounting our trip
to the party. The following conversation took place in Jelly's barroom about a month after the party.

> Herman and I laughed and talked with two other group mem-
> bers in the barroom. We sipped our beers, talked, and watched
> other people. Soon another of Herman's friends approached and
> spoke to us.
> "What's happenin'?" he asked.
> "You got it," responded Herman.
> This man was wearing a sporty overcoat and was neatly dressed.
> He and Herman talked for a while before Herman said,

"Eli, this my main man, Jimbo. Jimbo, this my cousin Eli. He
go to the University of Chicago."

"Aw, how you doing, Eli?" said Jimbo.

"Hey, how you doing?" I said.

"He intelligent! You know I don't be hangin' 'round with no un-
intelligent people, Jimbo. That's why I been hanging 'round with
you so long," joked Herman.

Everyone laughed. Herman then proceeded to tell the man how
we had partied together on his job. The man showed interest, as
I nodded in verification of the story. Then we finished our beers,
"hatted up," and started for the door.

Thereafter Herman referred to me as his cousin and introduced
me to others that way. In a sense this was the place I had lobbied
for, however unwittingly. We hung together and treated each other
as close friends, and the men followed suit. The more I hung with
Herman and verified his stories, the closer we seemed to become.
We began to "go for cousins," as the men say. Many of the men
knew, of course, that we were not real cousins, and, perhaps even
more important, Herman knew they knew. This was not a case of
deception. Rather, the fictive kinship term of cousin was used by
Herman, as it is by so many men on the streets around Jelly's, to
signify that we were close friends. We were "going for cousins."[10]

One of the important implicit aspects of this developing relationship concerned its protective nature. Herman and I would often hang
together and leave Jelly's together to go home or to a movie or somewhere else. Among peer group members, an unspoken rule requires
those who hang together to help or "take up for" one another in
times of need—particularly during physical fights, but also on general
social matters. My relationship with Herman gave me a certain implicit status in the group, a place interconnected with the "rep" and
rank Herman was sensed to have. A set of mutual obligations and
expectations began to form, so that group members expected us to
take up for each other.

My growing awareness of these developments contributed to my
own self-confidence around Jelly's liquor-store room, as I slowly

secured a right to be there. During the course of this entrée, I increasingly came under Herman's tutelage and guardianship. But why did Herman engage me in friendship at all? What was in it for him? After getting to know Herman better, I became aware that he regards himself as very knowledgeable about the ghetto streets. There is a certain amount of esteem to be gained by demonstrating that one knows his way around the streets, and Herman sees and presents himself as someone who has been "through it all."

Born and raised in Chicago, Herman has spent a good part of his life coming to terms with "the streets." He has been "through World War II," has been "a pimp, a hustler, a junkie" among other things —and has survived to talk about it all, something he does whenever "the streets" becomes an issue around Jelly's.

Because he carries this extensive and widely known personal biography, Herman is able to command a certain measure of esteem from the men who constitute Jelly's regular clientele. Other regulars usually agree with this definition of him and will work collectively to maintain it. At the same time, Herman wants to see himself as "decent." However, he knows that such an identity—about which I will have much to say later—is difficult to maintain for anyone hanging out at Jelly's.

As I said, in our relationship I provided Herman with a kind of verification of his identity and status on the streets and in "decent" society. Specifically, as I provided him with a "decent" pupil, one who had "all that education," I reflected well upon him and could thus verify his own claims to "decency." Of course I could also verify Herman's claims to street prowess by allowing him to teach me about the streets. And this really was important to me, since I needed to know the streets if I were to survive and carry out my fieldwork. By taking me under his wing, Herman could thus show that he knew the streets very well and at the same time could "be somebody" when "decent" friends became the issue.

All this fit nicely with the low-key, nonassertive role I assumed at the beginning of my study. I behaved in this way to prevent unwieldy challenges from those who might have felt threatened by a more aggressive demeanor, especially from a stranger. It is the kind of role any outsider must play—is forced into—if he is not to disrupt the consensual definition of social order in this type of setting.

Working at Sociability

At first glance the atmosphere of the liquor store is reminiscent of the ambience attributed to the old general store, with its pot-bellied stove and stereotyped, easygoing social relations. Relations among people of the liquor-store room seem effortless; the room buzzes with happy conversation, loud laughter, and play. The people here joke, shout, and argue from time to time. Unlike the barroom, this appears to be a place of spontaneity where friends and others who know each other well can really be sociable. Compared with the barroom, or what people of the peer group call "that side" or the "other side," relations here seem utterly unstructured.

But this view is deceptive. On examination, the initial association with the old general store fades. One begins to find that the sociability is not so effortless after all. People must work at it. Sociability here involves an elaborate set of subtle rules that emerge more clearly during interaction and that peer group members come to know and act in accordance with—or soon find themselves reprimanded.

On this side it appeared at first that there were no clear and stable seating arrangements—that people sat wherever they could find room. They sat on any old Coke or liquor case or leaned on Jelly's wobbly old counter. These places seemed to go to the lucky person. But as one spends time on this side of Jelly's he learns that the scarce seat goes to a person not so much because he is lucky as because the others feel somehow that he deserves it. On numerous occasions I saw people actively defer to others over seating. They did not need to be asked but would surrender a seat even at a look from a person who apparently had more right to it. To be sure, at times such assertions of right were made verbally or even resulted in arguments. For example:

On a cold and rainy Friday evening in January, Jelly's liquor store buzzed with the loud talk and laughter of about twelve men.

Friday is payday for many of those who work, and people seemed to be celebrating. Some periodically moved to and from the barroom, but most remained in the liquor-store room. Herman had just introduced me to Nathaniel, who was offering us a drink of his whiskey. But this was interrupted by two men who were arguing over the right to sit on a soda crate leaning against the wall. Attention turned to them. The argument became more heated, and one of the men "went in his pocket" and threatened to come up with a weapon. He just stood there glaring at the other man with his hand dug in his pocket. Then the other man deferred, saying, "Well, if the damn seat mean that much, you can have it! I ain't goin' to no jail over no seat!" He then went into the barroom. The man with the weapon took the seat, sat there for about ten minutes, then left for home.

This field note underscores the importance of something as seemingly trivial as a seat in defining social order.

Further, it seems at first that the people of this side play with just anyone. But on closer examination one sees that they play only with those who help them preserve and gain respect for their valued sense of themselves. One learns through involvements on this side that there is a complex social order that peer-group members have come to know during social interaction, that they collectively take as a basis of their continuing conduct, and that develops with their changing relationships. All of this became clearer to me as I grew more involved with the people of Jelly's.

Herman continued to sponsor my participation in the peer group. He still told people I was his cousin, a label that suggested that in times of trouble we would "take up" for each other. Yet the principle of reciprocity was at work in our relationship; Herman and I needed help from each other, but in different ways. Given our situations and positions in the group, Herman did not need my protection, and since I was the one defined as in need of such help, he probably would have been reluctant to accept it from me had the need arisen. On one occasion Herman demonstrated my need for his help by intervening in what could have developed into a troublesome situation.

It was a balmy Saturday evening in April. Herman, Leroy, Charlie, Tony, and I were standing in front of Jelly's liquor-store window. An ice-cold can of Budweiser, wrapped in a brown paper sack, changed hands. Each man took a swig and passed the can on. Cars and buses passed by and their passengers glanced over, but the men were oblivious to this. Pedestrians quickly moved on. An old flea-bitten brown mutt limped by. Tony was in a playful mood and began poking me in the side. The poking soon turned into shoulder-bumping. Herman, who had been watching this play, said to Tony, in a half-kidding yet firm way, "Why don't you cut all that weak shit, Tony." Tony stopped at what was taken as a warning from Herman.

This is one example of the way Herman gave help in situations that might have become problematic. In this instance I felt no tension between Tony and myself. But Herman, being very familiar with the social order of the group, understood that such "playful" games can quickly develop into trouble.

Equally important, Herman helped me learn what situations could lead to trouble by giving me information about the various men in the peer group. After introducing me to someone around Jelly's, for example, he would often pull me aside and give me a small biography, to inform me how I should treat the person and how I should allow him to treat me. In effect, Herman not only was introducing me to the peer-group members but was also informing me of his conception of their consensual agreements on rank and social order. Such information is regularly exchanged at Jelly's, often through actions and subtle gestures as well as words, and provides a way of knowing people without always having to "try" identities. For example, one night Herman introduced me to Charlie, still spry at seventy-two. We talked to Charlie for about a half-hour, then at the opportune moment Herman pulled me aside and filled me in on his record. At times, such an exchange of information would wait until the next day and at other times, it did not occur at all. In "Ol' Charlie's case," Herman told me that

"He's still gettin' pussy, stays sharp [dresses well], keeps a pocket full of money, keeps his shit [pistol] on him all the time, and he talks mo' shit than any one o' them jitterbugs out there. Charlie's got three grown kids, and he's a gangster from way back. That ol' stud still will blow a mug away [shoot] quick. So you can't play him cheap, and any mug up in here [member of the peer group] will cut yo' throat 'bout messin' with him. They all love him."

In effect, Herman was giving me Charlie's script and preparing me to accept and defer to it in the interest of social order.

Another of my early lessons from Herman concerned the importance of being able to "read the signs" people display during sociability. Most people value this ability on the streets around Jelly's and like to claim proficiency at it. As I mentioned earlier, "reading" involves paying close attention to a person's self-presentation to gain clues about how he deserves to be treated, especially if he is new. One notices the person's dress, his language, how he moves at Jelly's, the things he takes for granted, the kinds of questions he asks, even the way he formulates his questions. How much "room" he gets from others at Jelly's—that is, what certain others will allow him to get away with when he interacts with them—is also important. Such interactions can become behavioral cues signaling how he can be treated by still others in the setting. From all of this, others can gain some sense of how the person sees himself and what this might mean for their relations with him and others in the group. In effect, they learn how he deserves to be treated and thus are able to assess quickly the behavioral limits appropriate in their own dealings with him.

If the ability to read such signs is valuable, it is just as valuable to be able to display them to create the desired effect.[11] This was demonstrated to me one evening when Herman and I encountered Oscar, a fast, street-wise former street-gang member of thirty-three who is now a hustler of the streets. Herman went through an elaborate display for my benefit. As Oscar entered the liquor-store room and approached us, Herman said, "Hey, Oscar!"

"Hey, dude," said Oscar, in a slow, cautious drawl. This statement and its tone were enough to alert Herman to Oscar's mood. The tone indicated that Oscar felt a certain distance, Herman believed. It was as though Oscar had his "pistols on," perhaps only because I was a stranger.

Herman and Oscar exchanged a few words, as Herman moved astutely and almost effortlessly to Oscar's "level" by his speech and demeanor. Herman spoke "hip street shit," spiced with a few "mother-fuckers," "son' bitches," or whatever it took. I just sat at the bar with my beer in hand and watched Herman in action. Though he does not act this way in all circumstances, he seemed to sense the necessity for such behavior now to maintain Oscar's respect or, more to the point, to keep him in his place. To do this Herman knew he must in some measure meet the standards Oscar deemed important. Such standards are here expressed and met through adroit use of "tough" and "manly" gestures and street language, a posture Oscar could readily appreciate.[12]

After a few moments of this exhibition, which amounted to a kind of reestablishment of who was who, Oscar said,

"Who that you got with you?"

"Oh, Oscar, this is my cousin Eli."

"Hey, brother-man. What's to it?" said Oscar, as he extended his hand to me for a soul handshake.

"You," I responded, as I shook his hand.

In this situation Herman did not emphasize the side of me that Oscar might take as "square" by saying, as he so often did when introducing me, "Hey, this stud's gettin' his Ph.D." Herman just let that part of my status and identity lie dormant in this situation.

After a few minutes Oscar began to "hit on me" to buy some of the "hot" record albums he had tucked under his arm, with which he usually makes his rounds "hustlin' " from joint to joint.

Before long Herman interrupted, "Dig it, Oscar, Eli don't need none of what you sellin'!" He then tugged me away, as Oscar moved on. Herman and I retired to a corner of the liquor-store room, where he began to fill me in on Oscar. Considering Oscar a "bad egg," he said,

"I've known the boy all his life. I even raised him [meaning that he taught Oscar a good deal]. The boy ain't no good, no 'count.

He ain't nothing but a jive-time gangster. Just a li'l hustler who'd sell his own momma to get over. So you know what he'll do for me or you. The boy think he slick, always tryin' to get over, trying to test somebody, and if you give him any leeway, he'll try to beat you. That's what he was tryin' to do with you, tryin' you, seein' what you'd stand. You got to stand up to dudes like him, or they'll play you cheap. Then they'll always be tryin' to get over on you, you know? Dig me, you'll learn."

The ability to interpret a person's actions accurately and then to define the boundaries proper to place takes on special significance on the streets around Jelly's, compared with the relatively serene middle-class setting. One of the main differences is in what the participants in such interaction may have at stake—especially their sense of what is at stake. In the middle-class setting, when such boundaries are not taken seriously, or are ignored, ridiculed, or slighted, one stands to lose face.[13] Around Jelly's, a person not only stands to lose face, he may even lose his life—or at least come to sense a clear danger to his life. Awareness of the high stakes encourages people to pay close attention to their relations with others during interaction and sociability around Jelly's.

On another occasion Herman introduced me to Bill, a "decent" friend of his who is forty-seven years old and a janitor. Again, we were on the liquor-store side of Jelly's. As Herman and I arrived that evening, we saw Bill talking with some other men. As we approached Bill, Herman blurted out, "Hey, here's my best friend!" At this point, he hugged Bill and the two men just stood there grinning at each other. After a few minutes Herman said,

"Bill, I want you to meet my cousin Eli." At this Bill extended his hand to me. We exchanged greetings.

"Bill, this stud's gettin' his Ph.D," Herman said.

"Yeah?" said Bill.

"Yeah, that's right," said Herman, "he ain't like me and you. He done gone on and made somethin' o' himself. He gon' teach college, ain'cha, Eli?" Herman said this in a boastful, yet congenial way.

"Yeah, one of these days," I said, a little embarrassed.

"Well, that's al'right, son. Gon' get all that education you can get. That's what you need nowadays. Can't get far in this world without it," said Bill, seriously.

For the next ten or fifteen minutes the three of us talked about education and school. We talked about what a "decent" and "nice" thing education is and how people must have it these days to get a decent job. During this conversation Herman kept reminding Bill of how "heavy" and "intelligent" I was. Now and then he would throw into the conversation some big "intelligent-sounding" nonword that was supposed to impress us both, especially Bill. After a while we left Bill and moved on to the barroom. Later that evening, on our way to Herman's house, he filled me in on Bill. Bill was "decent, married to a good woman, got him a bad crib [meaning a plush place to live] with some nice furniture. Bill is really decent and ain't nothing I wouldn't do for him. We straight."

For Herman and others at Jelly's, there exists a variety of circumstances and situations during sociability that require different postures and strategies of personal demeanor. In the social setting of Jelly's both working and nonworking black people can gather among others enough like themselves to matter socially. Here they seek out certain others to spend their leisure time with—friends and companions with whom they can act sociably, talking, laughing, arguing, and joking. It is in this setting that they can feel themselves among equals, especially in relation to the wider society. In a fundamental sense, this setting represents their league, where they stand a chance to win in the competition for social esteem and rank. In this respect Jelly's serves as a kind of arena of social life. Here people present themselves in the roles that peers allow them. Here they engage in ritual exhibitions of deference and demeanor that, when properly reacted to by significant others, allow them a certain affirmation of self.[14] The people here create and work to sustain the principles and standards by which they can measure themselves and others. At Jelly's people can be somebody—and this is one of its main attractions.

2 The Elaboration of Primary Ties and Personal Identities

To convey an understanding of the social relationships at Jelly's bar and liquor store, I must say something about who the people are that gather there. At the time of my study, approximately fifty-five men frequented Jelly's, ranging in age from about twenty-two to over seventy. The people of Jelly's are by no means typical residents of Chicago's South Side or other ghetto areas. They represent a select segment of that population. In the first place, most are viewed as marginal or deviant within the larger black population, and in many circumstances they see themselves as deviant or as lacking in moral responsibility by wider community standards. These are men, after all, who hang out and participate closely with others they know to be drunkards, beggars, and thieves, though there are other men they are inclined to view as approximating the wider society's standards of morality and conduct. Most of these men are not involved in continuous responsibility for nuclear families. For many, their most important social and psychological supports are found in the company of peers on the corner at Jelly's. At times some of them refer to the peer group at Jelly's as "the family," and indeed some men who come here use fictive kinship terms like "cousin" to describe especially close relationships in the setting. To be sure, many who frequent Jelly's do have relationships with members of the wider black community, through real kinship or through halting friendship ties. But in the company of such people, many of those who frequent Jelly's are uncomfortable, "feel funny" and come up short with regard to "good jobs," stable nuclear family situations, and general "decency."

To the more conventional residents of Jelly's neighborhood, Jelly's and places like it are "rough" and "bad," and the people who hang out there are commonly regarded as "lowlife" or as "no 'count." To most such residents, many of whom encounter Jelly's clientele as they negotiate their way past the tavern, the men mean trouble. Some of the more conventional residents do buy six-packs of beer or packaged liquor at Jelly's, but they make their purchases quietly and leave quickly, fearful of becoming too involved with the men standing out on the corner or sitting around inside. To them Jelly's is a place to stay away from. They often hear their neighbors' accounts, usually exaggerated, of fights, cuttings, muggings, shootings, and killings in and around Jelly's, which makes for some self-doubt among those who do come and socialize. This is shown in the following interview with a resident of the area:

"I don't even now go near the place. Ain't nothin' but lowlife 'round Jelly's. One day when I did pass by, some of them boys up there said to me, 'Hey, man. Why don't we have some fun.' And they sittin' up in the alley, drinkin', buyin' one bottle right after another. Now, I'm goin' home from work. Now, they a get mad at me 'cause I wasn't interested in drinkin'. They got benches, stools, and things down there. You know, bricks, blocks, and things to sit on. All of 'em sittin' down there talkin' shit. Got they bottles of beer and stuff they drinkin'. Sometimes I get me a li'l drink, but I keep checkin' my watch, you know. Come time for me to cut out, you know. I be done worked hard all day. I say, 'Well, mens, I'll see ya'll.' And I'll go on 'bout my business. See, I don't hang around there. Nothin' but trouble waitin' to happen."

The people of Jelly's know how the more conventional residents view them and their kind—the kind of person who hangs around Jelly's; for it is a view they themselves partly share. They get reminded of how outsiders generally feel about them when motorists gawk at them from the safety of their cars and buses, or when pedestrians nervously hurry by. Some remind one another of what a "hole" Jelly's is, and some are reminded when their relatives complain about their "going to that ol' corner." The men sometimes come back to Jelly's explaining that they are the black sheep of their families, thus socially sacrificing themselves in favor of their relatives. The wives of some of the married men often complain about Jelly's, since they and their children must compete with Jelly's for the husbands' time and money.[1] They refer to Jelly's derisively as "that ol' tavern." Once in the setting at Jelly's, one can suffer from guilt by association, for outsiders are not inclined to make the subtle distinctions among men of various statuses that group members are usually quick to make. For example:

> One evening, after I had been hanging around with Herman and the others at Jelly's for about six months, while Herman and I were sitting around his house drinking beer his sister telephoned. Herman's common-law wife, Butterroll, answered the phone. After talking for a long time, she gave the phone to Herman. As Herman talked with his sister, he referred to me as his friend, Dr. Eli Anderson (exaggerating my status, since I was still a graduate student at the time). "Come on, Eli. Talk to my sister. Here," said Herman, as he handed me the telephone. After talking for a while, I gave the phone back to Herman, who then proceeded to brag about me to his sister. Then he returned the phone to Butterroll. She said, "Aw, Sis. Don't believe that mess. That man ain't no doctor! He ain't nothin' but one o' them wineheads that hang up at that ol' tavern with Herman." Embarrassed, Herman grew silent. Soon we left.

We can make some headway toward understanding the life situations of the men at Jelly's in relation to their self-identities and their statuses in the group by considering the concept of the *extended primary group*. For Charles Horton Cooley, the primary group was defined as a small ongoing, close-knit gathering of individuals engaged in face-to-face social interaction. Its members possess a "we" feeling, which they gain through their social interaction with one another and through their intimate involvements in the group as distinct from the external social world. As stated by Cooley:

> By primary groups I mean those characterized by intimate face-to-face association and cooperation. They are primary in several senses, but chiefly in that they are fundamental in forming the

social nature and ideals of the individuals. The result of intimate association, psychologically, is a certain fusion of individualities in a common whole, so that one's very self, for many purposes at least, is the common life and purpose of the group. Perhaps the simplest way of describing this wholeness is by saying that it is a "we"; it involves the sort of sympathy and mutual identification for which "we" is the natural expression. One lives in the feeling of the whole and finds the chief aims of his will in that feeling.[2]

This view is amplified in well-known statements by Mead, who argues that self-concept and identity are products of collective action.[3]

Although the group at Jelly's possesses these basic characteristics of a primary group, it is really something more than a primary group is ordinarily conceived to be.[4] It is a large and loosely interrelated group of men who, despite their loose association, "keep up" with one another. They all know one another, at least by sight or by name, and they all matter to one another. They visibly affect one another by their actions and words, for every member of the group cares what others think about him and what actions they attribute to him. The group is made up of smaller subgroups whose members, in proper circumstances, display a close feeling for members of other subgroups. All the men have an affinity for Jelly's in contrast to the wider society outside. The men of Jelly's are peers in this fundamental respect. But the large, encompassing group is socially stratified and segmented, especially when certain issues involving individual status and identity come to the fore.

Competition and conflict among individual group members lend a certain extended character to the primary group. Various crowd identities emerge during social interaction, and senses of personal identity and status are shaped. Group members become selective about whom they hang with and about the particular liberties of association they allow. They begin to find ways to draw distinctions between themselves and others with whom they do not want to be confused. At the same time, through a process of selective association, they align themselves with others they are proud to claim as "partners" or fellow crowd members. Through this process of selective association, members of the extended primary group find "their own kind of people" among those available at Jelly's. When they are able to find something in common, to support or to oppose, group members develop and maintain a sense of belonging. But more specifically, they work to gain a relatively secure sense of place at Jelly's that is communicated and made known by the way others treat them there.

The sense of personal identity and place is not immediately transferable to just any other street-corner. When group members travel to different areas of the city, they must negotiate a place anew. Their personal status as defined in the setting of Jelly's cannot readily be carried along into different social situations. Unlike the members of more formal secondary groups in our society, group members cannot take their credits for status acquired at Jelly's to other settings and cash them in for regard and social rank. That these credits are good only with others at Jelly's is one of the fundamental reasons they return: Jelly's is a place where they are somebody.

For those who come to Jelly's and "belong" to the peer group, this setting often becomes the thick of their social life. Here are the others they really care about impressing—the people who really matter and who count in their immediate views of themselves. It is this general audience of peers that gains the real capacity to accept or reject the selves exhibited, at times shaping them in important ways. An individual's personal sense of rank and identity is precarious and action-oriented. Status depends in part on what deference others are willing and able to grant while attempting to maintain their own valued sense of themselves in the group. It is here among intimate peers that selves on display may be meaningfully accepted, "shot down," "blown away," tried and tested, or simply ignored. It is during sociability that the reactions to one's presentation of self take on special significance. Simmel speaks to the point here:

> everything may be subsumed under sociability which one can call sociological play-form; above all, play itself, which assumes a large place in the sociability of all epochs. The expression "social game" is significant in the deeper sense which I have indicated. The entire interactional or associational complex among men: the desire to gain advantage, trade, formation of parties and the desire to win from another, the movement between opposition and co-operation,

outwitting and revenge—all this, fraught with purposive content in
the serious affairs of reality, in play leads a life carried along only
and completely by the stimulus of these functions. For even when
play turns about a money prize, it is not the prize, which indeed
could be won in many other ways, which is the specific point of
the play; but the attraction for the true sportsman lies in the dynamics and in the chances of that sociologically significant form
of activity itself. The social game has a deeper double meaning—
that it is played not only *in* a society as its outward bearer but that
with its help people actually "play" "society." [Italics in original][5]

Competition is important to primary-group identity because it is
through competitive encounters that subgroups and cliques are formed
and become prominent. Through competitive relationships, the men
come to place themselves and others within the various crowds or
subgroups. Through a kind of psychological jostling, the members
of the various crowds get reminded of "who they are" within the
larger group, particularly when they act socially "below" or "above"
their stations. The strength of a person's claim to membership in a
certain crowd—that is, of his claim to a certain identity—vacillates
as a result of the changing issues that come up through group conversation and action.

People of different ranks within the group relate on a very personal basis, looking to one another for social evaluation. A member
is careful about selecting which other members he will stand off; he
tries to keep certain kinds of people from getting too close. He fully
allows some others to do as they please and even totally ignores still
others. At various times the large group becomes delineated into distinct and opposing groups for which "they" and "we" and "us" and
"y'all" seem to be the clearest expressions. Sides seem to be chosen
each time group members talk about other group members as "yo'
people" or "my people" or "yo' crowd."

Not all group life, of course, revolves around explicit competition.
In certain circumstances, especially in times of group trouble or tri-
umph, the extended group can become characterized by an intimate
"we" feeling. It is during these times that the group most closely
resembles Cooley's ideal "primary group." For example, when group

members sense some threat from the outside, "all kinds of people" are likely to come together, rendering what assistance they can. They may use the word "family" to refer to the extended primary group and at times actually act as family members—sharing, helping, and nurturing their own. It is at such times that the "we" feeling of what I call an extended primary group is most clearly expressed. The most important reason the group at Jelly's exists appears to be the degree and kind of sociability it affords. In the words of the group members, the group is one people feel they can "handle." Simmel's words are again germane:

> Sociability creates, if one will, an ideal sociological world, for in it—so say the enunciated principles—the pleasure of the individual is always contingent upon the joy of others; here, by definition, no one can have his satisfaction at the cost of contrary experiences on the part of others. . . . Inasmuch as sociability is the abstraction of association—an abstraction of the character of art or of play— it demands the purest, most transparent, most engaging kind of interaction—that among *equals*. It must, because of its very nature, posit beings who give up so much of their objective content, who are so modified in both their outward and their inner significance, that they are sociably equal, and every one of them can win sociability values for himself only under the condition that the others, interacting with him, can also win them.[6]

This quotation stresses the idea that in pure sociability no one gains at the expense of another and that all parties to the interaction are equal; that everyone gains from the situation of sociability. The men at Jelly's are equal in the sense that there is a general shared status of peer-group membership. The fact of ghetto blackness contributes profoundly to the sense of shared status.

But within the peer group at Jelly's, the men show themselves to be utterly unequal as they assert their individuality by drawing distinctions among others with whom they share the social space. If anyone in the peer group is able to make group and personal distinctions and successful claim to a status as somebody, according to whatever standard is important to the group at the time, he does so at the pleasure of others in the setting, with their tacit agreement and deference. A person is somebody because others allow him to be —and only when those making such allowances are allowed to be somebody themselves. A principle of social exchange is operating as group members negotiate for status and identity. Through the sociability at Jelly's, the men manage to rank themselves into at least three rough and somewhat overlapping groupings *that they refer to as* regulars, hoodlums, and wineheads.

The regulars, more successfully than any of the other groupings, appear to act out and uphold the more general social, moral, and legal codes often associated with the wider society. They pride themselves on their ability to hold steady jobs, which they refer to as having "a visible means of support," and look down suspiciously on those who are unable or unwilling to do so. Central to their values is the notion of "decency," which includes a willingness to work and to be law-abiding, and they judge others around Jelly's accordingly. They tend to be older men, and most are either married or "shackin' up," approximating what they regard as a decent life-style.[7] Many of these men sometimes speak apologetically of their own presence at Jelly's, claiming it as a place mainly for recreation, although their behavior while there suggests it is really much more important to them socially, since much of their leisure time is spent there. The time they spend at Jelly's corresponds roughly to their free time before and after work, or to times when they are either unemployed or "on vacation."

A second grouping, the hoodlums, often exhibits disdain, or ambivalence toward the morals and values associated with more conventional society. They are intimidating to the regulars and others, for their activities are known to include stickups, burglaries, fencing stolen property, public gambling, and hustling or trying to make money by any means other than a steady job. Although some have legitimate occupations, the hoodlums usually survive financially by illegal means. These men are usually younger, and most are proud products of the Chicago street gangs. Many have jail records that go back to adolescence or "bad" discharges from the military. Along with the recurrent unemployment problems of the national economy, these facts help make it hard for them to gain and hold a "visible means of support" or to find other conventional means of making a living. The types of employers that black men with few skills and inadequate education are likely to seek out tend to pay close attention to personal records. These facts also make easier their ideological rejection of, or at least their ambivalence toward, the values and standards of conduct upheld and displayed by the regulars. Thus the hoodlums seem to embrace more firmly the values and standards they know their kind can meet. They most admire the militant black, the pimp, the successful hoodlum and the "big-time" gangster, or anyone who "gets over" the barriers they see as placed by the wider social system. Also, they like to see and present themselves as "tough" and as able to get "big money" without having to rely on conventional means; they constantly look for opportunities to exhibit their ability to meet these values.[8] The hoodlums hang around Jelly's corner at all times of day and night, and some stay from early morning to late at night. Members of this group frequently engage in various forms of street crime.

A third grouping, the wineheads, represents a kind of residual category within the larger group, which regulars and hoodlums can, and sometimes do, fall into. Wineheads have limited informal rights, which is effectively demonstrated by the personal liberties regulars and hoodlums take with them. Many of the men in this group have "seen better days" as successful hoodlums or regulars, but because of wine or age, or both, they now lack the personal organization and resources necessary for commanding deference as hoodlums or regulars. If the wineheads work at all it is only sporadically, to get enough money for wine or food. Like the hoodlums, they tend to spend their days and nights hanging around Jelly's corner, begging passersby and various hoodlums and regulars for money. Many have no idea where they will sleep from night to night or where their next meal will come from. A few work sporadically or draw unemployment compensation or social security payments, which their kin usually help them spend.

On occasion there are a few women socializing at the bar, but they spend very little time at Jelly's compared with the time most of the men spend there. When the barroom side of Jelly's closed down during the study, the number of women dropped off. When women do come around, they try to get certain group members to buy drinks for them, and then they stand or sit around with the men. They laugh and talk and pass information back and forth, adding a certain spice to the sociability. Although the regulars are usually quick to offer drinks and company to these women, they generally feel that Jelly's is no place for a decent woman; it is not a place they would like their wives to visit.

Most group members believe they have a chance to be somebody according to some standard important at Jelly's. This belief is perhaps the main incentive for their repeated trips to Jelly's. For example, there hoodlums are able to demonstrate their hegemony over the status hierarchy of toughness without being challenged by most others because of the risk involved in "behaving like a hoodlum." They also attempt to show their ability to get "big dough" without working, exhibitions that rarely require strict proof. Regulars are able to demonstrate that they have money and a "visible means of support" and can thus substantiate their claims to decency. Usually, when the values of decency became status issues, others in the group defer to them. And wineheads are able to just be the group's wineheads, although few would proudly claim such an identity. But within the group even the disadvantaged winehead status conveys some rights of membership—some expectation of others' care and concern. They are known, and there are supportive social ties even for them at Jelly's, thus giving them a stake in the status system.

The Closing

Perhaps the most important event that alerted me to a conceptual problem and brought me to the conception of the "extended primary group" was a temporary closing of Jelly's bar and liquor store about six months after I began my fieldwork. The closing, which at the time was not known to be temporary, represented a crisis for many of those who were regular customers of Jelly's, but particularly for those of the immediate peer group. The whole of the bar and liquor store closed for about two months. After that the liquor-store side of the establishment reopened, but the barroom remained closed for the duration of the study. It was during the closing that I had my first close and enduring association with members of the general peer group. The intensity of this experience pointed up to me the real segmentation, as well as the social and emotional closeness, that I have come to see as characteristic of the extended primary group.

The closing caused some apparent changes in the ways the men conceived of one another and thus attempted to treat one another. Before the closing, for example, wineheads would usually come into the liquor store on business, to buy their wine. After making their purchases, since they did not feel welcome inside, they would generally leave for the alley or the nearby park, where they could drink and be sociable among their own kind. The group members who spent much time drinking inside the liquor store did not have to remind the wineheads to leave, for they seemed to know where to go on their own. Others who had reputations as "bad" or as "hoodlums" were also reluctant to hang where they did not "belong." The "decent" group members generally associated with their own kind, at times drinking and socializing on the barroom side of Jelly's, but usually a core group of them could be found drinking and hanging in the liquor-store room. Sometimes members of all the groupings of the general peer group could be seen moving back and forth from the street to the liquor store to the bar. While the liquor store and bar were open, these arrangements were regularized and even expected, and members of the extended primary group seemed obligated to follow them.

During the closing, when group members were without their conventional props for expressing their rights to this or that "turf," they found such obligations and expectations somewhat weakened. Hence they began examining social arrangements and involvements they had been able to take for granted and have confidence in. Finding themselves in a situation that seemed somewhat unclear and unwieldy, people began groping for ways of dealing with one another. If there was ever a time when group members felt the need to coach and remind each other of their obligations about place, it was then. It was in this context that group members appeared to make the most use of such words as "crowds," "kinds of people," "yo' people" and "my people," to refer to various individuals and divisions of the extended primary group. With the normal rise and fall of various issues, the peer group, which to me had once seemed so unified, if not intimate, now took on a more obviously divided and extended character.

During this time group members continued to meet on Jelly's corner, in the alley outside, and in the park nearby, even though Jelly's was closed. For instance:

> I arrived at Jelly's corner on Sunday at 10:30 A.M. It was a chilly and overcast morning. Six men were standing near Jelly's doorway, socializing as they do when the place is open. Bemo stood in the doorway with his hands dug into his pants pockets. Oscar leaned against the big window. Duky dragged slowly on his cigarette. Mack asked Duky for a "square" (cigarette), but Duky said the lit "square" was his last, so Mack settled for a drag of that. The men laughed and talked about the events of the night before and watched the cars and pedestrians go by. We stood around there for more than two hours. New people trickled up and others left, slowly changing the character of the group.

Day after day, hour after hour, members of the group would intermittently come up to Jelly's. Sometimes they came in small groups of two or three, sometimes alone. While gathering and milling together to be sociable, the men would joke, argue, or play with one another, spending their time on the street corner. For many of the men, Jelly's was "the only place to go."

During the closing, the men often expressed their anger about it and looked for someone to blame for the inconvenience. Many times, in the afternoon or evening, a number of us would put our heads together and try to come up with some explanation. One man might speculate, "It's the city's fault. They been tryin' to close him for a long time anyhow." Someone might then suggest that "Jelly just couldn't drop that iron on the man," meaning that he was unable or unwilling to make payments to the "right people downtown." Or someone else might say, "You know a black man ain't got no chance in this city 'long as Daley up in there." And still another person might counter this with, "You know it's Jelly's fault. He never would keep this fuckin' place clean. Cat had all that shit [boxes and papers] stacked up all over the place. It's a wonder they let him stay open long as they did. The place was a fire hazard, and them honkies downtown ain't standin' for that."

One afternoon a number of us were gathered at Jelly's door watching the traffic and the people. The conversation turned to Jelly's closing.

"I thought Jelly was gon' open back up this week sometime," said Sam.

"Nah," said Red Mack, a person I heard others call a winehead. "He can't handle them honkies downtown. You know they be fuckin' wit' him. I bet he tried to stop payin' the man off. And the man ain't hearin' that shit, not from no Jelly."

"Yeah," said Jimmy Lee, "they don't wanna see no black man get nothin'."

"But you know, too, ol' Fisher [the grocery owner] been wantin' Jelly outa here for years. Maybe he did it. He want the place for himself," interrupted Tooney, a Puerto Rican.

"Well, if he do, I ain't gon' patronize him," proclaimed Red Mack, "I'll take my business elsewhere!"

"What business?" yelled Knaky, "You ain't got no business, Mack. How you gon' patronize somebody, when you ain't never got no money—wit' yo' beggin' winehead ass."

At this the others began to laugh. But Mack remained silent, checking himself, as he slunk away. He seemed to want to say something but lacked the confidence, fearing that Knaky might come down on him again in front of the others and make him look stupid. After a few minutes the group broke up and the men went their own ways. Some left in what the men referred to as "crowds" and some went by themselves. They had speculated enough for now. It was time to get the rest of the day and the evening together.

It was situations like this that alerted me to the distinctions group members made among the various "kinds of people" who made up the particular crowds at Jelly's. These units, however ephemeral their definition may appear at first sight, together make up the extended primary group. The following field note shows the process through which group members begin to join with others and set themselves up as distinctive entities:

At about 5 P.M. on a Monday, five members of the regular crowd stood around in front of Jelly's closed doorway. Though Jelly's bar and liquor store had now been closed for about three weeks, the men continued to gather there. Herman, T. J., Mr. Frazier, Bill, and Otis were standing in the doorway watching the traffic. When I arrived, they greeted me.

"Hey, Eli," yelled Herman, as he grabbed me.

"Hey, Herman," I returned.

The others chimed in their hellos. Then T. J. "hit on me" (asked me) for a dollar to help him on "a taste" (a bottle of whiskey), as he waved his own dollar bill at me. I then reached in my pocket and came up with a dollar and gave it to him, and he went off to fetch the whiskey at another liquor store about a block down the street.

But when T. J. returned the character of the group had changed. Curtis, Knaky, and Genie Boy, three of the "hoodlum" crowd, had appeared. Surprised at this development, T. J. began passing out the cups to those of us "in on the taste," excluding the hoodlums. He fumbled with the cups, as though he was nervous about the prospect of not sharing the whiskey with the hoodlums. As we regulars began drinking, the three hoodlums began to talk among themselves. Shortly, Smoke and Mooney, two more hoodlums, appeared. They began asking T. J. for a "hit" (a drink of whiskey), which he characteristically refused by saying, "There's just enough for us," meaning the regulars present. Refused, they first continued to hang with our group but slowly began to gather and talk with the other hoodlums. Two distinct groups were beginning to form on the basis of drinking. Five or ten minutes elapsed. Two separate conversations emerged—that of the regulars and that of the hoodlums. Just then Wallace, another hoodlum, and Red Mack, a winehead, appeared. Wallace produced a fifth of wine from his hip pocket and took a long swig. "Hey! Hey! Hold! That's mine, too!" shouted Red Mack, in mock concern over the wine. He grabbed for the bottle. Wallace pulled back. Good naturedly, Red Mack and Wallace struggled for the bottle. The others laughed and urged them on, but soon they stopped their play. Red Mack took his drink, then offered the bottle to the other hoodlums, seeming to know better than to offer it to the regulars, since they are known not to drink "that stuff." The hoodlums readily accepted the wine and passed it around. Now the talk became louder; there was more cursing and shouting. Soon the number of regulars began to taper off. First Mr. Frazier left, then Bill, and finally T. J., muttering something about how he had to get home to his kids. Within the space of twenty minutes the character of the group changed. Soon Herman and I left the corner to the hoodlums.

Group members tend to use the term "crowd" to refer to small, ideal groups of people who are active in the setting. At times they use it in a facetious yet meaningful way to remind certain people of "who they are" and to sort out people and render them more manageable as members of units within the larger group.[9] Crowds, as the men understand them, provide the members of the extended primary group with subgroups of others to "be with"—"marked" equals and nonequals with whom to associate. Through efforts to distance themselves from the "wrong type o' people," group members generally come to agree on who belongs to which crowd. But such agreement cannot always be counted on, for the men sense that relationships, issues, and resources for commanding deference easily change hands and at times are loosely held. Yet group members have collectively labeled the various crowds and their members and have assigned a relative informal standing to each. Hence their notions about crowds and about the values by which the crowds are assigned their relative status point up the segmentation within the group. The following experience that Herman, Pee Wee, and I had illustrates these points.

One evening Herman, Pee Wee—a thirty-three-year-old employed printer's aide—and I went to Jelly's for the express purpose of finding someplace else to go. We went there first "just to see what's happening"—a reason many of the members give for coming to Jelly's, though their behavior while there suggests they are also looking for sociability with the fellows. The three of us drove up to the corner and immediately caught the attention of a small group of men standing outside talking. The group included Sleepy, Uncle Rip, Mack, Leroy, and Stump.

After parking, we got out of the car and greeted the fellows. Herman greeted Sleepy with, "What's happening?" Sleepy answered, "You got it!" His answer implied that nothing significant had happened since Herman had last seen him, the day before. "Real news" might have been a shooting, a stabbing, a death, or some other event important to the extended primary group. Had he had any real news, Sleepy probably would have blurted it out, perhaps in an attempt to gain esteem for "bringing it to us."

In Herman's mind, as in the minds of the others of the extended primary group, Sleepy has a place. He is a winehead. He is known as someone who "drinks a lot of wine, don't work much, but don't mean nobody no harm." But also, he is known as someone who keeps close tabs on the others and on the daily occurrences around Jelly's. A few minutes after he greeted Sleepy, Herman said to me, "If there's anything you ever want to know about, Eli, just ask ol' Sleepy. He know it all." Sleepy, standing within earshot, grinned at this remark as though he had been stroked—which he had—for playing out a script everyone could approve of.

Later the men laughed and talked among themselves, reminiscing about the good and bad times they had had together. Some talked about what they intended to do the next day. One man bragged about his "nice li'l family" and flashed his family picture around. He was a regular. Another man talked about the night he had spent in jail a couple of weeks before, telling the story in an excited manner. The regulars consider this man a hoodlum. There were all "kinds of people" socializing at Jelly's on this day. Mainly, the men were having their fun by being with their friends—raising issues, arguing, play-fighting, laughing, and talking—then leaving the corner with members of their own crowds for other bars or joints inside or outside the immediate area.

Soon Herman said to me, "Let's go somewhere. Let's split, Eli." At this, Pee Wee looked up, as if at a signal, and walked over to us. The three of us then started walking toward my car. Sleepy, still

nearby but among the others, began to walk with us. Then Herman
looked at Sleepy and shook his head as if to say, "No, Sleepy. You
ain't goin' wit' us." Sleepy responded to this simple gesture by just
staying behind, not pressing Herman to say no to him aloud. Group
members have rejected him aloud before, and it embarrasses him.
Not wanting to risk this from Herman, Sleepy opted to stay behind
with no protest, acknowledging this reminder of his place. He simply
deferred to Herman.

On another occasion when a number of us were standing outside
Jelly's doorway, certain people again had to be reminded of their
places. On this day about ten men were milling about in front and
in the alley on the side of Jelly's building. Larry and Tall Joe, who
are considered wineheads, had been arguing for much of the time.
The argument was now becoming bitter. Larry threatened Joe with,
"I'll cut yo' throat, man. You just don't know who you fooling with."
Joe moved away, but Larry slowly pursued him. As their argument
became more and more heated, they moved closer to the space occu-
pied by the regulars. At this point Otis, a regular who was standing
in front of the door, shouted, "Now, why don't y'all ack like ya' got
some sense and stop all this mess!" Others who were standing with
Otis chimed in, "Yeah, why don't y'all carry that mess somewhere
else?" Bill, another regular, said, "G'wan back in the alley with all
that fight talk. We [regulars] tryin' to have some peace and quiet."
At these suggestions from "decent" people, Larry and Joe stopped
their arguing. Later, both were standing around in the doorway in
imitation of the regulars, "tryin' to have some peace and quiet." Attempting to listen in on the regulars' "heavy conversation," both men
seemed to have forgotten they had ever been at odds. The regulars
had reminded them of "who they were" and that their fighting was
disruptive. Larry and Joe clearly deferred.

Through such demeanor and acts of deference, which are common
around Jelly's, the social order becomes more clearly defined. It is
through this type of social interaction that the status system is often
tried and found out. Herman's place and Sleepy's place were both
effectively demonstrated for all who cared enough to pay attention.
And Larry and Joe pointed up the place of the regulars in relation

to the wineheads. Such actions help inform people about the informal status system operating at Jelly's, and the corresponding notions they express provide a general sense of who fits where, of who can do what to whom, and in what circumstances. At the same time, the men gain a sense of who is low, who is high, who is "fuckin' up" and who is "comin' along," and from where.

One of the most interesting features of the closing was the way the men managed their places without their conventional arena and the supports that went along with it. While Jelly's was closed, group members had to be out-of-doors in order to satisfy their need for sociability, and so they attempted more so than usual to manage sociability on the sidewalk and in the alley nearby.

But there they were all lumped together, with a certain social nakedness. Now, the men seemed more sensitive about their respective places. Gone were some of the important and relatively easy markers of one's place, such as demonstrating one's closeness to Jelly himself by being able to make full use of either room or to take certain liberties with seats in the liquor store. During this period some of the group members exhibited a need to find and to indicate new markers of status and esteem.

One way the men dealt with this was to rely more on the nature of their associations to uphold their claims about who they were. People seemed especially sensitive about who they associated with, as in the foregoing incident with Herman and Sleepy. Sleepy was trying to associate with Herman by "runnin' " with us, and Herman resisted Sleepy by reminding him of who he was—a winehead—and putting him in his place by treating him as a winehead.

The men also dealt with the threat to their social order through talk. It became apparent to me not only that people within the group associated only with certain others, but that one basis of the selective association was an ability to "talk about" yet other people. Through this talk, which was usually invidious, the men defined not only the members of other crowds, but also themselves. For example, "regulars" would gather and talk about wineheads; when a person they considered a winehead entered their vicinity the topic usually changed or the person being talked about would leave to be with men he believed were similar to himself or that he thought he could more readily handle—group members who were less willing or able to remind him of his shortcomings. Hoodlums often got together and talked about those they saw as regulars or as wineheads, and at times those even *they* saw as hoodlums, comparing notes on the activities of such people. When there were few or no regulars present, members of the other groups often attempted to claim this identity for themselves, but they would readily defer when "real" regulars appeared. The same was true for hoodlum status; when hoodlum traits seemed to offer advantages of group standing, some regulars attempted to lay claim to them until "real" hoodlums appeared, but then they returned to their accustomed social place. No one tried to assume winehead traits for esteem.

When Jelly's reopened after two months, the liquor-store area became a kind of functional bar used mainly by the men of the extended group. Women stopped coming around regularly, for there was no really decent place for them to sit and they would not stand around as the men did. Customers continued to buy packaged liquor, beer, and wine, but after their transactions they almost always left the premises. The visitors of the barroom side also stopped coming. The place was left to the members of the peer group, but particularly to the regulars, who continued to come to the liquor store, buy their "tastes" with their friends, and drink illegally in front of Jelly's wobbly old counter. They enlisted Jelly himself as "bartender." Now Jelly served up packaged liquor and cans of beer to be consumed on the premises, in defiance of the law. Concerned about the social control of his clientele, Jelly did not allow wine-drinking inside the liquor store, which excluded many wineheads and hoodlums.

As a result of the barroom's being closed, new rules emerged for the liquor-store room. When the barroom and the liquor store were open together, only group members able to claim "decency" or those "in good" with Jelly were allowed to drink and hang in the liquor store. But now, with only the liquor-store side open, almost anyone who "knew how to act right" was allowed to drink and hang around inside. Those who displayed "rowdy" and "boisterous" behavior, mainly wineheads and hoodlums, were discouraged from hanging around. When they persisted, and when their numbers grew too large, Jelly himself became somewhat nervous and would sometimes usher them out or demand that they leave. At times he would threaten them with the "piece" (pistol) he kept under the counter. But the order he wanted was usually not difficult to enforce, for most of the peer-group members would rally to his side against the "rowdy ones" and even help him put them out when necessary.

With this type of group enforcement of order and the general absence of visitors and women, Jelly's took on the character of a clubhouse whose members would hang inside or outside on the corner. The clubhouse definition was clearly evident as the peer group interaction inside the liquor store became all the more punctuated by the coming and going of Jelly's customers. For example, when customers entered the group's normal talk and behavior would stop at least for a moment. This sometimes happened on the initiative of the group members, but sometimes it was at the command of Jelly himself. The men understood that Jelly's trade deserved a certain degree of deference. But they also initiated the quiet in order to "check out" and identify the intruders so appropriate behavior could be enacted.

Appropriate group or individual behavior at Jelly's may take different forms depending on how the intruder is interpreted and defined or what he means to the group members present at the time. For instance, when the intruder is a strange customer, the noise level will sometimes automatically recede and a semblance of order and "good behavior" will be maintained until the person leaves, especially if it is a woman. If a group member accidentally swears or shouts too loudly in front of an outsider, he may put his hand over his mouth and say "excuse me" while others look at him with disapproval. At other times, when a customer is familiar to the group, the noise level and goings-on are interrupted only briefly and may be quickly resumed when the intruder passes inspection. On occasion, newcomers give off clear danger signs, and the group will judge them to "bear watching." When this happens the men usually stay quiet and keep their eyes on the strangers until they leave, then talk about them. They are said to "look like" strange gangsters, pimps, dope pushers, undercover policemen, or "jitterbugs tryin' to go for bad." The group views them as outsiders who may mean trouble and communicates this by their actions. Through their rituals of silence group members more clearly define their collective place at Jelly's as private. Their demeanor toward insiders and outsiders reminds group members that they do constitute a group and also reminds them who they are in relation to each other.[10]

By behaving in a particular way, according to some rule or standard group members hold important, people let others know what "kinda studs" they are. Every kind of interaction may be important in interpreting and defining the social order. What people say and do to one another is important, as are the tone of voice and the circumstances in which talk and interaction occur. Through interpretations and definitions of interaction, group members learn how to treat still others in the setting; what who can get away with from whom and what that might mean for their own future interaction with the persons involved.

In sum, it is through such interactions that group members remind others, and get reminded themselves, of "who is who." People are what others allow them to be. Moral support for the selves they present is sought and sometimes gained by accepting the agreed-on arrangement of relative statuses and at times by challenging such arrangements. Accordingly, they seek association with certain kinds of people and avoid the company of others, and they treat accordingly those whom they sense to be important to their desired self-conceptions. Thus, people negotiate for regard and social place within the extended primary group. Social order exists because people stay in their places, and they do that because other people help keep them there.

People who return often to Jelly's will somehow fit themselves into the peer group. They lobby for acceptance and through this process develop a sense of belonging. Peer-group members pay for the acceptance of their selves by taking on definite statuses and playing appropriate roles in the existing social order, roles that depend on the meanings their social characteristics have for the self-presentations of others. The kind of behavior others allow them in varying circumstances encourages them to adopt certain postures and

actions toward others in the group, and through this process of negotiation social characteristics become sources of esteem, envy, resentment, denigration, or praise. In effect, they become status resources.
The collective and the individual sense of the relative distribution
of these resources within the peer group helps determine social rank,
as a mental picture emerges of existing status arrangements. Group
members tacitly recognize the ranking system through the various
kinds of demeanor and specific deference they exhibit for deserving
others. They tend to act in accord with this ranking system, particularly their personal versions of it, and to gain some stake in what
becomes the social construction of these arrangements that constitutes a social order. They attempt to routinize and fortify their personal conceptions of the arrangements in the group by behaving and
encouraging others to behave "in line."

Yet the particular status arrangements are ever-changing and precarious. To a large extent status in the group depends on the impression the person fosters and on those his audience holds. To some
degree the quality of impressions is affected by the manageability of
group circumstances and situations. People compete for favored
positions within the group, based on the control they can demonstrate over the numerous and socially complex matters that here
become status issues. One's suitability for a given status or place is
judged by others who are competitors. Hence, there is a certain distrust of favored identities claimed, particularly identities associated
with the wider society. With their own sense of low status in the
wider society, the peer-group members at Jelly's have few grounds
for trusting such identities in one another. So status claims are most
effectively made through specific actions rather than by mere reference to a social position. Group members often demand visible evidence. Rank often depends upon what a person can prove he is in
relationship to, yet socially distinct from, others at Jelly's.

In attempting to develop some basis of trust for the identities
they present, group members have created their own local stratification system. They have created an incentive system of roles and
identities within which people can be somebody and establish a
more trustworthy social world. In line with this, the status arrange-

ments may best be described as collective action: people together are constantly lobbying for advantage by reminding others through meaningful conduct of the collective sense of who is who, who is what, and who and what stand in relation to whom.

The resulting identities and status distinctions are largely contrastive: a person knows who he is or to what "crowd" he belongs in part by knowing about the subgroups, statuses, and identities to which he does not belong and which others will not allow him to claim. He learns this, and his place, through the relative treatment he can give and receive within the extended primary group as others react to the self he presents. As explained above, the principal "crowds" that result from these stratifying interactions are, to use the men's own terms, the "regulars," the "wineheads," and the "hoodlums." Though it is possible to single out a core of members who "belong" to each crowd, it is important to recognize that these distinctions often depend upon prevailing circumstances. As we shall see in the following chapters, on some occasions even the most "regular" person in one collection of men may not be able to claim that identity in another collection.

3 | The Regulars

At Jelly's, all the men of the extended primary group are "regulars" in the sense that they come regularly to Jelly's and have a social stake in the establishment and in the group. But there has emerged a small group of men who consider themselves a distinct and identifiable category of the wider group. They refer to themselves and are referred to by others as "regulars." These are people who enact what they consider to be roles of respectability. They want to be treated as respectable, especially by those in other categories of the wider group. In general these men are older than the others, ranging in age from about thirty-five to seventy. They work regularly, which for them constitutes a primary social value.[1] More than any of the other groups, they are willing and able to maintain steady employment. Many see and present themselves as "hardworking men," who will jump at any chance to work long hours with as much overtime as possible. Some even hold two jobs. Also important, these men strive to "have something"—a nice car, a house, nice furniture —usually something material that they can work toward and pay for over time. Many of these men are proudly involved in stable nuclear family arrangements. And for their family members, especially their children, they tend to have "decent" and upwardly mobile aspirations. A few attend church with their families, perhaps even singing in the Sunday gospel choir. Compared to members of other groupings at Jelly's, they tend to be more stable both socially and economically. Their system of values might be summed up in one word—"decency."[2] Regulars judge others according to their notions of decency and reserve this term for those they consider like themselves. To meet their standards of conduct, others must work regularly, "treat other people right," be of "strong character" and "some 'count," and "worthwhile to be around." To have achieved such positive evaluation in the judgment of regulars and others is to be accorded the label of "regular" and, during social interaction, to be included among regulars within the extended primary group.

Some of the Regulars

T. J. is a heavyset, dark-skinned man of fifty-five. Born and raised in South Carolina, he arrived in Chicago some twenty-five years ago in search of a better life situation, especially steady and high-paying employment. His first jobs were in factories and steel mills and at construction sites. After about eight years he was hired by Commonwealth Edison, where he has been steadily employed for the past seventeen years. Around Jelly's this is an impressive work record, since many of the men are willing or able to work only sporadically or not at all. Proud of his outstanding work record, T. J. does not let the others forget it, for it adds credence to his sense of himself as "decent" and worthwhile. He is formally married and the father of three daughters, so his family life provides another distinction between him and a number of the other men. Like his "good job," the stability of his legal marriage and his "nice li'l family" and home contribute to his image of "decency." They are qualities that help others trust T. J. for being of "some 'count."

T. J. arrives at Jelly's almost every day about 4:00 P.M., a time that fits in nicely with the arrival of others of his "crowd." He usually arrives on the scene neatly dressed in moderately priced sports clothes. On summer afternoons at Jelly's, T. J. looks like he has just stepped off the golf course; he wears a straw hat "broke down" in front, cream-colored slacks, and white shoes. Consistently dressed in this style, he seems far removed from his job as a lineman, in which he had been so deeply involved only an hour before.

When he arrives, T. J. usually stands around posing and showing off his latest outfit. People pay him compliments, which he has come to expect and appreciate. The compliments reward him for dressing well and posturing and inspire him to continue, and T. J. seems almost obligated to show off. When he is not dressed and "clean," he will sometimes apologize to his audience.

While standing around posing, T. J. usually looks for members of his "crowd" with whom to get a "taste." If there are no regulars around, he will sometimes settle for members of the other crowds. Because of this, other regulars sometimes "talk about" T. J., accusing him of "trying to blend in with them young hoodlums" and reminding him of his place. It is not unusual to see T. J., with wrinkled dollar bill in hand, saying, "Hey, let's get this taste," or "C'mon, help me out on this taste," though he usually has more than enough money in his pocket to buy the whole bottle. Usually, through his or someone else's efforts, a group of regulars will get enough money together for a half-pint of Old Forester or whatever other whiskey they decide on. This effort will usually take care of his need for drink until dinnertime, at which point he will be off for his "decent" home. At times he hangs around and gets so involved in the activities that he will stay and "get tore up" (drunk), in which case he may not get home until very late.

When he does go, T. J., like most other members of the regular crowd, leaves the social involvements of Jelly's—except for a few other regulars—at Jelly's. He distrusts most of the men he associates with, fearing that they would "make him look bad" in other social settings or that some of them might actually "rip him off," given the chance. Thus he tries to leave the "streets" in the streets. But while there T. J. likes to posture as a man who can "handle" the streets and the people on them, even though others, as we will see later, are not always willing to accept this script from him.

Bill Porter is sixty-one years old, stands six feet three, and weighs about two hundred pounds. Mainly because of his age, but also because of his size and reputation, group members address him as "Mr. Porter." Group members tend to call older regulars Mister but they withhold this form of address from older wineheads. Mr. Porter is a native of rural Georgia. He arrived in Chicago at twenty-three and has been "workin' hard all my life. I'm's a hardworkin' man." Mr. Porter is proud of this image and demands respect for it around Jelly's. He is a stern man who is seldom seen laughing and playing with others, and at times he can be seen and heard "preaching" to the wineheads and hoodlums, and even to some other regulars, about being "right" and "decent." He "gets on" the hoodlums and wineheads for their "loud and boisterous" talk and their "nothin' ways." Sometimes, when with a crowd of regulars, he will try to make fun of some wineheads or hoodlums.

Mr. Porter is single and has no known kin in the area. He lives in a tenement not far from Jelly's. When he arrives, usually about 4:00 P.M. every day, he stands around with the men he feels are worthy of his company and association. As he likes to say, "I ain't got no time for no 'counts." Acting this out, regardless of whom he is standing with Mr. Porter shows that he is very conscious of the time and nervously looks at his watch as though he has some very important appointment to keep. This is his way of reminding group members of who he is, a self-consciously regular person whose time is valuable. After a short time he leaves Jelly's for his home, his work—or somewhere. Mr. Porter sees himself as "too decent to hang around a joint like this" for long. Yet he comes regularly.

Born and raised on Chicago's West Side, Nathaniel is a "hardworking" construction man of forty-two. He stands five feet nine and weighs about 215 pounds; he is solid muscle except for his beer belly. Nathaniel has a "good" discharge from the army and stays out of trouble around Jelly's. I have seen him walk away from a fight saying, "Aw man. It's too hot." But group members say he will fight if he gets angry and that he "hits hard." Nathaniel now works regularly for a construction company. Because he is "in good" with the owner, he is never laid off and is able to move around the city to wherever the work happens to be. He has this "in" because he is known to be a hard worker; he works long hours and some weekends. He often tries to remind some of the unemployed men at Jelly's that if they are good, he might get them "on construction," but he doubts that "many men could work like I do." He never comes through on his promises of jobs, and this has earned him the nickname "Mouth."

Nathaniel is legally married and the father of two little girls aged seven and eight. He is also the stepfather of two older girls, aged fifteen and seventeen. In line with the regulars' conception of "decency" and his own sense of manhood, Nathaniel "claims" the two stepchildren and tries to treat them as he does his natural children. One of the older ones, for instance, is about to go to college, a fact Nathaniel will not let the group members forget as he flashes her picture and brags about her achievements as if they were his own. His boasting about the young woman goes on until someone reminds him that she is not his own and really "belongs" to someone else. At this Nathaniel's "jaws get tight" (he becomes silent but perturbed), yet he quietly accepts the place presented him, acknowledging that he is not the girl's "real" father.

Sometimes Nathaniel arrives at Jelly's wearing his work clothes, usually still damp with sweat and covered with brown construction sand. He seems to wear them as a badge attesting that he works hard for his living. Now and again someone will remind him of how dirty he is, and he replies, "I'm a hardworkin' man. What'cha expect me to look like?" He then laughs off the matter and finds someone to drink with. Usually he will drink with almost anyone except one of the wineheads, for he detests their begging and "freeloading." "I work, they can work too. They ain't no better than I am!" Also, like many of the regulars, Nathaniel will not drink wine in public, since "that's what low-life people do," but he will drink "good stuff" in public. After drinking "good stuff"—whiskey, vodka, or gin—for two or three hours or until dinnertime, he leaves for his home and the dinner his wife has prepared. On occasion he will take a "regular" friend home to share his "good thing."

Pee Wee is a brown-skinned, thirty-four-year-old employed printer's aid. He is five feet eleven inches tall and weighs about 160 pounds. Pee Wee is happily married and has three daughters. Very proud of his family, he balances his time between Jelly's and home. Pee Wee says he got married "to try to have something." He grew up about a mile from Jelly's among the street gangs that dominated the area at that time. He highly values the "education I got out in these streets." After graduating from high school, a rare achievement for anyone hanging around the streets, the alley, and the corner near Jelly's, Pee Wee joined the army paratroopers and served in the

Dominican Republic. He was a "good soldier" and received an honorable discharge from the army, which distinguishes him still further. This background gives Pee Wee a certain amount of esteem both among the more street-oriented members in the peer group, many of whom regard toughness as a primary virtue, and among the regulars, who value formal education and decency. Pee Wee's posture in the group is that of a quiet but tough person. He "never bothers nobody" and "nobody never bothers him." From his posture and reputation, group members generally like and respect Pee Wee.

For the regulars, "strong character," being of "some 'count," and "decency" are the very important values. Regulars gravitate toward those who demonstrate decency through their actions and attempt, not always successfully, to avoid those who do not. They like to be around those who "treat other people right." They admire and trust those who can demonstrate a "visible means of support," which they often consider one of the primary characteristics of a decent person, particularly if the person is friendly and amiable with them. The people they consider "low class" and "no 'count"—wineheads and hoodlums—generally cannot offer evidence of a job or a secure place in the wider society, and thus they "bear watching."

The most impressive evidence of this secure place in the wider society is the nature of a person's visible means of support. Occupations that give the regulars their special relationship to the wider society range from factory work to janitorial service to truck driving. A few men work two jobs. The most important characteristic of a job is its regularity, but also important is the amount of money it pays and the status and identity it confers on the person as "a hard-working man." Just having a job lends the jobholder an aura of reliability among the fellows at Jelly's. Before group members are willing to grant their trust, they usually want to know if a man works. Hence, types of jobs regarded as worthwhile and decent can range across a broad spectrum, owing in large part to the men's appreciation of what limited types of occupations historically have been and still are available to lowly-educated black men. At Jelly's a large variety of work tasks can contribute to a respectable identity. The basic status issue is usually whether or not the man works.

That working regularly constitutes an important value within the extended primary group is borne out by the regulars' attitude toward unemployment. Unemployment insurance and welfare relief can sometimes provide as much money as some of the jobs available to men of the group. This might seem to be an incentive not to work, and for some of the men it is. But regulars look down on those who don't work. They distrust those who resort to welfare payments, seeing them as something less than full men. To be a full-fledged regular, or to be worthy of the esteem and respect of regulars, a man must work. For the regulars do not work for money alone; they also seek decency and respectability.[3] As L. C., a "hard-working man" employed at the local Ford factory, said to me one evening:

> "For a man to be al'right in my book, he got to work, or at least be tryin' to get some work. That's the first thing. Long as he workin' for a living, you know, out there doin' what I'm doin', well I got to respect him. Am I right or wrong? See, 'cause when we was comin' up, my daddy always told us, 'Don't be afraid of work. Don't be too proud to shovel shit all day, if you have to.' No matter what you have to do, you got to live, you know. When a man is workin' hard all day, 'stead of layin' 'round these here streets, well, he showin' me a good side of hisself. He at least *some* 'count."

Most regulars are in basic agreement with L. C.'s thinking, that a man is to be respected as long as he works for a living.

Although it is not an outstanding belief, regulars do seem to recognize some hierarchy among "kinds of jobs." This seems especially true as more kinds of positions have become available to blacks. People working in "sit-down" or white-collar jobs are viewed as "having it made." Group members regard them as "not working hard," especially in comparison with the "hardworking men" they know who work in the steel mills, on construction, and in other laboring occupations.[4] Yet though sit-down jobs are believed to be easy, they are thought to be high-paying and are esteemed by regulars and others at Jelly's, who strongly associate decency with such "clean" jobs. Though they are generally resigned to their own inability to get such jobs, they look forward to seeing their children do so. For most regulars, the means to these decent and clean jobs are job-training for a trade or formal education. That this is a strong feeling among the regulars is indicated in the following conversation of Pee Wee, a regular, whose wife, Sal, was in the hospital preparing to give birth.

About six of us, all regulars, were standing around outside Jelly's when Bill asked, "Hey, Pee Wee, Sal had her baby yet?" "Nah, she ain't come through yet," answered Pee Wee. At this, others present chimed in, showing interest in the topic. "I know you want a boy, don'cha, Pee?" inquired Ollie. "I'll be happy with whatever comes, 'long as it's alive and well. But I'll tell you one thing. If it do turn out to be a boy, he ain't gon' wind up like none o' you studs up in here," Pee Wee joked, shaking his head and grinning. "He gon' grow up and get educated and be intelligent. Gon' get him a good job when he get big! He gon' be somebody! He ain't gon' be like none o' y'all." Pee Wee and the others laughed along with this and the manner in which he said it. But it was a serious statement in that Pee Wee had underscored his desire that his prospective son acquire a "decent" occupation, not just any job.

The men easily understood Pee Wee's point of view, for it fits well with their own. Some of the men often brag about the "good" jobs their children are beginning to get. They keep a running verbal record of the jobs and other socially redeeming achievements and activities of one another's offspring. For example, Bill will not allow the men to forget that his son went to IBM school, now works in the Loop, and takes an "extra long" lunch hour in some "big shot" restaurant downtown. Then there's Otis, who brags about his daughter, who is "gon' be a schoolteacher." He keeps the fellows up to date about her latest activities "in college" and talks about the money he must send for her support. Many such tales about their offspring are accompanied by photographs that they show at the least opportunity. Most of the men of the regular group who have children will say they want them to have "the chance I didn't have."

For regulars, personal status and value are most ably demonstrated and expressed through the display of evidence of one's visible means of support. For them, and for others, nothing seems to speak more strongly about one's character than one's way of "making a living." This helps to define the person, to indicate "the way he is." When group members see a person going to work every day and coming to Jelly's at a regular time, they can begin to place some trust in him, particularly when he tries to associate or actually associates with those who work. Regulars can begin to assume that the person has something in common with them. He can be viewed as of "some 'count," for in some measure he does what they do. They can identify with him on the assumption that he can meaningfully identify with them.

When regulars find their own values expressed in another's behavior, they can begin to treat him as "safe." Around Jelly's, a person who "don't work" "bears watching," particularly if he hangs around and associates closely with others who don't work. The regulars generally feel that there are numerous members of the wider group who don't work and who will "rip off" others of the group if given the chance. Regulars don't want to become victims and as a precautionary measure they watch out for them. They try to keep them at a social distance and categorize them as hoodlums or wineheads.

Another expression of the regulars' values is sharing with fellow regulars. It is particularly important to have the financial ability to do so, for this is a mark of distinction and one of the criteria for inclusion in the regular crowd. Members are ready to assume that a person drawing a salary can carry his own when it comes to "getting a taste." They expect their fellow regulars to be able and willing to share, not to "always be bummin' off people." What one is able to share, of course, is based upon what one claims as possessions. Regulars give one another various forms of help, particularly social favors. It is part of the relationship among regulars to look to one another for financial and other types of support that only working people are considered able to render. For example, the working person is considered an asset to other regulars when they need a loan. It is the custom for them to borrow money from one another, usually with few questions asked. For example:

On Tuesday evening, Bill, Otis, T. J., Mr. Thompson, Jelly, Red Mack, Sleepy, and I stood around in the liquor-store room. Red Mack and Sleepy were the only wineheads present; the others were regulars. At one point Otis said, "How much money you got, Bill?" "Oh, 'bout a couple million. What, you want some?" Bill replied. "Yeah," said Otis, "Lemme hold twenty dollars." With no further questions, Bill took out his wallet, picked out a twenty-dollar bill, and handed it over to Otis. Everyone in the room observed this transaction, but no one commented. It was not unusual for regulars to behave this way.

Regulars appear to deserve favors from one another. A principle of social exchange is involved in these relationships, as regulars give and expect to receive various kinds of help. A regular will give support to another regular with the understanding that the support will be reciprocated. Wineheads and hoodlums of the extended primary group are rarely, if ever, in a position to pay back such favors to those who successfully claim to be regulars. And no self-respecting regular would put himself in the position of asking a winehead or a hoodlum for a favor, especially a financial one. Thus the exchanges help define and affirm the solidarity of regulars as a collectivity in which each member is a partner in the definition of being a regular.[5] Further:

I had just bought a half-pint of bourbon to give to Spider, a marginal person in the group, for helping me out of a tight spot with some hoodlums I did not know well at an early stage of the fieldwork (see pp. 202–4). Spider was not around, and I had to leave shortly. So I gave the half-pint of bourbon to Herman to give to Spider. "Now be sure to give it to him, Herman," I said. "I am. I'm gon' give it to him. And that's gon' buzz the shit out o' that nigger [pleasantly surprise and confuse]. See, 'cause li'l shit like that'll put something on a cat's mind. It might make him treat other people right. It might make him get up and get him a job, no tellin'."

For the regulars, the ability to be trustworthy and dependable in reciprocating social favors comes first and foremost from a strong financial base. Being a good and decent person is often equated with having a job and the ready money that is expected to go along with it. Because they lack a strong basis for believing one another when money and stable jobs become an issue, regulars often grant their trust only after the visible means of support and its good use have been demonstrated over time. People are indeed required to prove themselves on this issue.

Even then, the proof is often considered by peers to rest on "shaky" grounds. Regulars often feel it necessary to talk about their jobs, comparing the kinds of tasks they perform and, at times, their salaries. If a person gets a raise, he is likely to let the others know. Then he may have to produce his job description for those who question him. To affirm themselves as regulars, some people feel the need to display convincing items that will engender the trust of peers when jobs become the issue. Those who are very uncertain of their identities as regulars will attempt to demonstrate not only that they have a job, but also that they are able to use their money properly. Some defer to other regulars by attempting to buy drinks for them, which are sometimes refused.

At times certain men attempt to demonstrate their worth and belongingness by literally whipping out evidence that proves them trustworthy associates of regulars. They try to meet a "show me" standard, often with crumpled, wallet-worn paycheck stubs or paid telephone bills, auto repair bills, and other items. For example:

One Saturday at about noon, eight men, including Jelly, stood and sat around in the liquor-store room. The conversation concerned the events of the previous night. People exchanged funny stories about group members who "got tore up" the night before. T. J. argued good-naturedly with Nathaniel about how much liquor each could hold. At one point during the argument, a bored Jelly shook his head and waved them away. Topics of conversation arose and passed. People entered and went out. Some made purchases and left, others bought beers and stayed in the room. The number rose to ten, and then fell to seven. After about forty-five minutes, Willie came in with an armload of packages. After greeting us, he moved to the soda-pop cooler. He said, "C'mon, Nathaniel. See what I got here!" This was really an invitation for all of us to come and take a look at Willie's goods. He began spreading his purchases over the top of the cooler. Others, including Jelly, gathered around Willie, who was now beginning to show his goods and tell the price of each item. He had a pair of "expensive" Stacy-Adams shoes, socks, shirts, and a new sports jacket. T. J. disputed the price of Willie's sports jacket, and Willie defensively reached for his wallet and searched for his receipts. During the course of his "search," he displayed his paid monthly house note, his paid car note, his paid phone bill, and at least four old paycheck stubs. Before producing the receipt for the sports jacket, Willie took the opportunity to show us a number of uncalled-for items attesting his financial ability.

Because they have a sense of their worthwhile relationship to the wider society, especially as they compare themselves with others on the corner, regulars can see themselves as the most "decent" and socially accountable people at Jelly's. They easily view the wineheads —people who spend most of their time begging for money for wine and food—as far below them on the wider society's social scale. And when they look at those they call "hoodlums"—people often engaged in various shady schemes to make money, from burglaries to stick-ups—they are very sure that their own values are "better" and that the others are in need of correction.

In this perspective the regulars hold members of the other groups accountable for not being as they want to see themselves—"decent" and worthwhile. Their notions of accountability may result in real attempts to ignore wineheads and hoodlums, but they cannot fully do so, for these groups are very much a part of Jelly's and the extended primary group. There is thus a process of negotiation through which places within the larger group are distributed. In a certain social exchange some get to be regulars, others get to be hoodlums, and still others are defined as wineheads. At times there may be disagreement and even some friction among members of these various groups, but when decency, ready money, and a visible means of support become issues, the members of other groups usually defer to the regulars. It is in this way, at least in part, that the subgroup of the regulars is created.

Becoming a Regular

The regulars are given deference because of the honor the other subgroups accord to the wider society with which the regulars claim a connection. The regulars are thus actually "created" by a process that includes attempts to demonstrate their connection to that wider society through verbal accounts or behavior and personal effects that can stand as evidence of such a relationship. In an effort to gain esteem and respect, regulars often resort to exaggerated self-presentations that may include reports of their vacations, of parties they have attended, of their jobs, of the upwardly mobile achievements of their relatives, especially their children, of the clubs they belong to, of the fancy restaurants they have visited, and of their good times in other parts of the city.

While such accounts may suggest decency and social accountability, they become meaningful for regular status only when others accept and believe them. The following field note illustrates this.

After being at Jelly's for about twenty minutes, Herman and I decided to "go somewhere." After letting the others know, we left for a fancy bar and restaurant frequented by black and white middle-class people on the far South Side. When we arrived, Herman wondered aloud if "they" would let us in, since we were not dressed up. After getting in, we ordered drinks at the bar. Though we felt somewhat self-conscious, we did stay long enough for me to drink two beers and for Herman to drink two whiskeys, after which we tipped the bartender and left. . . . The next afternoon at Jelly's, Herman bragged about our going to the fancy place, telling how "Me and Eli went to this place where real people hang out. Ain't no squares and wineheads there. Ain't nasty and filthy like this place, neither. Nothing but foxy chicks and decent folks go there, nothing else allowed. None o' this drunk shit all around you," he said, pointing to some of the wineheads present. Herman was a bit high, and he went on and on. Finally, his tirade became too much for Roosevelt, a sixty-six-year-old winehead. He said, "But Herman, you ain't nothin' but a goddamn janitor. All you do all day is slang them filthy, stankin' mops and clean the white folks' shithouses. That's what you is." At that Herman shut up, feeling unable to say anything in return. He knew Roosevelt was right.

Being believed is a problem for many of the regulars at Jelly's, particularly when the wider society's values are at issue. Holding down a steady job is one major way of laying claim to regular status; being the head of a nuclear family strengthens one's claim. But not all the men at Jelly's who are considered regulars have these qualifications. For example, having no family has not made it impossible for Bill Porter to be treated as a regular and to be called "*Mr.* Porter," for he meets the standards of regularism in other important ways and thus his claim to decency is believed. Other regulars will associate with him, but certain wineheads and hoodlums know they must not presume to do so. In what ways do Porter and others like him, who are occasionally out of work or do not have families, come to be included in the category of "regulars" by the others at Jelly's?

Whether or not a person has steady employment is perhaps the most important part of his claim to decency. But other aspects of his life-style and ways of behaving in public can make that claim more or less believable. There are no permanent rules for judging a person's distance from the top of the social hierarchy at Jelly's, for there are many ways of displaying one's identity as a regular, in personal and group circumstances in which such displays are deemed appropriate. One can become a believable regular by acting as a regular should act in situations where decency becomes an issue.

Regulars often take a participatory interest in politics. Unlike many of the wineheads and hoodlums who seem to have lost faith in the established political process, the regulars feel it their civic duty to vote. They believe that their vote will make a difference in deciding who occupies government office, on both the national and the local levels. Some regulars have proudly served as precinct captains or as voting-day marshals at local polling places. On election days, some of these men come around and remind the others to vote. In accordance with these beliefs and activities, regulars try to keep up with the latest political and social events and often discuss public affairs they think are important. But during these exchanges, the expression of certain items of information and opinion may suddenly reflect on the rank of an individual within the group. This is illustrated in the following statement by Ollie, a regular who is treated as the group intellectual.

It was Saturday afternoon when eight of us, six regulars and two wineheads, stood around in front of Jelly's. The day was overcast and a light rain was just beginning. Suddenly Ollie appeared. After the men greeted and acknowledged him, he asked,

"Hey, Herman, by the way, you was high when you said this, but did Curtis [Herman's brother] get married again?"

"Yeah, he married. Been married a month today. A month today," answered Herman.

"This make his fourth time?" asked Ollie.

"Uh-huh," answered Herman.

"Now, I know I'm a single person and ain't never been married, but I'm under the considered opinion that that's one of the things that hurts the society we live in— lot of people don't know, but we as black people have always suffered under this thing about the broken home. We always have. We've always suffered under this. But I say this, no civilization will ever exist for any length of time without a strong base of family life. And the family structure in America is gone to pot. In other words, like I don't mean reefers . . . ," said Ollie.

"I know where you comin' from!" interrupted Herman.

Ollie continued, ". . . and the thing is that I done read a lot of history and noticed one thing that stands out in history most of all is that most successful civilizations always have strong family ties. Maybe that's why we as black people—as individuals we might be a success, but on the whole, the black people in America are a failure.

"Hey man, you sho' is wise, Jack. 'Cause I always felt this here, but I never been able to express myself or never could express myself . . . ," said Herman, affecting a very proper tone of voice in deference to Ollie's show of intelligence.

". . . But see, like we in America, we Americans—see like I spent thirty-one months overseas and I found out one thing that we Americans got going for us that no other people have is that we Americans, no matter how bad things get, we always have the tendency to blame somebody else for it," said Ollie, interrupting Herman. At this, others began to laugh, supporting Ollie's presentation and urging him on.

"Look at Nixon," continued Ollie, "All the shit he done. It wasn't his fault! It was a conspiracy to get him and all that type o' shit."

"Damn, Ollie. You a hunnert percent right!" said Herman, approving of Ollie's display of the knowledgeability and "intelligence" that everyone knew he had.

With this presentation Ollie identifies himself not only as a "heavy" intellectual, but also as an upright citizen, an identity that implicitly distinguishes him from the wineheads and hoodlums of the extended primary group. The other regulars who are listening find no reason to reject or feel outraged at the substance of Ollie's speech. For they tend to follow him by thinking of themselves in much the same way Ollie thinks of himself—as an American citizen.

Another factor in the regulars' ability to see themselves as citizens arises from the nature of their personal experiences with various formal institutions of the larger society and the way they are ready to define and interpret such experiences. On the whole, their experiences have been relatively nonalienating and nonstigmatizing compared with those of members of the winehead and hoodlum categories with which they are so familiar. Most regulars, for example, have received "good" discharges from the military, whereas wineheads and hoodlums tend to have "bad" discharges. Within the extended primary group, a "good" discharge is an honorable discharge or a general discharge under honorable conditions. The other possible types of military discharges, the undesirable, the bad conduct, and the dishonorable, are considered "bad." For group members, such designations are important not only because they reflect upon a person's character around the corner, but also because they can and often do make a difference in terms of a man's job opportunities.

Unlike many of the wineheads and hoodlums, regulars generally are able to speak of their military service and citizenship with a certain sense of pride. They often spice their conversation with references to World War II or Korea, invoking the name of some famous general they claim to have served under. They often remind others that their military service time was beneficial both to "our country" and to "ourselves," as they speak of the marketable skills and the wisdom they gained "in the service." It is not uncommon to hear regulars relating specific personal war experiences that glorify the country and the military, whereas the wineheads and the hoodlums find such statements difficult to make and obnoxious to listen to, as they think of the trouble many of them faced in the service. To be sure, wineheads and hoodlums do talk about their own military experiences. But their bragging usually concerns the "toughness," the violence, and the trouble they faced while associated with the military. Their concerns usually are not with the aspects of service that regulars are so ready to appreciate—"decency" and "citizenship."

Further, unlike the wineheads and the hoodlums, the regulars are generally able to point to "clean slates downtown" at the police department. In conversations on the corner or inside Jelly's liquor-store room, they sometimes "talk about" the jail records of certain wineheads and hoodlums, indicating at the same time how they stand superior on this issue. They derogate those who are "only able to talk about what the county jail look like." Regulars on the whole have spent relatively little time in jail compared with members of the other groups and thus have been able to avoid becoming statistics with the formal agencies of social control. Further, the regulars tend to be fearful of the awesome power of the local police, whereas the hoodlums and some wineheads act unimpressed by the police. More-

over, regulars not only tend to show a great amount of deference to
legal authorities, but also have a general high respect for rules of
law. Indeed, they tend to display an almost blind belief in "the law."[6]
Supporting their belief in the law is their knowledge of what happens to those who go against the law. Very simply, people who go
against the law get "in trouble," something regulars wish to avoid
at all costs. By contrast, some hoodlums view a possible encounter
with the police as a chance for personal affirmation, as some boast-
fully relate their past running and shooting battles with the police.
For regulars, people who get in trouble usually wind up in Cook
County Jail, gain a record, and later find it difficult to obtain what
the regulars seem to cherish most—"a visible means of support."
The regulars know that the employers most likely to be sought out
by members of the extended primary group tend to place great emphasis on the nature of a person's record with the formal agencies
of social control. They realize that to be black, with few marketable
skills, and with a jail record or a "bad" military discharge or both
is to face heavy odds against finding a "decent" job. At Jelly's and
on the ghetto streets generally, they easily find evidence of this. They
see living proof in the persons of wineheads and hoodlums. Whenever this issue arises, among themselves or in mixed company, they
will sometimes point out the need to be law-abiding. They will also
point out how they've managed to keep their records clean, both "in
the service" and in civilian life. They feel proud of this achievement,
given the "hard times" they have been through with reference to the
general unemployment situation, the police, whom they generally
distrust, and military experiences.

While regulars at Jelly's are men who have managed to stay out
of "trouble" with legal agencies, they do participate at times in some
activities defined by the larger society—and by themselves—as illegal.[7] For example, some regulars are known to carry "pieces" (pistols) for protection, which are usually "hot" (stolen) and unregis-
tered. Also, many of the regulars buy stolen goods from hoodlums
of the group, which regulars define and simply dismiss as surviving
or as "getting over." Though they engage in "crime" at this level,
regulars draw a sharp line at personal involvement in stealing or

robbing, or at instigating crimes against persons and property. Having such limited involvements in crime, they usually avoid the attention of the police.

While their participation in crime at this level may appear to fly in the face of their sense of "decency" and citizenship, protecting oneself with a pistol or "getting over" seems not to bother regulars as being contradictory to their commitments to abide by the law. Regulars view the area around Jelly's as dangerous. People of the neighborhood have been mugged, robbed, raped, and shot at, while the police seem to them not to care, or at least to be ineffective. For regulars, as for others in the neighborhood, it is right to protect oneself by any means necessary, while to do less than this is to carry oneself improperly. And such activities as buying stolen property are seen by certain regulars not as bad or criminal, but merely as helping oneself survive financially. As one regular told me, after buying "hot" property from a fence inside Jelly's, "I might as well do it. If I don't, somebody else will. I'm out here just like the next stud, tryin' to survive. Hard as times are? I'm lookin' for every bargain I can get!"

As the regular struggles to be decent and law-abiding in the social context of Jelly's, he gains and displays a peculiar orientation toward "trouble." This orientation suggests that although the regular must contend with the trouble-filled social world of Jelly's and the streets, he must also somehow prove himself above it. In attempting to do this, the regulars make constant references to and comparisons with others in the setting, drawing invidious distinctions, usually vis-à-vis the hoodlums and wineheads, but sometimes among themselves. They point to others' trouble with the law, or to others' behavior that will lead to legal sanctions if continued. When such distinctions are made in agreeable company, the regulars place themselves above trouble, a chief concern among them.

This concern with staying above trouble is illustrated in the following exchange between The Terry, a hoodlum, and Otis, a regular. Here The Terry brags about a fight he was involved in a few days earlier and the stab wounds he received. During the exchange Otis refrains from rewarding Terry for his posture and past actions by simply refusing to acknowledge them as worthwhile. Rather, he puts down Terry's behavior and invokes regular beliefs and values, then proceeds to instruct him about what is "right." The conversation changes from Terry's bragging to a lecture by Otis and confirms the real places of both in the social order.

"The motherfucker grabbed me 'round the collar and caught me right here on the neck with his knife. But I got the son of a bitch," opened The Terry, pointing to the wound on his neck.

"Now, I ain't had a fight since I was eleven years old, and I'm sixty now," countered Otis.

"That's been a many moons," commented Terry.

"Terry, you got to stop all that fightin' and shit. That ain't no way to be. Wh'cha gon' fight for? Show me the point? Two fools don't make nothin'. Somebody got to have some sense. I would just leave if somebody wanted to fight me. You should have just gone on 'bout your business, shit! You ain't got to stand there and argue with him. Just walk away. Fightin' don't make no sense!" advised Otis.

"But I call myself walkin' away from him and found out, god-damn, that the man had a knife," explained Terry.

"If you walk away, that prove you braver than he is. You a brave man if you can walk away," answered Otis.

"Yeah, you right. It take a fool to fight and a man to walk away," agreed Terry. [Here Terry seems to agree with Otis's definition of the situation.] "I was walkin', god-damn, and I got hit [cut]."

"It was you and another brother, huh! We fight and cut more than anybody on earth, don't we? You can say 'bout Whitey what you want to say about him. I don't love him, now. Never will give a damn 'bout him. But they have a different system than what we have. Whatever it is. We don't do nothing but fuck with who? Each what? Other! Break in each other's what? House!" explained Otis.

"That's what Whitey want you to do!" said Spider. (Spider is a person who hangs out with wineheads, hoodlums, and regulars. Group members see him as marginal.)

"That's why they gon' separate you and keep you that way long as they can. You can believe that. If they let you over there [in a white neighborhood], they done investigated you, ha-ha. You can believe that, now. Down from the top to the what? The bottom! I mean that's pitiful. I been in this city fifty-five years. I used to live at 3377 Wentworth. On the east side of the street wasn't nothing but dagos. On the west side of the street wasn't nothing but pollacks. You know how many niggers lived in that block? Two. My family and another family. Went to Horace Mann School at Thirty-sixth and Shield. They later changed the name to Framer Branch #1. Shit. I went over there.when it wasn't but three niggers. It's pitiful. I don't know whether Whitey got to wake up—or we got to wake up. I think we got to wake up—a little bit, anyway," answered Otis.

"We got to wake up to reality and use yo' motherfuckin' mentality, and stop all this fightin' and cuttin' and shit," said Spider.

Otis's lesson on "behaving yourself" voices the regulars' concerns with "trouble" and "decency." These are concerns to which they are strongly oriented, especially when confronted with men who are admitting to and bragging about not "behaving themselves." Regulars find that the men they define as wineheads and hoodlums do not uphold their orientation toward trouble, yet they continue to share the social space of Jelly's. To survive as a regular, one must keep a constant vigil, watching those who "bear watching," not only to protect oneself from becoming a victim of "trouble," but also to uphold one's own interests and values in the setting and not allow oneself to be drawn into the collective definition of hoodlum. Hence regulars look for the proper orientation toward trouble when checking out people around Jelly's to determine whether they are worthy of association.

The regulars observe degrees of association in their relations with others of the extended primary group. Through their selective associations, they can affirm themselves to some degree as models of the "decency" they associate with both the wider society and their own social order at Jelly's. Aside from the "regular" ways of behaving mentioned above—telling stories about experiences in the social world beyond Jelly's, carrying out one's civic responsibilities, staying clear of jail, and avoiding violent confrontations on the street—one also strengthens his claim to regularism by associating closely with others who are successfully meeting the standards of decency. By following the selective associations that occur, we can trace out a kind of chart of the social hierarchy at Jelly's. The associations involve such deceptively simple social transactions as group drinking, borrowing money, speaking up or "taking up" (physical fighting if necessary) for one another, or even just borrowing cigarettes. The following field note illustrates aspects of the process of selective association, particularly the grounds on which the associations may be based. The speaker is Wigfall, a regular who is just barely hanging onto his regular affiliations.[8]

"Now, I happen to be a pretty strong man, myself. Or I could be a lushhead. A lushhead's a guy who has just give it up, and decides to just drink liquor.

"Just like you see out in the park there. The guys just all go out there, sit on the park bench, and they chip in and they buy a drink.

"There are guys out there who don't never have the money, but there are some who have some money once a month. But everybody know everybody, and everybody gon' drink when one drink. When one drink, everybody drink, you understand? If you in.

"Now I can go there, I don't care who it is out there, anybody out there, they're gon' give me a drink, if they got somethin'. Now, what make a person . . . what put a person in that position? He get disgusted with life. It come from way back, slavery times. Far as black people are concerned, they've always had it real tough. They've never been used to a lot of money, and you know, and all this. They had to work hard for everythin' they got. But some youngsters can see from right here to far in the future, it's the same old thing as it was in slavery times, only with a different face. Let's put it that way.

"Now, like me, I'm at a point now. The lowest point I've ever been in my life. Really. So, I worked and worked and worked at my job. Now, I been on this job for ten years. Now, I'm gon' show you somethin'.

"I work in school maintenance. Al'right. I started workin' for $1.85 an hour, now I only make $4.00 an hour. Now, but the cost of livin' done went up so much. I shoulda started at $3.25. Now I should be making $5.35 or somethin'. I'm just making $4.00. That just go to show you what's going on.

"There's a lotta people done experienced all kinda jobs. Everythin', and couldn't make enough money to live. But see, they couldn't make it by workin', so they done give up. They've give up! They say it don't pay to work. That you can live without workin'.

"Now, I been depressed as a result of this. We hire a lotta people at $1.80 an hour. Right now, my job. They start them out at that, and boy, the turnover is rough. People come and go. They work two or three weeks, till payday, and they gone. Now, recently we hired some people and the union try to come over and try to talk to everybody, etc., etc. Want you to join the union. Most of us decided, well, we only have to pay a hundred and fifty a year. What we really need is just a decent salary so we keep up with the cost of livin'. We can adjust, you understand?

"You don't make enough money to live, to pay rent, buy groceries, with the high price of groceries and everythin'. So, you go get on some type of aid. The women get on ADC. You can't make enough money to support your family in the right order. So you give up after a while. And you say, 'Aw, the hell with it. I'll draw unemployment compensation, till that give out.' The money get shorter. You might have been a whiskey drinker [a regular]. Well, you wasn't a lushhead. You was socializin' with certain people in a category that was perhaps beyond your means.

"Al'right. After a while, you get so you can't go out there and keep clean, buy clothes and buy whiskey. So, you come out and your change is short in your pocket. And you decide, 'Well, I'll drink with these guys [wineheads].' You give 'em a quarter, you know. And you have a drink of wine. So you drink wine today, and so on. You don't go to work. Whoever you livin' with, they feed you today, and after a while, and so on.

"Then you go back out on the corner there and stand around. You not workin' now. You standin' around on the corner. One of the boys say, 'Gimme a quarter. We gon' get a bottle.' They get a fifth of wine. You take a drink of wine. You get ready and you eat. But after a while, you keep drinkin' the wine. Then you can't eat. Done lost your appetite for food.

"Well, you get up the next mornin', and you kinda shaky. You know. You wants to go out there and have a drink of wine. Things settle down. You cool, got fifteen cents in your pocket. You say, 'Well, let's make it up and gon' get us some wine.' They [wine-heads] get one. And this gets to be a habit. Just like smoking cigarettes, or anything else. First thing you want to do when your eyes open in the mornin', you want a drink. You don't want no breakfast. You want a drink. You don't want no food. You get the drink, and you sho'nuff don't want no breakfast then. So you drink and you drink.

"But then, this is what happens. People are depressed. They can't live like they want to live. They see people cruisin' by in nice cars, see people got nice clean apartments. And all this. And he can't cope with it, without workin'. But he don't want to work for this little bit of money he gon' get. 'Cause the little bit of money still won't put him where he want to be. You understand? Here's a guy with a El Dorado that's a friend of his. This hurts a man, when he see a friend of his can drive a El Dorado and got a nice clean apartment and a beautiful lady and two or three kids. And he can't do it! Even if he work. Don't care how he work and how he save. He can't handle it, and so he give up. Then he find him a different group to associate with. He got to associate in his category.

"Now take me. I know all the heavy people and I know all the light people, see. But, I know I can't handle that group where I go to they place and they got wall-to-wall carpeting—in the base-ment. They got a bar in the basement. They got liquor stacked up as much as one of these taverns up here. But they're friends of mine. But sometimes they can invite me and I won't go. Know what I'm talking about? I be sittin' out here on the park bench, chippin' in a dollar [the amount regulars usually chip in] on some whiskey, drink that, and feel pretty good. Feel in place, you know.

" 'Cause I can't invite these people to my house. Now, like I want to invite my boss to my house. Now, I been supervisor on my job two times. Now look. Now, another supervisor, he from Argentina. He and his wife, he got married year before last. He invited the boss to his house. Now, he got everythin' so beautiful and nice. But I would like to invite the boss to my house, but I can't do it!

"All these things I think about! This is what I'm talkin' 'bout. Now see this is what make people like they are. Now, I'm a hard-workin' man. And I can work everyday, and it still won't let me do what I want to do."

Wigfall's story illustrates the feelings of the group members about their crowd affiliations within the extended primary group. It indicates the social pressures that impinge on people at Jelly's, encouraging them to seek out and hang with this or that crowd or, as Wigfall says, their "category." When major events occur that affect a person's evaluation of himself, he may begin to feel he ought to be hanging with a crowd he can handle—say wineheads rather than regulars, or vice versa. The crowd may be higher or lower, in some sense, than the person's original crowd. People of the group rise or sink to their "own levels"; they gravitate to the crowds in which they feel comfortable, given the nature of the personal judgments being made by others. The idea of reciprocity is important here, as was shown in Wigfall's story, especially the personal and group feeling that to be included one must have the social ability to return numerous favors. People somehow know what they are capable of in rendering such favors to peers, and they know what group of people is appropriate for them. They learn their capabilities during social interaction.

About a month later Wigfall lost his job. And sure enough, he began hanging with a different group. Later he moved away from his family.

Tiger: A Case Study in Mobility

Tiger is a forty-year-old, brown-skinned man with thick, greased-back hair, a slight paunch, and well-developed muscles. He is about five feet nine inches tall and weighs about 190 pounds. Tiger grew up in Boston and left school in the eleventh grade. He then enlisted in the army and was released about fifteen years ago with a "bad" discharge. Up to the present he has been sporadically unemployed. He has worked here and there as a dishwasher, a parking-lot attendant, and a construction laborer, and currently he works full time as a janitor at a local hospital. At one point Tiger was a prizefighter, a part of his past he does not let others around Jelly's forget. For instance, he often interjects the names of "big-time" prizefighters into his "conversation," as if to claim he knows them. When talking with others, he will sometimes go into a fighting stance, putting his fists up and planting his feet as though he were in a boxing ring. Part of his need to remind others of his worth stems from the fact that his publicly known personal biography is checkered with hard luck, setbacks, and ups and downs, with very few triumphs. But through all of this he sometimes boasts to the fellows, particularly the regulars, that he has never resorted to sticking up people for survival money.

Over the past two years Tiger's life has been especially checkered. He did a stint in Cook County Jail for public intoxication and vagrancy. He has had bad luck finding and holding jobs, at least the kind he would like and that certain group members would call decent. Before finding his present job as a janitor, Tiger was pretty much down and out, often wondering where his next meal would come from and where he would sleep. During this time group members saw Tiger as a person who bore watching, for he did not have a visible means of support and would hang out with others who did not work. Much of his time was spent with the wineheads and hoodlums. He often begged around the corner and on rare occasions ran errands for Jelly with the expectation of receiving change. On occasion Tiger could be seen standing around on the corner eating a doughnut or some cheese and crackers, sharing this with other wineheads or keeping it all for himself. Some of the more fortunate members of the group would take pity on him when he seemed pitiful enough.

Group members, especially the regulars, call this condition "carrying the stick." In his study of Chicago's "hobohemia," Nels Anderson discovered the phrase "carrying the banner." He states, "It is not uncommon for men who cannot find a warm place to sleep to walk the streets all night. This practice of walking the streets all night, snatching a wink of sleep here and a little rest there, is termed, in the parlance of the road, 'carrying the banner.' " At Jelly's this variant is used.[9] For regulars, this is one of the most serious violations of the value of decency. As Herman once told me: "It takes a *man* to get out there and hit that clock on time and work eight hours. A decent person ain't got time for a cat who don't wanna do nothin' but carry the stick."

For regulars, a man is supposed to be responsible, to be able to take care of himself. He should "work for a living" and not "freeload" off others. Consistent with this expectation, a man is supposed to be of "strong character," which is usually demonstrated by his ability to get and hold a job. Work is of crucial importance for a sense of place within the extended primary group. A respectable man is a hardworking man. From this viewpoint, if a man is down to "carrying the stick," his very character is at issue, for he has failed to meet the group's general standards of decency. And the failure is usually assigned not to the wider social system but to the man himself. But not all regulars see things entirely this way. One afternoon, Mr. Porter, an older regular, and Wigfall debated this issue.

"These wineheads out here bring it on themselves, see. See, a record follow you. I don't care if you ain't but twelve, thirteen years old, it mean somethin' for you later on. Even a juvenile record can follow you," said Porter.

"It's the economy that make things so bad. See, in this United States, the white people, the Caucasians, they've got what we call the establishment. Now, it was established a long time ago, during slavery times, a certain way to keep you economically down. And that system is just as good today as it was before," said Wigfall.

"Aw, I don't agree with that. You know what you do? You keep yo' own self down!" exclaimed Porter.

"No . . . Mr. Porter, no," answered Wigfall.

"It bugs me to hear you talk about the white man keepin' you down. The white man can't keep you down. The white man is tryin' to help you up," answered Porter.

"There might be some possibility . . . but please believe me, Mr. Porter . . .," rambled Wigfall.

"Cause if he wasn't tryin' to help you up, then how would you survive?" exclaimed Porter.

"Please, Mr. Porter!" exclaimed Wigfall.

"Now, that burn me up when a black man keep talkin' 'bout the white man is keepin' you down. You keepin' yo' own self down because if a black get hold to a little somethin' then what they gon' do? They gon' be in this area, and every time they think you got a little money, they gon' knock you in the head, drag you up in a alley somewhere, and take what you got!" answered Porter.

"But if you run it all the way down, Mr. Porter, you'll find that . . .," said Wigfall.

"See, that what wrong wit' these kids right now, today! These older guys is always tellin' 'bout what the white man have done. And 'he had you under slavery.' The white man ain't never had me under slavery, he ain't never had my mother and father under slavery—he ain't never had my grandparents under slavery. So how the hell he keepin' me down? Now, my way foreparents, way before any of us was even thought of, now they might of been under slavery. But hell, ever since I been workin', when I work, I get my paycheck," said Porter.

"You under slavery right now, Mr. Porter, but you just don't know it, see," answered Wigfall.

"Aw, man, shit. You oughta hush. What kind of slavery?" asked Porter.

"You don't know it?" exclaimed Wigfall.

"What kind of slavery?" repeated Porter.

"But this is slavery. Economical slavery," said Wigfall.

"Shit. What kind of slavery is I'm under? Wha'cha mean about economical slavery?" asked Porter.

"Everything is programmed to keep you in a certain position. You ain't gon' never get out of it, and I guarantee you that," said Wigfall.

"Well, just look at how many rich people, Negroes, done worked themselves up. Some of 'em ain't even finished high school. Look at some of the rich Negroes, some of them didn't go but to the sixth grade or grammar school. Well, hell, they come to be multimillionaires," pointed out Porter.

"But you got to be a hell of a man to break out of Charlie's system, the way he got it set up for you," said Wigfall.

"But look how many well-to-do Negroes that own buildings and all that kind of stuff. If you gon' make yo' money, and blow yo' money, and buy wine and pussy off yo' money, and whatsoever you gon' buy, well now that's yo' business. Don't blame it on the white man just 'cause you ain't got nothin'. Some of the people out here make it and they blow it. It's they own fault. You carry the stick, well that's you, ain't no white man. Talk about the white man got you blocked and all that," said Porter.

"Well, he sho'nuff got a whole lot of tricks for you," declared Wigfall.

"I tell these wineheads every day I'm out here, the white man can do without you, but you can't do without the white man. 'Cause the white man got everythin'," said Porter.

"It's designed that way! It's designed that way. You think that's accidental?" asked Wigfall.

"You know what it is. It ain't designed. You know what it is, Wigfall?" questioned Porter.

"But you s'posed to be the same as he is! Only difference is color," said Wigfall.

"How I'm gon' be the same as he is, how we gon' be the same as he is when we both black. How?" asked Porter.

In reference to Tiger's predicament, Mr. Porter said, "I ain't got no time for no 'counts like him. Next thing I know, he'll be trying to knock me in the head to get my little money. He could find a job if he wanted one, but he just don't want to work. I work for a livin'. Other guys out here work, so why can't he? He just ain't no 'count."

The positions and arguments of Porter and Wigfall illustrate the polar ideological extremes within the group, either of which may be used by regulars when they are thinking or arguing about visible means of support.

Tiger, though, has had special problems in getting work. When he was released from the army he received a bad conduct discharge, which has made his career on the streets of Chicago and around Jelly's difficult. His record also reflects a variety of brushes with the law. Taken together, these obstacles have made it almost impossible for him to get what regulars define as a "good job"—a steady, regular, and legal occupation. When he is fortunate enough to find employment, Tiger's position is usually precarious, because he has to lie about his past to get the job. If he is found out, which for him is a constant concern and which usually happens within a week to a few months, he is almost always let go.

But Tiger faces group obstacles too. Even if he is not found out, he often becomes unhappy with his work because the job is labeled "shit work" by others in the group, including some regulars. Other wineheads may rib him and call him a fool for working, even though they want to share his money. Some of the wineheads will stand around in front of Jelly's and brag about how they are "getting over" without "slavin' for the man." Then some of them will talk about Tiger as a "cat who bustin' his ass workin'. Not me!" In his attempts to deal with such pressures, Tiger often takes days off without permission. He will call his work "too hard," quit the job or get fired, and come back to the streets around Jelly's. He then draws unemployment compensation, resumes begging, and "carries the stick" with the other wineheads.

During the summer of 1971 Tiger "carried the stick," spending his days socializing with other wineheads and his nights roaming the streets and sleeping in parked cars or in the parks with his drinking buddies. He led a vagabond existence: he would find a meal here, beg a drink there, and snatch some sleep whenever and wherever he could. He begged money from regulars, hoodlums, and whatever passersby would venture close enough. He and his buddies did obtain enough to survive, but just barely.

During this time Tiger often acted and behaved as though he had a dual personality. In the company of regulars, people who had money to give and "decency" to flaunt, Tiger would sometimes come on as very meek, quiet, and deferential. Though this was not always the case, it occurred often enough for me and others to take note. For example, even when the topic of discussion was something he knew about, like prizefighting, he might nevertheless "be quiet," deferring to others present. Later, he might "hit on" the same people for money, to which some would respond, "Fuck you! Go n' get yo'self a job, you lazy, good-for-nothing no 'count." At this he would simply lower his head and walk away. But some regulars, after making such a tirade, would give in and "loan" Tiger a dollar or two. When regulars lent money in this way it was not really a loan but an attempt to "buy off" Tiger. They would let him have an amount of money they knew he would be reluctant to repay even when he had it, since money was so scarce for him. After he received the money, they expected him to stay away from them, lest they embarrass him by asking about the "loan," thereby proving he was not a good risk. They simply wanted to be rid of him. Also, when a regular buys off a winehead in this way, the winehead may become obligated to run errands or otherwise serve the regular. On numerous occasions I have watched Tiger studiously avoid the company of certain regulars. At times when he was the only winehead around, he would move on when too many regulars appeared. Many regulars used this "buying off" tactic to deal with the constant begging of people like Tiger. After seeing it work they would often whisper and laugh among themselves at the winehead in question.

One evening six regulars, including Herman and myself, were gathered in front of Jelly's liquor store. Tiger and Mack were the only wineheads there. Tiger was trying to "get up the money" for some wine. He asked me, "Eli, lemme hold somethin'. I'll see you straight when my check comes" (meaning lend me some money and I'll repay you when I get it). I then went into my pocket and came up with fifty cents. I gave it to him, and he went inside the liquor store. I asked Herman what he thought of the loan I had just made. Herman laughed matter-of-factly, "He sold himself cheap."

Tiger understood that the regulars were not his "kind of people." The crucial distinction between them and himself was the "visible means of support." They appeared to take almost any opportunity to remind him of the difference, and he would usually accept their definitions by behaving "in line." Around them, he would act like a winehead. His awareness of his basic shortcomings in their eyes made him uncomfortable around the regulars, even though they were the kind of company he really wanted. Although Tiger felt a certain resentment toward the regulars, he tried very hard to gain their approval, which they were almost always reluctant to grant.

In the immediate presence of the wineheads, there was quite a different Tiger. This Tiger was not so taciturn. He was more self-assured, drinking and laughing, talking, and even instructing and advising some of the others about their personal problems with the law, or women, or the "sissies" (homosexuals). Sometimes he could be found arguing with one of the wineheads about the part of the "taste" he didn't get. Or he might argue about a loan he had given one of these men. With a different group of people, who also lacked a "visible means of support," Tiger could feel more self assured. It was clear that he was more comfortable in this group, in which the other members could not readily presume to remind him of his "shortcomings."

Although Tiger and his winehead buddies survived the summer easily enough by sleeping in parks and parked cars and by begging, the fall and winter presented serious problems. Many of the group members lamented the coming cold weather, for it brought a different life arrangement for many of them. Instead of hanging outside on the corner, they now found the liquor-store room of Jelly's more inviting. But Jelly and the regulars do not usually encourage the wineheads to share the space of the liquor-store room; they must behave or leave. Further, it is much more difficult to "carry the stick" during the winter. People have died from exposure on Chicago streets.

The wineheads develop ingenious survival strategies to deal with the cold weather. Some find "sissies" to live with, trading their sexual favors for room and board. Others commit petty crimes just to be caught by the authorities so they can be kept in Cook County Jail for the winter. A few wineheads seek out, or fortuitously come upon, employment that will see them through the winter. They usually intend to quit the job when milder spring weather comes along.

Tiger happened to come across a janitorial job that winter, which for him was a matter of luck. First, his new employer, a local hospital, turned out to be relatively easy to get along with and did not put him through a lot of red tape and questions. By contrast, most wineheads are prevented from getting jobs by stringent employment practices and must then resort to some other strategy for survival. Also, this was the kind of job Tiger could do well, yet it did not make great demands on his time around the street corner, which is usually a primary consideration for wineheads. He had to work from 6:30 P.M. until 2:30 A.M., a shift that left his days relatively free for hanging around with the fellows at Jelly's.

This development in Tiger's life brought important consequences for his identity and status around Jelly's. When people asked him about going somewhere or "doing something," he could proudly answer, "I gotta go to work pretty soon." He would now pester people about the time, mostly regulars, since these were people he most wanted to impress—not that impressing the hoodlums and other wineheads was unimportant to him. The place buzzed with Tiger's voice, "What time you got, Sleepy? Is it six yet? How long I got before I gotta go to *work*?" In this way he reminded those who cared enough to listen that he now had a job, "a visible means of support."

After receiving a few paychecks, Tiger began flaunting his money and check stubs around Jelly's. Whenever the issue was money, he would be right there. At times he would try to even up past debts with the regulars, for now he too was a "workin' man." Among his winehead buddies Tiger began to buy the whole bottle of wine, whereas before he had only chipped in the few pennies, nickles, and dimes he could spare. He even managed to buy drinks for some of the regulars who had for so long been supporting him with "loans." Tiger now felt he could approach such people, a feeling that had important consequences for his own place at Jelly's.

Perhaps the most important consequence was that Tiger now began to see himself in a different light. Contributing to his new self-concept were his new routine, his money, his visible means of support, and his new reception by the other people around Jelly's, all of which helped set the stage for defining himself as a "new" Tiger. Others began to see him as a "new" person. But also, he was beginning to see the various groups at Jelly's in different terms, particularly wineheads and regulars.

Tiger began to put his winehead buddies down. Many of them had now become a nuisance to him, as they begged him for more and more money and for contributions to this or that "taste." The wineheads became for Tiger the "kind" of people to avoid. Many of the wineheads, some of whom had been drinking with Tiger only weeks before, started to bad-mouth him. They began to define Tiger as "stuck up" and as "too good to speak." They accused him of what they call "crossing the track," which refers to a winehead who gets "some money" and does not share it with his former drinking buddies but attempts to take up with a new group. For Tiger, the "new group" was the regulars.

Regulars became, for Tiger, people to be with. Their "ways" seemed to grow more and more appealing to him once he had a job. He could now meet their expectations for reciprocating favors. Some of the regulars, particularly Herman, Wigfall, and Pee Wee, allowed Tiger to drink with them on the implicit condition that he pay for his share of the "taste." For them, "winehead Tiger"—as he had been called—was slowly becoming just plain "Tiger." This change of name was also catching on among other regulars. Tiger seemed more and more acceptable as regulars began to treat him more and more like an equal. For example, T. J., who used to "signify" at Tiger, rubbing in the belief that Tiger was a winehead, now began to accept Tiger's association. One evening just before six, the time when Tiger had to get ready for work, T. J. said in the presence of other regulars:

"Hey, Tiger! Come on, let's get one before you go on that job of yours. You with us, now. C'mon, man, let's get some o' that good stuff. How much you got on this taste?" Quickly Tiger came up with a ruffled old dollar bill, then quietly waited for the others (regulars) to put in their shares. After getting a bottle and some cups and orange drink, we split up the taste, each man getting as many hits (a drinking portion of liquor) as the bottle would allow. T. J., who held the bottle, offered Tiger an extra hit. But Tiger refused, answering,

"I gotta *work* tonight!" The others laughed at this, encouraging Tiger to break up. Tiger then said, "I guess I'm man enough to stand one mo' hit." Here Tiger seemed very much included in the regular crowd.

Many of the regulars, who only a few weeks before would not even take up time with Tiger, let alone drink with him, were now drinking "good stuff" (scotch, gin, bourbon, and vodka) with him from the same bottle.

To be sure, not all regulars in all circumstances were fully accepting of Tiger. His acceptance was situational and depended in part on the values and standards others wanted to uphold, if only for the moment. This is indicated in the following note.

One Thursday evening Willard and Herbert, two regulars believed to have "big dough," were sitting in Herbert's late-model Buick, "digging the scene." Both men have nuclear families and own "fancy homes." And they are known as "hardworkin' men." The men were parked near Jelly's front door and could be seen passing a bottle of liquor back and forth, taking hits. Ten or twelve men, mostly wineheads and hoodlums, were milling about in front of Jelly's door, not far from Herbert's car. Willard sat on the side of the car nearest the men. Spying Herman, Willard called him.

"Hey Herman. C'mon over here." Herman was talking with Tiger, but stopped and walked over to the car.

"Get on in," said Willard.

"Just a minute. I gotta get some cigarettes," said Herman.

"We got some cigarettes. Get on in and get you a hit o' this Jim Beam." Herman got into the car. After about fifteen minutes, Tiger walked over.

"What you want?" asked Willard, a man known to be suspicious of wineheads.

"A, uh, I want a talk to Herman," said Tiger.

"Wha'cha want, man. Talk," demanded Herman impatiently.

"Aw, man. It's somethin' personal," said Tiger.

"Aw, man. It ain't nothin' personal. Wha'cha want? Some money?" asked Herman.

"Yeah," answered Tiger. "Lemme hold a quarter."

"Aw, man. I ain't got no money," said Herman.

After that Tiger had nothing else to say, so he left and joined the others standing in front of Jelly's.

At earlier times, when Tiger apparently was more committed to his identity as a winehead, he would have had no qualms about asking for money in public, and I had seen him "begging" others for wine money. But now that he had a job and appeared to be gaining a commitment to being a regular, he seemed constrained about his begging, particularly in the presence of those who might censure his conduct.[10] In commenting on Tiger's current situation, Herman said the following:

> "See, 'cause Tiger somethin' like a phony. See, now, Tiger can't stand them wineheads. He's workin' now. He feel like he's independent. Feel like he more than the next one of them cats. But yet his attitude and character. Most times I don't even wanta be around him. He's loud. He's talkin' all *this* talk and ain't qualified to live up to nothin'. Only thing he can talk about is some money he's won. And the girls he got with the money. That's his total conversation. He talk about that or he talk about the time he used to throw leather [box]. He say he know Sugar Ray Robinson, Bobo Olson, Freddie Dawson, Ike Williams, Johnny Bratton [big time prizefighters]. That's all he know to talk about. And then he argue and talk loud and can't nobody hear nothin' but him. And it's all gon' be 'bout boxin'. Like he used to be hell of a boxer or somethin'. But he don't bring it to me too fast, 'cause he know I'll tell him, 'Aw, man. G'wan get outa town, man. You don't know nothin' about them people.' See, and I done rubbed it so much that he know better than to come to me with all that jive."

Not all wineheads are as socially mobile as Tiger, and it is obvious that his status as a regular was precarious. Slipping back into the status of winehead would be only too easy, and this happens from time to time when others deny him association and remind him of his biography. But Tiger's new routine allowed him a basis from which to distinguish himself from most other wineheads. The regulars were quick to pick up on this difference, but as a group they were not fully convinced that he would be able to maintain his new routine and his "visible means of support." Some regulars closely observed his "progress" and bet secretly among themselves on his chances of retaining his new job. Tiger had been through similar changes before, as have other wineheads, only to quit when things got very tough, when he had earned enough money to see his way clear, or when milder spring weather arrived. But maybe this time would be different, as Tiger seemed to be taking his new job very seriously.

4 | The Wineheads

The winehead category at Jelly's constitutes a kind of social residuum within the wider group. It is made up of men who range in age from thirty-three to seventy. Some have lived within the area of Jelly's almost all their lives; others have traveled widely and have "done everything and seen everything." Wineheads usually do not hold jobs, or they work only sporadically to get enough money for wine, food, and a place to sleep. What they appear to value most is "gettin' a taste" and "havin' some fun." They spend a good portion of their time around Jelly's drinking wine or trying to obtain money for wine or food, usually by begging from other group members and from outsiders. The label winehead is used mainly by people who do not consider themselves closely affiliated with this group and is a symbol of denigration. Those considered members of the disvalued winehead category seldom if ever verbally admit belonging to it. Yet they usually accept the treatment generally accorded to wineheads. Often they defer to others by moving away from the larger group and gathering with their own kind. Or they may remain in the company of members of another group but defer when the group's values are at issue. Thus they must keep their place. The wineheads not only are victims of group labeling, they actually engage in a relatively stable pattern of activity that is disvalued by others with whom they share the social space of Jelly's.

At almost any time of day a group of wineheads can be seen gathered in the alley or in the park near Jelly's. They sit on a bench or on the ground or lean on the side of Jelly's building waiting for something exciting to happen. For instance, they wait for a "main man" to come along or even for the rain to begin—or stop. Any such event can act as a catalyst for other things. While they wait, some member of the group may come up with enough nickles, dimes, and pennies to "put on a taste"—usually a bottle of wine or a can of beer, but sometimes even toxic cough syrup. Since many of this group do not have a means of support, they must beg from others, particularly regulars, for money to get the taste, and also for subsistence. Sometimes when they have been able to "get up" enough money, they celebrate as though they have won a victory.[1]

One early weekday afternoon in May, I was in the park with six men the regulars commonly referred to as wineheads: Red Mack, Jocko, Green, Spider (who is marginal), and two others. Red Mack said, "C'mon, Eli. Help us on this taste."

"I don't drink that stuff," I said, following Herman's instructions on how to handle wineheads. Mack then moved on to Jocko and asked, "How much you got, Jocko?"

"I got a quarter and a nickle," answered Jocko. "What you got, Mack?"

"I got forty-five cent. We need thirty mo' cent to get one," said Mack.

"Here come a stud. Lemme hit on him," said Spider. He then walked toward the sidewalk while the others watched, talking among themselves and wondering whether Spider would score. Spider walked up to the perfect stranger and boldly asked for fifty cents. The stranger looked over at us, then dug into his pocket. He came up with only thirty cents, the amount Spider really needed to make the price of the wine. Then, I heard Spider say, "Thanks, man. Sho' 'preciate it." The stranger hurried on his way, and Spider swaggered back to the group, smiling confidently. When he approached us, he held out his hand for a slap of recognition for his successful performance. All the men, including me, slapped his hand, telling him, "job well done." Jocko then went to get the Boones' Farm Apple Wine.

This scenario is repeated many times during the course of a day, and the results supply conversation at times when there is not much else to talk about. The tale may be told by other wineheads or by a regular who witnessed the transaction, particularly if something novel happened. Often the person making the loan or gift is seen and talked about by the wineheads as a "mark," a person taken advantage of.

When enough money has accumulated, someone—usually a person who has not made a major contribution—will be appointed to purchase the taste. He dutifully goes to fetch the taste and returns to pass the bottle around the group. Usually, in acknowledgment of his limited contribution, he will defer by waiting for all the others to drink what they want. He drinks last, "after" the others, thereby deferring to those who really "own" the taste. This complex cooperative activity, which contains many opportunities to go amiss, involves the winehead group in differentiating itself from others who are more "proper." Yet all members of the extended primary group are susceptible to being drawn into and identified with this collective process. Therefore the others, especially the regulars, require ways of dealing with and distancing themselves from the wineheads and those who act like wineheads. Their solution to this problem is usually self-serving.

Begging for money on the streets is one of the distinguishing characteristics of the wineheads. They always seem to be "broke," with barely enough money for food and shelter, let alone for drinking. One of the important reasons wineheads characteristically have barely enough money to keep alive is that most simply don't value work. Many will say outright that they enjoy themselves by not working. To be sure, some draw welfare payments, unemployment compensation, or military disability, but the amounts they receive are hardly adequate. For many the money is received one day and "drunk up" with buddies the next. Sometimes even their buddies rob them while drinking together; and the next time, the person robbed may rob his buddy.

If wineheads must work, they will frequently work only long enough to satisfy immediate needs. Whereas the regulars are often very much involved in retaining and bettering their jobs, the wineheads seem neither to desire nor to be able to begin—let alone maintain—a stable pattern of employment. Whereas regulars often praise and respect those with a visible means of support, the wineheads, particularly among themselves, often put such people down. It is not uncommon for the wineheads to talk about an employed winehead who has "crossed the track" as being foolish for working. This was shown in the case of Tiger. Such group considerations make getting and sustaining a job difficult for those who desire it. Because of a lack of marketable skills, poor work records, jail records, "bad" military discharges, and general racism, most wineheads are unable to work at regular jobs, which tends to dampen their desire to do so.

If the wineheads as a group approximate the regulars' values of work and decency, they do so mainly through talk about what they "used to do," "used to be," and are "gon' do." A winehead may often talk about the jobs he used to have and the "times" he used to have when he worked here or there. Some talk about the families they used to have and worked to support, though few families can actually be traced. And they often talk about—and exaggerate—the amount of money they used to earn. In terms of the future, it is not uncommon to hear wineheads talk about joining job-training programs or about plans to go to auto mechanic school or whatever. Yet the plans never seem to materialize. They simply serve as something to talk about and laugh about. When certain men talk in this manner others will laugh in their faces and say, "You a barefaced lie," or "You should be 'shamed."

Most wineheads lack the ability and motivation to hustle the streets as many hoodlums do. They do not possess the personal organization necessary to steal and then fence the goods, and most also lack the will, the nerve, and the cunning to be a good stickup man. But there is also a question of general motivation toward crime of this nature. The winehead is either on the verge of uncontrollable alcoholism or is very much an alcoholic. He needs alcohol. Thus he seems motivated mainly toward "gettin' a taste," not toward acquiring "fast and big money" like the hoodlums. To be sure, at earlier points in their careers some wineheads have been creative hoodlums. It is not uncommon to hear them critique someone's version of a "hustle," a stickup, or the proper use of a pistol or knife. But now, between the law and their thirst for alcohol, wineheads usually lack both the skill and the motivation to be successful criminals.

Thus, people of the residual winehead category are often viewed, both by hoodlums and by regulars, as "has-beens" without enough "order about themselves" on the streets and in the wider society to entitle them to deference. This view conceives of wineheads as "no 'counts"—people with few informal rights within the extended primary group. Though they may once have been active regulars or hoodlums or "gangsters," now they will associate with almost anyone who will have them, especially if there might be a drink involved. They are seen as casualties of the streets, as social "nobodies," as people who lack that "order" that is so important for both survival and positive regard, either in the street or in the outside world.

Regulars and others "talk about" wineheads and claim that "when a winehead's eyes open up in the morning, all he wants is a drink of wine." The typical winehead is known to "do almost anything for a bottle of wine." His main activity around Jelly's is "getting some wine" or some "wine money." Even his needs for food and shelter are seldom considered in terms of the future but are mainly to be taken care of in the present, to be immediately replaced by and washed down by wine, then laughed off and talked off in the company of those he can claim, at least for the moment, as "drinking buddies." This condition serves to frustrate almost any effort toward achieving a "visible means of support."

Some of the Wineheads

Roosevelt is a tall, dark-skinned man of sixty-six. Over his relatively long life, he has been many things. At times he talks of the days when he was a "hardworking railroad man" or when he was a church-going family man who "got tired of taking care of somebody else." At other times he would talk of himself as a "bad actor," meaning that he was good at gaining the confidence of adversaries in order to take advantage of them and that he was a good hustler. Also, he has been a shoeshine boy who knew "Chi when it was Chi." With great felicity and charm, Roosevelt can talk about the days when Duke Ellington and Billie Holiday played the clubs of the South Side. "In them days I was a tough young stud. Oh, but I was," he would say, cocking his head to one side and strutting a few steps down the sidewalk. Even the regulars and hoodlums find such stories entertaining and sometimes buy him drinks. Roosevelt is loved by the group, especially when he does not act threatening. He knows all the group members well and seems familiar with their personal shortcomings and failings, which he tends to reveal when he thinks a person is "gettin' too big for his britches."

On most days, unless he is ill, he may be found on the street, in the park, or in the alley near Jelly's, drinking wine or "tryin' to get a taste" with his winehead buddies, or hanging in front of Jelly's window "showin' out." He is known for his begging around Jelly's, and when some people see him coming they know what he wants. Roosevelt lives on his social security check, which usually is spent before the next one comes, at which point he has all the more reason to beg regulars and others for money for a "taste."

Jimmy Lee was a twenty-nine-year-old, dark-brown-skinned man who lived a few blocks from Jelly's with his aunt until he died in his sleep. He grew up among the street gangs not far from Jelly's. He liked to talk about his "education" in the gangs and how he learned to fight at an early age. Like many men of the winehead group, Jimmy Lee joined the army when he was old enough, served in 'Nam, and was released with a "bad" discharge. He was very bitter about his experience with the military and would often walk away in disgust when regulars began telling stories glorifying the army. On many occasions I heard Jimmy Lee describe with great bitterness his difficult relationships with "noncom" southern whites who had given him a hard time, which he would say contributed to his "bad" discharge and to his social demise on the ghetto streets. About the time of his death, he was complaining of a "hurtin' " in his side that many, particularly the regulars, dismissed as the inevitable result of drinking cheap wine rather than the "good stuff" they drink. It was widely known in the extended primary group that Jimmy Lee was carrying the stick, and some regulars would ask how he was feeling, or say "How's that hurtin' you got, Jimmy Lee?" At that time his diet consisted mainly of cheap wine and lunch meat or cheese and crackers.

Jocko is a tall, thin, light-brown-skinned man of thirty-seven. Like Jimmy Lee, he is an ex-army man. But unlike Jimmy Lee and a number of other wineheads, Jocko received a general discharge, which, though not the most desirable type, is considered "good" by the extended primary group. Owing to a shrapnel wound in his head, Jocko has a "service-connected" nervous disability and must live with a metal plate in his skull. From time to time he gets painful headaches and drinks wine to ease his pain. He uses the headaches to rationalize his thirst for wine when among regulars. Some of the regulars are very sympathetic to Jocko's predicament, for he has convinced them that he wants, but is unable, to meet their standards of work and decency. He is unable to hold onto a regular job, so he spends a good deal of his time on the corner with other wineheads, trying to get a taste. Jocko lives near Jelly's with his sister Sugar, a divorcee, and her three daughters. When his "army check" arrives, Sugar usually goes with Jocko to the currency exchange and cashes it, keeping most of it for their home expenses. She gives him a small allowance, which he easily runs through in a few days, only to be left to begging from the regulars and others until his next check comes.

In their pasts, many of the wineheads have had a more important social stake in the wider society. Their ranks are filled with men who have seen "better days." Some have been happily married at one point, as Roosevelt was, working regularly to support wives and children; they frequently bring up these aspects of their pasts in conversation around Jelly's. Some wineheads have been through the military, which for many has left social and emotional scars. Some have had "nice" apartments and "nice rides" (cars). Old Roosevelt, for instance, used to work regularly but is now retired and drunk most of the time. Red Mack is "educated" and was a paratrooper, as he reminds all who will listen. Tall Jocko used to be in the army. Johnny Ray "used to be with Job Corps." These known personal biographies help others of the extended primary group to see members of the winehead category as people who have failed at life. Viewed in this manner, the winehead group becomes a kind of residual category.

Group members try to keep their personal friends from falling into this group. When a person of another group, especially a regular, seems to be getting too close to the edge of the winehead category he will be warned or even, on occasion, offered help. Particularly when the person in danger of falling would reflect poorly on the status and identity of other regulars, they come to his assistance. But this may also happen when group members sincerely care for the person's welfare. Usually he will be coaxed back on the "right track" or at least encouraged to hold himself in the "right way." These actions preserve the sense of the established social order and the sense that his potential benefactors care about him personally. This is illustrated in Herman's experience.

During the fall of 1972 Herman and Butterroll, his common-law wife of fourteen years, were having problems with their relationship. Members of the extended primary group, especially the regulars, knew about the trouble, since the whole group is usually in on what happens to most of its members. At the same time, Bea, Herman's old flame, began to show him some attention.

When Bea and Herman stopped going together some years before, she began to "take up time" with a well-known "gangster" of the South Side and has since gained the reputation among Herman's regular friends of being "expensive," a woman who is known to spend time only with men who will help her financially. Bea's association with the gangster, who is reputed to have "big dough," has contributed to this reputation. Among group members she is known to hang out "up on Sixty-third"—not close to Jelly's. With the renewed association of Bea and Herman, at a time when Herman was having problems at home, other regulars, including some of his closest friends, became very concerned about his personal and social welfare.

When Herman's home problems began he mentioned to a few people—me, Pee Wee, his brother Curtis, and a few others—that Butterroll was "raisin' sand" at home, that she was "at it again, on

my case, and won't gimme no slack." Herman threatened to leave
home. Some of the other regulars dared him to do so, implying he
was not man enough to stand up to Butterroll. As this news went
around the group, some began to question Herman's image as a
manly "master of his house," which is the role working men, particularly the regulars, are supposed to play. This situation presented
Herman with a challenge to prove himself, to demonstrate that where
women were concerned he deserved to be highly regarded.

Group members became more confident of Herman's manly ca-
pacities when he spent the following weekend with Bea. By this
action Herman demonstrated a certain independence that many of
the married regulars often strive to display even while maintaining
their images as participants in a stable home life. Herman's ren-
dezvous with Bea began on a Friday evening after he had been
paid. Normally, on Fridays Butterroll drives up Jelly's alley to meet
Herman and get his money, as the wives of some regulars do, before he is robbed or drinks it up—or before he can use either of
these possibilities as excuses for not giving her money to manage
the household.

On this particular Friday Butterroll drove up, but Herman was nowhere to be found. She asked, "Spider, you seen that man of mine?"

"Naw, I ain't seen him. Lemme ask some of these other guys,"
said Spider. He went inside Jelly's and said, "Hey, it's Butterroll.
What should I tell her? Any o' y'all seen Herman? What should I
tell her? I don't wanta get involved!"

At that point Jelly said, "Tell her you ain't seen him, man. That's
the truth. Herman ain't been 'round here. You know that, man."
Spider did as Jelly instructed. Having this answer from Spider, Butterroll seemed satisfied and left. The men didn't know yet that Herman was really planning not to come home that evening; in fact,
most believed he was only bluffing.

On the following day, Saturday, Butterroll called Jelly's first thing
in the morning, inquiring about Herman and reporting that she had
not seen him at all the night before. With this bit of news, the air at
Jelly's buzzed with talk about Herman, and some of the men were
impressed by what could be taken as a show of independence.

After spending the weekend with Bea, Herman returned to Jelly's and attempted to show the group some evidence of what he had done over the weekend. Right away Herman mentioned that he had gotten into "some strange leg" (new sex) over the weekend, which helped confirm some of the rumors about his "creeping" (sneaky infidelity). For most of the extended primary group, such behavior is a way of meeting the male street ethic of "find 'em, fool 'em, fuck 'em, and forget 'em." Because of his actions, and his report of them, Herman seemed to gain some status. Many would give Herman their undivided attention, but not everyone was convinced or impressed by Herman's talk of his exploits. Sensing this, Herman threatened to repeat his weekend performance.

On the following Friday, Herman again went to visit Bea and stayed with her for the weekend. This time Butterroll was furious. She called Jelly's repeatedly during the weekend in search of Herman. On the following Monday Herman came home to Butterroll. On Tuesday he was back at Jelly's bragging about what he had done. But this time, to back up his story, he displayed the woman's "piece" (pistol), which he had "borrowed" from her dresser drawer. For that whole week Herman was the talk of Jelly's.

As if all he had done were not enough, he threatened to visit Bea again the following weekend—and he did. Only this time Herman took "breathers" at Jelly's, while the woman supposedly lay in bed waiting for him. While he was in the liquor-store room, Butterroll called. L. C., a regular, answered the phone and asked loudly, "Is Herman here?"—although he was looking at Herman when he answered the phone. Herman made a face and gestured that he was not there, as he looked at the others with a smirk and a look of confidence. L. C. then told Butterroll Herman was not around.

But she somehow knew he was around, for she said to L.C., and in a sense to the rest of the group, "Al'right, now. Herman messin' up. He messin' up. Now, I ain't gon' be standin' for too much more o' his shit. Good-bye!" L. C. hung up and relayed this message to Herman and the others present. Herman raised his hand and waved at the phone, as if he didn't care about the message. Then he walked outside and soon left.

Herman's behavior had now begun to worry some of his friends among the regulars. Many feared he might be losing control of himself. Had he "gone off his rocker"? Now some of the regulars began to discuss seriously whether Herman would lose his "good thing," a concern that really pointed up the men's sense of the important role Butterroll played in Herman's life and in his personal and social welfare. This concern was expressed in a number of conversations around Jelly's, especially among the regulars, who felt they were in a position to comment on Herman's situation.

Such conversations were revealing of the social order of the group. For example, on Sunday of the third weekend that Herman went out with Bea, T. J. wondered whether Pee Wee, a close friend of Herman, should speak to him about his behavior, to remind him that he was "fuckin' up," as the group members say when one of their own appears to be losing ground in meeting the standards they deem important for him.

"Herman better cut all that funny shit out, or he gon' sho'nuff lose a good woman," said T. J.

"Yeah, Butterroll ain't gon' be puttin' up with too much mo' o' the shit he puttin' out," said Sleepy.

"The nigger better straighten up and fly right. Seem like when a man get him a good thing that he a want to keep it. Now, Butterroll a good woman. She burn for him [cooks well], take care o' the house. Shit, she even now keep Herman together. He a be lost without that woman," said T. J., turning to me. "Eli, now you and he s'pose to be tight, why don't you pull his coat? [alert him]" At that point Pee Wee, another good friend of Herman's, approached and the group's attention turned to him.

Red Mack, a winehead, spoke to Pee Wee, "Pee Wee, you better say somethin' to yo' boy. He fuckin' up. You know, Pee Wee, I hate to see what'll happen to Herman if Butterroll cut out on him. 'Cause if he lose her, he a soon be carryin' the stick just like one of these wineheads out here."

Sharply cutting Red Mack off, Pee Wee said, "Best be taking care o' yo' own damn self, Mack. Leave Herman to take care of Herman! You better be tryin' to keep yo' own shit together. That's what you better do. How you gon' talk about anyone carryin' the stick, Mack? Herman got a whole gang of order to himself compared to you, Mack, and any one o' yo' buddies. Shit!"

This statement put Mack back in his place as a winehead and helped take up for Herman's place as a bona fide regular. But equally important, it spoke for the place of regulars in relation to wineheads, making clearer the distinction between the rights of wine-heads and those of regulars. Within a few minutes of this talk, which T. J. soon joined, along with Sleepy and Spider, both of whom are marginal, Mack eased away, leaving the scene to the regulars present.

After Mack, the least regular of the group, was made into a scape-goat, the regulars—who had somehow reaffirmed their regularity through dismissing a person who clearly was not one of them— went back to the "serious" discussion of Herman's situation. They talked about how Bea was "good for nothing," a woman who did not deserve their friend Herman. They also spoke of Butterroll as the kind of woman Herman needed, one who had proved her worth by sticking with him in times of trouble. They felt that Bea, who was now used to good times and lots of "fun," would leave Herman after she took his money.

In commenting on the situation, Blue, a regular, said, "You know this bitch he fuckin' with done gave everybody some pussy. You know all she gon' do with Herman is take his money. That's just what gon' happen."

And Sleepy, a marginal, who had become more regular than Red Mack, agreed, saying, "You know, yeah. He gots to be droppin' some iron [money] to spend that ho's time," seeming to affirm his own position of the moment as a regular.

Then T. J., in an act that seemed to exclude the two marginal people, whispered to Pee Wee and me, "Tell me. What Herman gon' do with some bitch like that. All the ho gon' do is take his money. She don't give a fuck about him, 'cause if she did she would have never put him down fo' that gangster. I hope he get hep. Seem like the boy done lost his mind. You really ought to talk to him Pee Wee, you or Eli, one."

After this, the conversation drifted to some other topic in which the more marginal people were allowed to participate. This action again reminded those present, however subtly, of their respective places in the social order of the extended primary group. There appeared to be certain rules about who regulars and nonregulars could talk about and with whom.

Later that same evening, Herman's brother Curtis and I shared a bottle of Old Forester with orange juice. "Eli, I want you to say something to Herman. Now he really think a lot of you, I mean you educated and all, and you can talk to him in ways that even I can't. Now you know he fuckin' up at home, runnin' 'round with this other woman. Just tell him what a good thing he got with Butterroll. You know, you hep, put a bug in his ear. Pull his coat," said Curtis.

"Yeah, the cats have been talking about him. Have you tried to talk to him?" I asked.

"Nah, he ain't gon' listen to me no way, but I think he'll take your word seriously. He really thinks a lot of you, you know. You know he can't make it without Butterroll. You saw him when she went in the hospital for them two weeks. Herman almost came apart." Here, Curtis was referring to a time a few months earlier when Butterroll had gone into the hospital for an operation. Without Butterroll at home, Herman began eating sporadically and going about somewhat unkempt. At that time, also, members of the group had made an effort to "take up" for Herman as one of their own: T. J. and some of the others sometimes went over to Herman's house to cook for him, and some of their wives sent "dinners" to his house or to Jelly's. During this two-week period Herman lost weight and seemed to be losing the "order about himself" that many regulars value so highly. It was then that other regulars attempted to come to his aid, trying to support him and keep him from falling into the winehead category.

At Curtis's request, and after assuring him that I had faith in Herman's ability to take care of himself, I decided to make an inquiry. The next evening I ran into Herman at Jelly's liquor store.

We greeted each other as we usually did. "What you drinking?" I asked, as is customary when wanting to buy someone a drink at Jelly's. On numerous occasions Herman and I had bought drinks for each other, and we felt very free in using each other in this way. It was one of the ways we demonstrated our closeness in the presence of others.

"I'll take a tall Bud," said Herman. "What you drinking?"

"I'll take the same," I said.

"Hey, Jelly!" shouted Herman, in a joking manner, "Get off that fat ass o' yours and get us a couple of tall Buds." Jelly then fetched the beer, and I paid him for it. He grumbled something at Herman, as is customary in their relationship, which invariably involves casual joking, arguing, and grumbling. We then took the beer and moved over to a corner of the liquor-store room where we could be away from others. Again, this was not unusual when we met and wanted to exchange tales about what had been happening in our lives. After we had talked for a while I said, "Say, Herman. What's been happening with you and this new lady? You know, you've got everybody talking 'bout you. The boys [regulars] are beginning to worry about you. Even Curtis is concerned. He asked me to talk to you."

"Yeah, I know," said Herman, "Pee Wee brought it [the regulars' concern] to me last night. See, Eli. I was just puttin' the shit on these squares' minds. Sometimes these cats up in here don't know who I am, and I have to let 'em know. You know, make 'em know. See, 'cause quiet as it's kept (just between you and me), I ain't goin' nowhere and Butterroll ain't neither. But sometimes, see, I got to put somethin' on her mind so she don't take me for granted, you dig."

"Well, I felt you had it together, but the cats kept on bugging me about talking to you . . ."

"You know Butterroll's the best thing that ever happened to me. She loves my dirty drawers. She good to me, even if she do argue sometimes. What two people that live together ain't gon' argue sometime? Huh? But see, I had to let these squares know that I ain't no square. I'm just playin' these studs, you dig. But don't you get all concerned. Ol' Herman ain't gon' do nothin' foolish. Besides, I been out in these here streets a long ol' time." Herman winked and grinned at me when he said this. We then had another beer, laughed and talked with some of the other fellows, and left to see a movie.

The foregoing story illustrates not only Herman's personal understanding of the social order of the extended primary group, but also —and most important for this discussion—the regulars' sense of their place in the group in relation to wineheads. Moreover, it indicates the respect in which the wineheads represent a residual category within the extended primary group. The regulars' view of themselves as above and distinct from the winehead category is what they most want to protect and maintain, even to the point of "taking up for" fellow regulars when they approach the edge of the winehead group. The story also points out how precarious their status is. Because of this precariousness, the regulars, who seem the most concerned about their own standards, have developed a need to set themselves apart. In their various attempts to fulfill this need, they in effect help to create not only their own group solidarity, but also the residual category of wineheads.

The Problem of Distancing Oneself
from the Wineheads

Regulars, and men who would like to see themselves as regulars, create this residual category by pointing out others who have become "victims" of the social order. The regulars use these "others" as scapegoats in a process of realizing their own sense of place in the extended primary group. They label the victims wineheads and, among themselves, "talk about" their failings and shortcomings. Regulars and others believe and find the typical winehead to be "ignorant" of the wider society's values and standards. He is to be pitied for not being able to carry himself properly. Such labels and explanations allow regulars to "help" wineheads by offering them correction or instruction about how better to meet public standards. But at the same time, the labeling, the explanations, and the instruction seem to make the value of decency even more difficult for members of the winehead class to meet, especially as it is defined by regulars judging them. This is indicated in the following story.

One weekday evening in late October, L. C. and a small number of regulars "cracked" a bottle of Jim Beam in the liquor-store room. I bought a pint of orange juice and shared it as mix for the whiskey. We all drank and talked, as issue after issue came up. Dicky began talking about his wife and children, telling us his wife wanted to work and that this might make trouble in his home. "It's hard enough keepin' a wife and kids in line," he said, "without addin' a job for her to it. Pretty soon she might feel like she can get by without me." Others brought up arguments indicating why she should be allowed to work, and one person told about his experiences with a "workin' wife" and about how her work started his own troubles in married life. No sooner had this issue been raised than it was dropped, to be replaced by Mr. Porter's speech about the tune-up his car needed before the cold weather set in. After this matter had worn itself out, L. C. and Albert argued about the roles each had played in various overseas theaters during World War II.

Topics like these rise and fall very quickly in the liquor-store room. At times heated arguments may develop over minor points of information about someone else's talk. Many feel a real need to express themselves by making some verbal contribution to the gathering. The conversation I have just described evolved for about two hours before it turned to talk about the wineheads. L. C. raised the topic by expressing to Dicky, another regular, and to the others present, his concern and sorrow for the situation of Bemo, a winehead, who was clearly "carrying the stick" as the winter was beginning to set in.

"The boy Bemo sho' got it tough. Ain't got a pot to piss in and he barely eatin'," said L. C.

"I just saw him 'bout a couple of hours ago, him and Cleo [a retired regular] was together. I don't know where they went," said Dicky.

"He probably tryin' to beg some food out o' Cleo, and Cleo ain't got that much hisself," said L. C.

"Well, somebody ought to help him," entered Mr. Thompson, another retired regular.

"Yeah well, you know, all the average one of 'em will do is piss you off and make you sorry you tried to help 'em. Now take just the other day when I took Bemo to a cafe over in Hyde Park. Now me and Bemo go in this pancake house. I call myself doin' a good turn [apparently blushing], I mean, you know [explaining], the man barely eatin' and I figure I been blessed with a good job and my family in good shape. So I figure I'm gon' help 'im get 'im a little somethin' to eat. [This is a practice many regulars will follow when trying to be "decent" to their fellowmen in need of help. In helping a winehead in this manner, they make sure their money is spent for food instead of wine.] Now, see, I done told Bemo ahead of time to have hisself fixed up a little and I would get 'im somethin' to eat. So I meet 'im and take him over to this pancake house. Now, we go in there and decent black folks and white folks sittin' around eatin' and stuff. The waitress sits us down, now. People lookin' at us, now. Me and Bemo. I say to Bemo, 'Bemo, we inside here, now could you please take off yo' hat?' Bemo just looks at me. And we sat up there for awhile, till the waitress bring us our food. Now, I'm starting to get a little warm [perturbed]. So, I say to Bemo again, 'Bemo, you makin' me look bad, sittin' up in here eatin' with your hat on. Why don't you be respectful and take off your hat and do like these nice folks do?' I tried to explain this to him, 'cause this is how you s'pose to do when you out someplace eatin'. Now, I said this in a nice soft tone of voice. But the cat's jaws got tight [mad]. And there I am with this winehead, and see, what make it so bad is that it seem like everybody lookin' at us. Him and that old raggedy assed coat of his'n. You know, the winehead wanted to fight me for askin' him to take off his hat. Boy, I'll never do that no more."

At this, Dicky added an explanation for Bemo's behavior. "Well, what you expect?" said Dicky. "He ignorant! He ignorant!" The label "ignorant" is one of the important words regulars use when talking about the "failings" of wineheads. They also use it to describe other regulars in circumstances they feel warrant it. The word serves as a kind of catchall explanation that helps the regulars dismiss flagrant violations of the norms and values they believe in and want to uphold. By explaining wineheads and others in this way, the regulars attempt to distance themselves socially from men who pose threats to their own interpretation of the social order of the extended primary group.

Through their acts of social distancing, they indicate a residual category of the group. Once this residual category has been created, pointed to, and talked about as distinct from the category of "regular," the regulars may relax their own standards of conduct somewhat. Thus they often engage in conduct indistinguishable from what in different circumstances—and from a different perspective—they would themselves readily label "winehead" conduct. "Regular" conduct, then, may be viewed as a posture "regulars" may assume when they sense a threat to their own identity or when they sense an opportunity for successfully presenting, defining, and, most important, distinguishing themselves as regulars.

Late one July afternoon The Homey, a winehead who had arrived from the South some years before, and a number of other men, including wineheads, regulars, and hoodlums, were gathered on the sidewalk in front of Jelly's. Some of us were standing in the alley, while others were sitting on wooden soda crates and leaning against buildings on either side. T. J. took a few swigs from a can of Budweiser wrapped in a brown paper sack, the "regular" way of drinking beer in public. Jocko, Jimmy Lee, and Red Mack were busy trying to get "a cold one" and hence were standing around begging change from various people, including occasional passersby.

Wigfall and I shared a tall can of Bud, while we talked about an upcoming Cubs ball game. The cool breeze felt good, and the rest of the afternoon promised to be pleasant.

Then The Homey came up and leaned against the side of Jelly's building and "passed his water"—the regulars' euphemism for "pissed." Some of the men simply moved away and continued doing what they had been doing. Others shook their heads as they joked, pointed, and hunched one another. T. J. said, "Damn, Homey. Why you got to act like a nigger? Why you got to be a nigger and piss upside the man's building?" Some watched seriously, while others laughed and still others mumbled among themselves. Through all this The Homey, who was somewhat high on wine, appeared stoic and indifferent. After a long while, he began asking various people for bus fare to the West Side. None was forthcoming. Soon, with a look of disgust, he pulled from his pocket a bunch of old bus transfers that he uses to get around the city, physically intimidating bus drivers, who won't risk putting him off their buses. Then he left.

After The Homey left, a number of the men "got on his case"—that is, they talked about him and his behavior. The group included a mix of wineheads, regulars, and hoodlums. Though T. J., a regular, took the lead in the talk, he was soon joined by wineheads and others. Taking this as an opportunity to uphold regular values, wineheads here colluded with the "regulars" against The Homey. Red Mack, an outstanding winehead, called Homey "good for nothing." Others tried to explain Homey and his conduct as "ignorant." Even Jocko, a winehead who sometimes gets drunk with Homey but was relatively sober at this time because he had no money, wondered aloud, "I don't see how come the man couldn't go and use Jelly's toilet like all the rest of *us* do," as he included himself in the running for regular status values. There were other similar comments. Through much of this talk about The Homey, it seemed that these group members were conducting a kind of purification ritual. The Homey was the group's scapegoat—and in a sense represented the whole class of wineheads. Not one person came to his defense. Nor did any "regulars" complain about the moves being made by the wineheads present. In these particular circumstances, this group was preoccupied with the collective disparagement of Homey, which for them improved their own group standing.

Later, in a parallel but contrasting situation, T. J., a bona fide regular, had the chance to become the group's scapegoat, though it never happened. After more members of the extended primary group had arrived, people began breaking off into their own crowds. As evening approached, different regulars, wineheads, and hoodlums came and went, apparently changing the definition of the group.

Topics of conversation changed rapidly. About four hours after Homey had left, a number of regulars, including T. J., Herman, Pee Wee, Blue, and me were standing around in the park not far from Jelly's. As we shared a bottle of whiskey, we all laughed, talked, and just had fun with one another. At some point amid all the fun, T. J. felt the need to "pass his water" and did so against the nearest tree. Though there was a slight pause, the group members appeared inattentive to T. J. When he finished, the conversation and the fun continued as though nothing significant had happened; as if no violation of regular standards of decency had occurred. There was no invocation as when Homey was the center of attention a few hours earlier. On this occasion the group seemed not to have the need—or the right—to victimize one of its own, as it sometimes finds the need to victimize relative outsiders.

Begging or "passing water" in public helps qualify a person for the label "winehead," but such acts do not necessarily determine winehead status. They must also be situationally defined as personally distinctive winehead attributes. It is through the collective action of "talking about" a winehead that group members not only define the person and indicate the nature of the social order, but also define their own group standards. By implication they work to consolidate their group position.

By "explaining" a person with reference to this label and by being able to point out men who act like wineheads, the regulars and others who can avoid being counted as wineheads help create a class of people that becomes in fact a status group distinct from themselves. For the social order is in part defined by who is able to talk about whom in whose presence. At issue here is the question of informal rights. Someone who can "get in on" a certain side of the talk can simultaneously make some claim on status values and on the identity that others he is colluding with are believed to possess.

It was 10:30 A.M. Monday when I arrived at Jelly's. Two retired regulars, Mr. Butler and Mr. Lewis, were sitting on wooden crates near the counter in the liquor-store room, and Jelly was standing behind the counter. I greeted all of them as I entered. In a few minutes Pope, another regular, entered. We all greeted him. Soon Mr. Lewis asked Pope, "You on vacation, ain'cha, Pope?"

"Yeah, Mr. Lewis, I'm off for a while." We engaged in small talk. Jelly read the morning *Sun-Times* and interjected interesting bits of news as he read. Time passed. The potato-chip man drove up and delivered a fresh carton of potato chips. Silent, we attentively watched him do his job. Our eyes followed him to his truck as he got in and drove off. We seemed not to have much to do at that time of the morning. Mr. Lewis then looked over to the park and said, "Them wineheads out there already. They a be drunk directly," referring to their early-morning arrival at the park, which is really quite normal. Jelly looked up from the paper and laughed.

"Yeah, one of them son' bitches with some Boones' Farm. They done started already," laughed Jelly.

Then Mr. Butler said, "There oughta be some law 'gainst people like that. They don't do nothin' all day 'cept hang around in that park and drink that cheap wine."

"They ain't gon' work, don't wanna work. Just a bunch a no 'counts. That's all they is," added Jelly. Outside, the wineheads were oblivious to anything being said about them. They seemed to care little for the opinions of those outside their group. Red Mack was singing at the top of his lungs while Jocko sang the background. Jelly shook his head and laughed again. The others laughed along.

In this way the regulars and any others who would like to have the regulars' apparent social distance from the winehead category indicate who is who by simply "talking about" the wineheads, thus making important statements about themselves as well. Regulars and others further indicate these social differences by telling "winehead stories"—"funny" or "sad" tales of particular wineheads' failure to meet regular standards of conduct. The stories, and the way they are told, have a judgmental character.

One winter evening Otis, a postal worker who is considered a regular, arrived in a shiny new Chevy. After parking directly in front of Jelly's, he bounced into the liquor-store room where there were a number of other regulars and a few wineheads and hoodlums. Beaming with pride he confronted the men. "There it is! There it is," he said to the group. Meanwhile some group members had already gathered around his new car, looking it over and checking it out. Jelly and Pee Wee had been engrossed in an argument over city politics, but they stopped and looked out the front window at Otis's "new ride." Others also stopped what they were doing, and some went outside for a better look. After the excitement had died down and the crowd had dispersed, Otis returned to the liquor-store room and told Jelly to "set 'em up." Whenever someone buys a new car, it is customary for him to christen it by treating his friends to drinks at Jelly's. In addition to this, the person usually takes the men closest to him for a kind of ritual drive. On this particular occasion Otis, who is regarded as "tight" with his money, drew invidious distinctions among members of the extended primary group. For instance, when Jelly began serving up the drinks, The Homey, a winehead, and Clay, a hoodlum, put up their cups for drinks. But Otis immediately refused them by snapping, "Hey, what you think you're doing? Ain't no wineheads drinking off a me"—thereby putting the men back in the places he considered them to have. Then he turned to T. J., a regular, and said, apparently for the benefit of all present, "Next thing you know these son' bitches a be wantin' to get in on the drive." The Homey and Clay seemed to know in advance what to expect for their "pushy" behavior, and as "outsiders" they eased off to separate corners of the room. Then Mr. Thompson, a regular who is a retired Pullman porter, interjected, "You 'member what happened to Bill when he let a winehead get in his new car, don't you?" "No. What happened?" I prompted. "Well, Mickey was the winehead's name. He don't come 'round here no mo'. But anyway, this fool got into the backseat of Bill's car, and Bill took some of the cats for a spin, you know. Well, when the winehead got in, he had to take a shit, and he shitted all over the man's floor. Ha-ha. That's sho'nuff what he did. And Bill was mad for weeks. He wanted to kill that winehead." The men, including Jelly and some of the wineheads present, broke up with laughter at the way Mr. Thompson told this story. Then, Blue, another regular added, "That's a winehead for you. That's a winehead for you. Ha-ha." The others continued laughing.

Another instance of such judgmental conduct occurred on a Friday evening at Jelly's. Friday is payday for many of the regulars, and they usually pour into Jelly's to celebrate the end of the week. Normally, by six o'clock on Fridays there are thirty to thirty-five men in the liquor-store room. During this time they drink, smoke, laugh, yell and shout at one another, and generally let off steam. Also, they discuss their personal lives and relate the troubles and triumphs of the past week to the sympathetic, and sometimes unsympathetic, ears of buddies and others who congregate at Jelly's. On this particular Friday evening there were about four or five wineheads in the room, but Red Mack and The Homey were the real standouts. Mack was drunk and doped up, nodding out while sitting on a Coke case against a wall. The Homey sat next to him and begged regulars and others for money. Most of the men he asked refused him flatly, but some reminded him of back "loans" he hadn't paid, and just a couple gave him money.

Mack, a thirty-three-year-old winehead with a ruddy, very light complexion and straight brown hair, nodded back and forth, appearing ready to fall to the floor at any moment. He was dressed in blue jeans and an old green army jacket, and his hair was greased and plastered down on his head. The regulars reluctantly see Mack as a winehead, for he is "educated" (high school) and hence does not fit well with their own conceptions of what a winehead should be. But they treat him as one anyway, though seeming to hope that he will someday grow out of his winehead ways and "get himself together and get some order about himself."

Once during the night Mack almost fell over, thus catching the attention of T. J. and Albert, both of whom are usually regarded as regulars. Both men stopped drinking their scotch for the moment and pointed at Mack, focusing their attention on Mack's failure to carry himself properly. Meanwhile Mack continued to nod and rock, unmindful of the attention he was now beginning to get from a growing number of regulars who had taken an interest in his disorderly conduct. He seemed more ready than ever to fall to the hardwood floor. The men waited and some pointed at Mack and laughed. Then T. J. stepped back in a grand gesture and shook his head from side to side, fully aware of his performance. He turned up his cup and said, "It's a shame 'bout that boy. He works just enough to get a little money, just enough to get sloppy drunk on, and just like that . . . ," snapping his fingers. Just at this moment Mack crashed to the dirty floor. The men roared with laughter as some of them pointed and gestured, hunching one another as they did. Mack jumped to his feet, looking as though he had just awakened from a deep sleep, his eyes red and glassy. He looked around for a moment at his audience, then nervously walked outside into the cool night air. T. J. continued shaking his head and laughing. Albert looked at T. J. and said, "Such a young man, too. Ruined on that juice [cheap wine]." Then Spider, who can be seen almost any day hanging with the wineheads and the hoodlums but who will attempt to associate with regulars when he is given an opening, got in on the put-down, saying, "The boy got a education, too. Got mo' 'an I got." He thus passed judgment, taking the opportunity presented by the collective disparagement of Mack to identify himself as a regular. He was attempting to shore up his own regular credentials by pointing to someone who had indeed spoiled any chance for being seen as regular. "Too bad," said Spider, again in agreement with T. J. and Albert and the other regulars. For that time Spider could feel himself as regular, joining in on the derogation of Mack and by implication upgrading himself.

Spider's talk illustrates not only how certain marginal members of the extended primary group are allowed to see themselves as regulars, but also how members with relatively few status resources or informal rights may be used by others as props for their own status and identity. The standards of conduct deemed important appear always to be shifting, for they are invoked by people who are competing with others in varying circumstances and who themselves in some measure contribute to those circumstances. Thus something akin to musical chairs operates, and the prize in the game is status. Status in the extended primary group goes to the person who is better able to convey the impression that he has the group attributes certain others lack.

However the attributes of status are not perfectly fixed. They are precarious and are situationally influenced, if not determined. One way of dealing with the precariousness of group status is to gather with people who will make one's notions about one's own status and identity more credible to whomever one wishes to impress, including oneself. One attempts to collude with others one wants to identify with against those one wants to be distinguished from, particularly when the latter have flagrantly violated group standards. By gathering together, group members publicly indicate, to themselves and to others, the nature and roughly the degree of rule infraction or standard violation. Men who exclude others simultaneously attempt to place themselves on the "better" side of the line, among the upholders of the rules. It is partly in this way that the crowd of wineheads is cognitively and actually created by regulars and by others who might like to be regular.

In such instances little attention seems to be given to the known personal biography of the now-colluding regular-to-be. Attention focuses upon the specific act and its implications for status. At this instant and for this particular status issue, the person campaigning to be regular is out to find others who will agree with him about the standards of the group. He often asserts his sense of the standards in exchange for being accorded a position on the "right" side when the judgmental social act of status construction has been completed. However marginal, he may be regarded as regular at least temporarily. The subgroup of regulars that carries out the constructing may be viewed as being "short of help" for the time being and hence in need of temporary allies. When "better regulars" come along who will serve as less flimsy props for the definition of regular, firmer, more exacting standards may be employed, thus increasing the number of persons considered wineheads or marginal.[3]

The Wineheads' Place in Social Interaction

Because of their built-in inability to meet the "decent" standards of conduct that regulars seem especially inclined to invoke in their presence, most wineheads gather with and stay among their own kind. When interacting with regulars and others, they tend to be quiet and not say much, lest the regulars complain and remind them of their place. Most wineheads come into the liquor store only to purchase their wine, then leave to join their drinking buddies. Ordinarily no one needs to tell them to leave. Through such acts of deference, the wineheads exhibit a certain respect for the justice of status arrangements in the extended primary group.

I have often seen wineheads leave a spot in the park, in the alley, or on the sidewalk when "too many" regulars and others appeared. For instance, many times I have seen Bemo, whom I knew fairly well, move away whenever regulars began to congregate. One day I decided to talk with him about this, so I joined him on one of his walks away from the regulars. The two of us walked away from a gathering group of regulars toward a group of wineheads about thirty yards down the alley. At first we talked about various things other than the issue I really wanted to know about. But at an opportune moment I asked him, "Bemo, why do you always leave when T. J. or Bill or Dicky or any one of those cats comes around?"

"Well, I'll tell you, Eli. I just ain't got nothin' in common wit' them studs and they ain't really got nothin' in common wit' me," he said.

"What do you mean?" I asked further.

"I mean, well, they talk about me behind my back. Them studs don't really dig me. They prob'ly laughin' at me right now. You get 'round them and they got to start talkin' all that heavy shit. Man, I don't always be wantin' to hear that shit. Now, I ain't one of them. You know T. J. got big dough [money], least that's what the cats be sayin' 'bout him. Them cats just ain't my kinda people," he said.

"But I see you laughing and talking with them sometimes anyway," I said.

"Aw, yeah, I mean, they'll laugh and talk with me, and even now lay some bread on me, but that's 'cause I got a decent conversation [intelligence] and don't never bother nobody. Now they al'right when you get 'em alone—but when you get them all together gangin' up on you, you know, all that 'I got this and you got that' shit, then I got to move. See, I know I ain't got shit, and I don't get all upset about that. But as soon as one of them studs get around me, they come out o' this ol' 'why can't you find yourself a job, Bemo' bag. Then I got to say later for 'em. And you know, Bemo a sick man, Eli. Bemo ain't gettin' no younger."

"How's your stomach?" I asked, referring to his well-known ailment.

"Oh, I'm doin' al'right now, but a few days ago I was sicker 'an a dog. I was spittin' up a little blood, too. But I'm doin' al'right now," he answered.

"You better get to a doctor," I advised. "Have you seen one?"

"I'm seein' one. I'm seein' one, but he just say stop drinkin'," said Bemo.

"You should take his advice," I said.

"I have cut down, but that's my pleasure and my fun. Can't take that all away. Uh, say, Eli. Could you lemme hold a quarter?" asked Bemo. At that point, I reached into my pocket for loose change and gave him all I had—about sixty cents. After that we joined the wineheads and hung with them for the rest of the day.

One reason many wineheads move away from regulars is that they somehow know their places within the social order and apparently believe in the justice of it. Seldom do they question the assessment of the regulars: that wineheads are not as good as regulars. They know that decency is very important in the general social order of group standards and principles of status, especially among the regulars. And they generally know, though some must be reminded from time to time, that they lack the resources for commanding deference and making successful claims to decency. They know they don't have jobs like regulars have. Some wineheads work for regulars. Others beg from regulars and others in the group. Most realize that they could be reminded only too easily about their shortcomings with respect to the regulars' definitions of decency. These definitions are usually not disputed by wineheads; they may simply move to be among those with whom they can feel more comfortable.

For the wineheads, such "decency" is practically an unapproachable standard: the more a winehead reaches for it, the more elusive it seems to become. Regulars regard the typical winehead as a person who cares little for public proprieties. Whereas regulars, for example, pride themselves on, and even form as a group around, the activities of buying and drinking "expensive good stuff," like Old Forester or Jim Beam or Jack Daniels, and of drinking it behind the closed door of Jelly's liquor-store room, they know the winehead thrives on drinking cheap wine—for which he usually must beg—on the public streets and sidewalks. Similarly, the typical winehead is known to have no compunctions about "passing his water in public" against the nearest tree or the side of Jelly's building. There are other "failings" as well, all of which the regulars consider offensive to their own sense of decency.

With regulars, wineheads are often reminded of their comparative "failings" and shortcomings, both through the treatment regulars mete out to them and verbally, as the note above makes clear. Wineheads are often referred to, even when they are present, as "ignorant," as "no 'count," and, equally important, as "wineheads." Such language reminds them of who they are and of the kind of treatment in store for them as part of the extended primary group.

Wineheads have limited informal rights in the group. The average winehead is not allowed to remain in Jelly's liquor store for long after he buys his wine. Few are ever treated to a meal the way L. C. treated Bemo, for such ventures often confirm the regulars' conceptions of wineheads, as occurred in that case. Very few wineheads are ever invited to the homes of regulars. And whereas wineheads often ask regulars to hold portions of their incomes for safekeeping, it would be unthinkable for a regular to ask a winehead to hold money for him. Moreover, when a regular demonstrates an uncommon degree of trust in a particular winehead, it is usually a special occasion for the winehead.

On a hot Saturday afternoon in July, Jelly was running low on ice. Jocko was standing around outside the door of the liquor store. Jelly, who is usually "hard" on the wineheads as a group, and harder on Jocko in particular, thought he would "try" Jocko by asking him to fetch some ice for him. Jelly said, "Hey, Jocko. Want you to do something for me." For a winehead to be asked to do something for Jelly is often seen as an honor, even if the two are temporarily on bad terms.

"Wha'cha want, Jelly?" said Jocko.

"I need some ice. Can you do it for me?" asked Jelly.

"Sure," answered Jocko, and became quite excited. He had been stroked and was anxious to please Jelly. It was clear to everyone that Jocko was happy about being able to do Jelly a favor. Jelly reached into his pocket and came up with a ten-dollar bill that he gave to Jocko. Then Jocko left for the ice. Jelly winked and smiled at the others present. Two hours passed before Jocko returned with the ice.

While he was away, the others wondered what "the winehead" had done with the money. Most guessed that he had found some of his boys and gotten drunk on Jelly's ten dollars. But the truth was that Jocko had searched out his friends to show them the ten dollars as "proof" of Jelly's trust in him. After fetching the ice he went back and displayed the ice for them. Of course, by the time he returned to Jelly's, the ice was somewhat melted. But for some time after, Jocko beamed with a new sense of self-worth and pride. He was proud of Jelly's confidence in him.

Even when they know what treatment is in store for them, most wineheads seem to accept what the regulars mete out. In fact, through their actions, they often actively support the others' view of them as subordinate. Here the wineheads show a sort of slave mentality. They tend to pay for association with regulars by becoming "their wineheads." This was indicated on numerous occasions, for instance, when a number of regulars were standing around outside Jelly's one afternoon talking about another "joint up on Thirty-fifth." In describing the place as "rough" and "low-life," T. J. said, "Yeah, most of the studs up in there are worse off than our wineheads." No one disagreed with this assessment, not even the few wineheads present.

One way the wineheads pay the social debt for being allowed in regular company is through their deference. They listen without complaint to the epithets regulars apply to their kind. They continue to hang around, seeming to pretend that they are "in on" the talk. At times they work to deny their status as wineheads, yet they readily accept the telling treatment handed them by regulars. Their denial helps them to think they are not being "talked about," not being colluded against, and thus not being included in the winehead category.

But they know they can be reminded only too easily that they lack the resources regulars possess. Thus in regular company a winehead will be quiet, not wanting to say too much and incur the challenges of regulars. At such times wineheads may go through personal degradation ceremonies, even at the hands of regulars who, in different circumstances, seem marginal. They do all this in exchange for the informal rights of inclusion such conduct promises. Yet the promises are seldom really fulfilled. To gain the company and association of "regulars," people with winehead attributes must agree to *be* wineheads. If they act as though they don't know their places, they risk provoking regulars to put them there. The following story of Red Mack illustrates these points.

Red Mack

As mentioned earlier, Red Mack is a very light-complexioned man of thirty-three. He is about six feet tall and weighs about 150 pounds. Group members often refer to Mack's color as "bright." From a distance he may be taken for white, which makes special problems for him when he is confronted by strangers on the ghetto streets. Mack is single but sometimes lives with a sister in the neighborhood. When she puts him out he goes to live with various friends or homosexuals, with whom he is known to exchange sexual favors for room and board.

Many regulars view Mack as a winehead who is trying to meet their standards of conduct but failing. His "failing," which often seems spectacular in the context of the regulars, helps make him the ready butt of a number of winehead stories. The regulars sometimes gang up on him and make him a victim and scapegoat who is by definition unable to meet their standards of conduct. All of this, including his own interpretation of his role in the group, has worked to make him a "character" around Jelly's.

After graduating from a local high school, which is rare for a winehead, Mack enlisted in the army paratroopers at the encouragement of The Terry, a hoodlum who claims to have "raised" Mack and continues to influence him. Mack served with the army in the Dominican Republic during the United States involvement there, then was released with a "bad" discharge. He returned to the neighborhood and began hanging around Jelly's with his old buddies, many of whom were spending a good portion of their time on the street corner. It is known that Mack used to spend a large part of his army severance pay and his unemployment compensation to support the fun and drinking of his friends.

At that time, according to reports from group members and from Mack himself, he conceived of himself as "somebody." He had just returned from the paratroopers, and in the street-oriented crowds around Jelly's that status is highly regarded. Mack saw himself as a "trooper" in the present tense. He would often borrow from his former status in an attempt to satisfy his current need for self-esteem. Many of the group members still respect this aspect of his biography. In particular, the younger, toughness-oriented group members listen attentively to his war stories and service-related experiences, which he continues to tell with great relish.

When his money began to "grow thin," Mack found various jobs, from parking-lot attendant to dishwasher to foundry worker. But usually, after working from a few days to a few weeks he would quit or be fired or laid off. Sometimes his "bad" discharge would be the issue. At other times he would attribute the loss of his job to his own inability to stick to "the man's routine." Now and again he would be out of regular work but would manage to get "some kinda day work." Regulars see Mack as a person who "quit working so he could be with his crowd." As Mr. Thompson said, "He just quit all them jobs so's he could run the streets with these other wineheads out here." From the time that he was discharged from the army until the present, Mack has worked only sporadically on this job or that, somehow controlling himself enough to survive, though barely.

Also important for his known biography around Jelly's, Mack has been in and out of Cook County Jail. Over the course of his career around Jelly's, he has at times gone to jail intentionally. Like many other wineheads, Mack has committed petty crimes with the intent of being caught and put in jail so he would have a place to live during the winter months or at other especially hard times.

Mack has also been jailed unintentionally, for public intoxication, disturbing the peace, and assault and battery, among other petty crimes. Unlike the average hoodlum, Mack tries to draw a line between crimes against persons and property and the petty offenses that earn him short periods of detention. But on occasion he cannot avoid getting into scrapes and real fights, which often land him in "County." As the regulars say, "Mack might drink and fight and talk all that bad language, but that boy will not rob someone. The biggest thing he want is to get high on that oil [wine] and have some fun. That's all he want." But his "fun," as the following field note illustrates, not only may get him into jail, but also tends to give the regulars something to talk about. In fact, much of Mack's conduct around Jelly's provides the regulars some help in creating and reaffirming their own standards. Comparing themselves with wineheads like Mack makes regulars proud of who they think they are themselves.

One Wednesday evening in October at about 5:30, Red Mack and Jocko staggered along the sidewalk. Both were literally "falling down drunk." First Mack fell, while Jocko just stared at him. Mack lay on the ground for a long three to five minutes. Jocko said, "C'mon now, Mack. Get up off that ground. Get up! Gimme yo' hand, man!" Pedestrians stared as they cautiously passed by. Meanwhile, from across the street, regulars were pointing and laughing, as a crowd of them gathered. Though not able to hear all that Jocko and Mack were saying, they were able to fill in, for this scene had occurred many times before. Finally Jocko pulled Mack to his feet and the two men held onto each other. But then both tumbled to the sidewalk, Jocko on top of Mack. They lay there on the ground for two or three minutes. Howls of laughter came from the regulars on the other side of the street. This show was made all the more funny for them by the puzzled looks on the faces of passing pedestrians and motorists. After about fifteen minutes of this Jocko and Mack made their way to a tree about fifteen yards away. Here they sat and rested for about twenty minutes before trying it again.

This kind of experience, often repeated around Jelly's, gives regulars and others something to "talk about" and is just the kind of event that confirms their own conceptions of the wineheads. It provides data for winehead stories to be told to regulars who were not around, or to be retold among those who already know about it "just for laughs." Such a story is usually told in a way that affirms and collectively defines the regulars as a "decent" group of people and may also enhance and make more secure the place of the person telling the story.

Although such behavior is usually enough to gain Red Mack the ready label of winehead, there are times when he may be viewed as marginal. These are the times when he has just arrived at the corner sober and has not had time to begin drinking. Also, he may be "clean" and, for a winehead, dressed up. Being "clean," for a winehead like Mack, may require only combed hair, freshly washed blue jeans, and shiny black shoes. With such a self-presentation Mack stands out as someone special. Thus, when sober and clean, he may be more easily seen by regulars as "trying to be like us." Comment and debate may thus focus upon what it takes for someone like Mack to "be like us," for it is at just such times that regulars may feel themselves threatened. They may feel a need to impose more exacting standards for someone so unlike what they themselves want to be —and to be seen as. It may very well be that they then see Mack as the kind of person for whom they could only too easily be mistaken. Thus it is under just such conditions that some regulars most urgently feel the need to voice real and imagined differences between themselves and a person like Mack. Jelly himself, for instance, often points to Mack's failings by saying, "The boy try to work and be decent, but the moment he get some of that oil in him, then he gone. He like a different person."

To be sure some regulars show sympathy for the plight of the wineheads and even pick out certain "favorites" to help along. Acts of help from regulars tend to work as a kind of sanction on people like Mack. Sometimes, after what some call "showing out" (for instance, the drunken episode of Mack and Jocko described above), the wineheads involved may not come around for a while, lest they must face the men who had invested undeserved confidence in their decency. Some wineheads work for these sympathetic regulars, helping with janitorial work in buildings in the general area of Jelly's. Mack, for instance, has worked for a number of janitor-regulars, taking garbage cans down to the alley. Also, when some regulars want rooms painted in their own homes, it is not uncommon for them to gather a group of trustworthy wineheads and pay them with a case of beer or some wine. This kind of employment, or exploitation, serves as a social control by allowing certain wineheads to associate in limited degree with people they often consider "better."

Because of his liking for "the oil," Mack tends to frustrate a number of regulars who see themselves as trying to help him, including Jelly himself. Though Jelly tolerates Mack's conduct, he becomes disturbed when he sees Mack, or any other winehead, "nodding out" in his liquor store, for he deems such behavior as "looking bad for my place." Jelly allows regulars, who buy "good stuff," act "decent," and carry themselves properly, to stay as long as they want. But he is usually quick to yell at Mack, threatening to throw him bodily out of his store or to call the police. Mack's informal rights, like those of others who have been defined as wineheads, are limited. When Mack, or his kind, swears or talks loudly, Jelly is quick to scold him, whereas he allows regulars to talk as loud as they want—within reason, of course. His treatment of Mack is especially rough, and his barbs and yells are shrill whenever Mack is involved in a slight infraction of his rules.

Sometimes Jelly even puts his place "off limits" to Mack, since he considers wine the main cause of Mack's problem and wants "the boy to do right." When Jelly sees Mack at the door he will yell, "I thought I told you to stay out o' my place. Now I mean that. Now, get out before I call the police." If Mack persists, Jelly will pick up the telephone behind his counter and pretend to call the police, winking at the regulars. Intimidated, Mack curses Jelly under his breath and leaves the store. But he manages to get some regular or a winehead in good standing to get a bottle of wine for him.

Actions like these affirm the relatively high place of regulars, and their attendant patterns of deference remind group members of the limited rights of wineheads and of those who act like wineheads. But also, these contribute an incentive for the wineheads to do better. At the same time, these processes contribute to the construction and affirmation of the social order.

5 | The Hoodlums

The last crowd of the extended primary group is made up of men other group members commonly type, label, and treat as hoodlums. The group members defined as hoodlums are most obviously alike in their ages and in their values as expressed through personal demeanor. Comparatively young, they range in age from twenty-one to forty-five, although most are under thirty-five. Most hoodlums have grown up in this part of the city, if not this neighborhood, and have emerged from the ghetto street gangs. The mere attributes of youth, including particular styles of self-presentation, are usually enough to qualify one for the identity of hoodlum until one proves otherwise by one's actions, associates, or both.

The values of the hoodlum are indicated by his presentation of self.[1] Generally hoodlums value "big money" and "being tough." Accordingly, when money becomes a status issue they often attempt to present themselves as "slick," adept at tricking unsuspecting strangers—or other group members—out of their money. According to the other group members, hoodlums most admire and "pattern themselves after" successful hoodlums who "get over" or "live good" without having to work at a regular job. In line with this, the hoodlum venerates the "big-time" hustler, the pimp, and well-known successful gangsters. Yet around Jelly's the hoodlums are "small time"; their activities include petty theft, stickups, burglaries, and fencing stolen goods. Some even work regularly. Those who work gain a cautious measure of trust, especially among regulars. Those who don't work, or work only sporadically, are not to be trusted and "bear watching," even among their own. They are known to live by what they can "hustle."

Some are able to obtain public aid, unemployment compensation, or help from their kin. They spend much of their time hanging outside Jelly's or "runnin' the streets" with buddies. Occasionally they engage in street fighting. At times members of the hoodlum group may take a proprietary interest in the area around the corner—in the spirit of their gang days—and make verbal and sometimes physical defenses of the area against "outsiders" they believe are threatening to the extended primary group and to themselves.[2] Their primary role in the group is to be tough. These activities and the values they express help earn members of this group the reputation for "being bad" or "being tough" or "being mean and ornery." Within the extended primary group they are marked out as the "wrong type o' people," as "people who don't treat other people right" and thus "bear watching."

Hoodlums, unlike the regulars, tend to exhibit a high degree of alienation. Many feel wronged by the system, and thus its rules do not seem to them to be legitimate.

The accompanying styles of self-presentation among hoodlums are best exemplified by a posture of readiness to meet "trouble" head-on and to do almost anything for money—except work hard at a regular job. These actions and their perception by other group members help shape their identities within the wider group as well as within the subgroup of hoodlums. In meeting their standards of conduct, they negotiate for a degree of deference and social regard.[3] If regulars mainly value a "visible means of support" and "decency," and wineheads care about "getting some wine" and "having some fun," then hoodlums appear to care mainly about presenting themselves as "tough" and able to "get big money." It is primarily along these principles that people others define as hoodlums are allowed a chance to be somebody within the extended primary group.[4]

Some of the Hoodlums

Five feet eleven inches tall and weighing about 150 pounds, Tyrone is a forty-nine-year-old self-proclaimed "dope fiend." Tyrone grew up in Gary and arrived in Chicago about five years ago. He quit school in the eleventh grade and joined the army. He says, "They gave me a choice between going to the army and going to jail, so I chose the army." Later, Tyrone was released with an undesirable discharge. When he returned to Gary he "lied about my discharge so I could work in the steel mill." He has a former wife and two sons living in Gary, whom he talks about from time to time. In Indiana he was convicted of armed robbery, burglary, and a host of other criminal offenses and consequently has spent much of his adult life behind bars or, as he says, "dodgin' the police." Currently he claims he is a part-time pimp and a hustler of the streets. Occasionally, he works for a Chicago tree nursery or works on construction. When in great need of money he has been known to hire himself out for day labor, but usually he hustles and pushes dope to satisfy his "terrible motherfuckin' dope habit."

Tyrone claims he has been involved with a local methadone program, which he bitterly criticizes as a "hype," as a "game run on blacks and po' whites." He says, "They don't know nothin' 'bout this shit [the long-term effects] they motherfuckin' self, but they'll use this shit on people like me. It just a maintenance thing. Look at me. When I first got on the program, I thought I was gon' kick [become cured]. I wanted to kick! I wanted to work and be a productive citizen. That was five years ago, and just look at me now! My jaw's all sunk in, my hair's fallin' out, my teeth are loose and comin' out. I spit up blood sometimes. Look at me. I'm all fucked up!"

Around group members, Tyrone's "total conversation" consists of talk about his days in prison, his fights with the police, his stable of prostitutes, street violence, and his "more than a hundred dollar a day dope habit." Among members of the extended primary group he wears these aspects of his biography as a kind of badge attesting his social worth. The regulars become somewhat intimidated by him and his stories and move away whereas the "hoodlums" are attracted and hang around him to be further charmed. Usually armed with some concealed weapon, Tyrone is generally thought of as "dangerous" and "cold-blooded." Group members say he "bears watching."

Born in Chicago, Oscar emerged from a relatively stable home where his father was usually employed as a steelworker and his mother as a domestic. Oscar stands five feet nine and weighs about 150 pounds. He is thirty-three years old, single, and has many girl friends who regularly telephone him at Jelly's. Oscar has two brothers and three sisters, all of whom grew up in the city and now live on the South Side not far from Jelly's neighborhood. Around Jelly's, Oscar often speaks of his "family" and his "parents," emphasizing these words with some pride. He continues to see his sisters and brothers regularly. When things are not going well for him, say when someone is "after him" or when he is in need of money, he will go and live with his kin until times are easier. Few of the hoodlums around Jelly's are able to claim such family resources, for many have "put their people [family] out with them," or their family members are reluctant to trust them for fear of being "ripped off" by the "hoodlum" or by "hoodlum friends and tramps" he might bring to the house.

Like a number of others the group members view as hoodlums, Oscar grew up amid the street gangs of Chicago's South Side. He boasts of his "education" among the gangs and attributes to it his ability "to handle" and to "live off" the ghetto streets. At seventeen, Oscar quit school and joined the army, from which he later received a general discharge. He returned to Chicago to work in various factory jobs and to "hustle the streets." Many of the men he now hangs with are former fellow gang members, some of whom are spread out over the West Side and the South Side. He has told me that he "looks up my ol' cronies 'cause everybody else too slow for me." Those who will hang with Oscar are seen as friends, but also as challenges to exploit financially and "beat" mentally.

Around Jelly's, Oscar often expresses his desire for "big money." He is usually hatching some scheme to get "some quick money" with a friend from the corner. Sometimes he will whisper to one person about his designs on another. He might say, "Psst. Hey, Eli. Watch this. Hey Sam, lemme hold a dollar till payday?" If Sam, a friend of his, will "loan" Oscar the money, Oscar will then wink or hunch another person, to communicate how "smooth" and "slick" he is. With money in his pocket already, Oscar feels he has "beat" the person making the loan.

Unlike most hoodlums, Oscar does work regularly. He is now employed at a local automobile assembly plant, working the shift from 6:00 A.M. until 2:30 P.M. Oscar usually dresses "sharp," in the latest fashions. Some describe his appearance as the "pimp look." He sometimes wears patent-leather shoes so "shiny you can see yo' eyeballs in 'em." He wears expensive "gangster hats" and bright-colored slacks and silk shirts and attempts to derogate those who dress more conservatively. Also, he wears several rings, including a flashy and expensive-looking "diamond" on the small finger of his left hand. When he talks excitedly his left hand gestures wildly, showing off his ring.

When he arrives at Jelly's, he usually stands for a while looking for members of his crowd. When he finds them he socializes, but he watches them, for they "bear watchin'," and they watch him for exactly the same reason. If his crowd members are not around he may settle for certain regulars he figures are "fast enough to keep up with me." While there are some regulars he avoids "because they're too slow," there are certain ones he seeks out, thinking he may learn from their "heavy conversation." Seldom if ever will he settle for wineheads, unless he wants one of them to run an errand for him.

For a short period after his arrival he is almost always very quiet, preoccupied with what some call "diggin' the scene." Sometimes he stands and poses, apparently aware of his performance and of his audience, as he checks out his reflection in Jelly's big window. His first words of any substance are usually questions about the whereabouts of some person who allegedly owes him money. He reminds others of this by saying something like, "You seen Sonny? I wish I could find him. The stud owe me a dime [ten dollars]." After this he may take out his dice and begin to roll them together, shaking them in his fist and asking various group members to "shoot a quarter" or whatever amount he feels like wagering. After a while Oscar and several others he has been able to persuade to join him may be seen on their knees in the alley or on the sidewalk. They shoot dice or pitch pennies for money, or they may find some other public spot in which to play Poker or Bid Whist. Such activity can gain the label hoodlum for many in the group.

Aside from gambling, Oscar is a kind of entrepreneur of the ghetto streets. Around Jelly's and other joints, he makes his rounds attempting to sell "hot" record albums, rings, watches, and other items that may not really be stolen but that are often represented that way to make them sound more appealing. When the goods really are "hot," he will display the Sears or Marshall Field labels and price tags, attempting to sell the items at "half" the price marked, though ordinarily he gets less than half. Group members call this kind of entrepreneurship "hustling,"[5] a term that may refer to anything from robbing and sticking up others to gambling, fencing, and "sellin' dope." Group members use it most often to describe a person who seems always to be "out to make some money off o' somebody," a phrase that fits Oscar. Although he denies stealing from others around Jelly's, many group members believe he will if given the chance.

Like other hoodlums around Jelly's, Oscar lives and actively participates in what might be described as the subculture of violence of the ghetto streets.[6] He is commonly armed with his .38 caliber pistol, which he occasionally flashes. He expects others to be "carryin' somethin'." Frequently he may be seen standing with his hands dug into his pants pockets, as though he were ready to come "up with somethin'" at any moment should the need arise. He says this posture will "make anybody think twice before they try to do somethin' to you." He refers to his weapons as "my li'l equalizers that keep me alive" and that allow him to make his rounds. Among group members he is known as someone who can "really go," meaning he is considered a good street fighter and will not hesitate to fight. Oscar has fought often and has threatened to cut people around Jelly's. Although I have never seen him do it, some say he has drawn his pistol on others around the corner more than once.

Oscar often brags about his exploits with violence, apparently assuming that it gains him social regard within the extended primary group. In the presence of others at Jelly's he mentions matter-of-factly the "bout I had the other night with that gang of jitterbugs,[7] when I fired and hit least one of 'em, I hope." Whereas an audience of regulars may look askance and be intimidated by such talk, an audience of fellow hoodlums may be impressed. Oscar knows what he is doing by telling such stories; they are among the elements making up the known personal biography that helps define him as a hoodlum.

Clay is a tall, muscular, dark-complexioned man of thirty. Upon arriving in the neighborhood and at Jelly's some two years ago, he claimed to be from Detroit, but most group members did not believe his tale. Most of his background is a mystery to others of the extended primary group, yet they do not push him to explain himself. Group members tend to talk about him behind his back. Within the group, it is rumored that Clay shot and killed a man in Los Angeles and is now wanted by "the law."

When Clay began hanging at Jelly's, he was inclined to be quiet and reserved, talking with only a few people and seeming to have no friends. Group members began thinking of him as a "nice quiet guy who don't bother no one." After about two months, Clay "cut into" (or attempted to become friends with) Oscar. They began hanging with one another. Soon the two were seen together almost all the time, and others began referring to them as "tight." After about six months, when Clay arrived at Jelly's he would inquire after the whereabouts of his "cousin," thereby informing others that they were "going for cousins" and were very close. Oscar often did the same, asking for his cousin Clay. The two "ran together," "hustled together," and attempted to "look out" for one another. Others respected this relationship.

Because of this known biography, which now includes his relationship with Oscar and others they hang with, Clay is increasingly considered by group members to "bear watching." He has "changed" from being a "nice guy" to being "the wrong type o' person." It appears that group members, for lack of anything better to go on, have borrowed from their conception of Oscar and have applied aspects of it to their notion of Clay. Clay has also contributed to this notion by engaging in what others see as hoodlum conduct. Now he threatens and "jumps on" others he considers less than himself. But most of all, associating closely with Oscar and other hoodlums has been enough to make him appear a hoodlum. His "running buddies"—

other hoodlums—tend to support him in this "bad" role, and the
regulars merely accept it.

But hoodlums, like men of the other groups at Jelly's, are defined
not only by the company they keep but also by the quality and
nature of their associations. Associations help make a person's claim
on certain status values credible or incredible. For association is
more complex than simply "who hangs with whom." Beyond that,
it refers to the manner of hanging, or what one is allowed to do with
particular others—the range of liberties people are allowed to take
with one another. For example, some people—but not all—will be
allowed to take a drink from one's bottle or to bum cigarettes and
even money. Exchange of favors helps mark out friendships and also
status relationships. Men who publicly allow reputed hoodlums to
take certain liberties with them thus run the risk of being regarded
as hoodlums themselves. Status is derivative, as the following incident dramatizes.

One Wednesday afternoon in December at about 3:30, I arrived
at Jelly's and encountered Bill, Sleepy, T. J., Calvin (whom group
members consider marginal), Mr. Thompson, Jelly, and a few
other regulars. I greeted the fellows and joined them in listening
to Bill's talk about the hoodlum Oscar. When I arrived the men
were talking about crime and the "rough streets." Then Bill entered with, "Naw, I don't like to be 'round guys that do that kind
of stuff. It's just a cryin' shame that we have to put up with all
this mess. Just like, well now, you see. That gun he had coulda
gone off and everybody in here woulda been hurt. It coulda been
a real shootout at the OK corral."

Not knowing what the conversation was about, I asked Bill
what he was referring to. He said, "You heard 'bout what happened yesterday didn't you, Eli?"

"No, what happened?"

"Yeah, well we all was sittin' up in here yesterday 'bout this
time when 'long come Oscar and asks Calvin to hold this pistol for
him. Well, no sooner 'n Calvin puts the roscoe [gun] in his pocket,
here come two more of *them* with pistols drawn out like they
ready to shoot somebody. Had them pointin' right on Oscar. So,

now Oscar come out wit' his own gun, and they all stand one another off. Now while all this is goin' on, all us guys [regulars] was sittin' round here like we do, only everybody is scared to death. Man, you talk about somebody bein' scared. I ain't never been so scared in my life. Thank the good Lord that none o' them guns went off, and they finally cooled off and left. Took Oscar with 'em. They say Oscar was shootin' craps with them boys over in this alley over here and got to arguin' 'bout the money, so he grabs one of they pistols and takes off," said Bill, recounting the events of yesterday.

"Who was they?" asked Sleepy.

"I don't know who they was. Probably some o' them hoodlums from Thirty-fifth Street. No tellin' who you liable to see Oscar involved with. You gotta watch that boy. He a get his ass killed, and you too. Boy, you talk about guys movin' out o' here. Guys was really movin'," commented Bill.

Then T. J. laughed and pointed at old Mr. Thompson. "Did you see how ol' Mr. Thompson moved? Mr. Thompson, I never knew you could move so fast. Ha-ha." The others smiled and laughed good-naturedly, bringing a smile from Mr. Thompson.

Then, returning to the seriousness of the situation, Bill said, "But you know it's a shame that the boy Oscar got to carry on like that." The others present, including Oscar's friend Calvin, just shook their heads in agreement or breathed sighs of relief that nothing worse had happened or that they were fortunate enough not to have been around while Oscar was making trouble or "startin' somethin'." The men's conversation focused on Calvin, who had kept the pistol in the incident above. Perhaps in anticipation, Calvin began telling a hoodlum story about Oscar.

"That's Oscar for you, I mean he always into somethin'. If he ain't tryin' to gamble with you, then he tryin' to sell you somethin'. I don't understand him myself," said Calvin, appearing to attempt to dissociate himself from Oscar and his kind.

"But Calvin, you be with him a lot," entered Mr. Thompson, helping to blur the distinction between Calvin and Oscar and to make the distinction between the regulars and the hoodlums present even clearer.

This comment apparently frustrated Calvin, for he proclaimed, "But I don't be with him! Just 'cause I be talkin' with the cat sometime don't make him no partner o' mine." Calvin seemed angered by Mr. Thompson's tone of voice and his associating him with Oscar. Treating the comments as accusations—which they were—he remained silent for the next five minutes, as the conversation moved on to other subjects. Finally Calvin made his exit without any announcement except his movement toward the door and a fake punch at Spider, a person not involved in the previous conversation, who was leaning on the cigarette machine near the front door. Outside the big front window of Jelly's, Calvin could now be seen tending to his German shepherd dog, Smut; he rubbed and patted the animal. Shortly, he untied Smut from the light post and walked him down the street, bantering with a group of "hoodlum" types and daring them to "mess with" him while Smut was around. Smut barked loudly at the men, while Calvin patted him approvingly yet held onto him tightly. They moved on down the sidewalk.

Though Calvin is considered a hoodlum by many group members, he nevertheless is believed to have a certain amount of "regularism in him." One reason for the belief in his part-time "regularism" is the "crowd" Calvin tends to hang with. Depending on the situation, he might hang with the hoodlums, the regulars, or at times even the wineheads. But again, one's company is not an infallible indicator of one's place in the extended primary group. Rather, it is the quality of the interaction with one's company that is important for the designation of status. The ways a person can draw distinctions between himself and others who represent particular values in the larger group, and the ways such distinguishing acts are received by others who have vested value-interests, are the real determinants of rank within the extended primary group.

For example, owning a vicious dog allows Calvin a certain commonality with the regulars. When Calvin travels on foot he is seldom without Smut, whose qualities he advertises to ward off potentially troublesome hoodlums. Regulars are able to identify with this. They can sense that Calvin is on their side and against the hoodlums, whom many of them fear and really want to be rid of. Further, whenever the opportunity presents itself, Calvin attempts to associate with the regulars and to dissociate himself from the hoodlums. He attempts this most often by "getting in on" the talk about some hoodlum behavior. As T. J., a regular in good standing, told me, "That boy'll talk 'bout a hoodlum like a dog." (Meaning that he "signifies" or tells funny hoodlum stories.) But such attempts at distinction sometimes fail, particularly when regulars and those who aspire to be regulars take advantage of an opportunity to distinguish themselves from Calvin himself. He sometimes presents them with the opportunity they need to remind him of who he is—a hoodlum.

The Problem of Distancing Oneself from the Hoodlums

Even though he may in certain circumstances be regarded as a hoodlum, Calvin usually attempts to pass himself off as a regular. That he must make an effort to prove himself in this way may be revealing about his real concept of self. When in the company of someone he considers a regular, he may choose to exhibit his regular side, as is indicated in the following story.

One evening Calvin asked me to give him a ride to a South Side shopping center "to pick up a birthday present" for his common-law wife, Mae, and some window decorations for their apartment. I agreed to take him to the shopping center, and as we drove up Thirty-fifth Street Calvin began. "I just gotta get Mae somethin' for her birthday, somethin' nice, you know. Wanna get somethin' for them front windows, too," stated Calvin.

"What'cha gon' get?" I asked.

"I don't know what I'm gon' get for her birthday, but I know just what she want for the windows. You know them funny li'l glass hangin' decorations that go for curtains. They got diamond shapes and V-shapes to 'em, you know? And they stringy. You know what I mean, Eli?"

"Yea, I think I know what you mean. Maybe we can find them."

As we neared the shopping center we engaged in small talk. For instance, Calvin saw what he thought were some "gangbangers" and "jitterbugs"[7] and pointed to them. This led to talk about his own "gangbanging days" and about an instance where he and his friends were required to demonstrate toughness and daring in their gang. He asked me if I had belonged to a gang. I said no, that the town I had grown up in was too small for sustained gang activity. We then talked about the town and the "kind of people" who lived there. The talk continued until we arrived at the shopping center. At that point we went into one of the stores looking for the things he wanted. We found the decorations for the window but were unable to find a gift for Mae. After looking for a while, we gave up on the idea and left. We headed south on King Drive for Jelly's neighborhood and Calvin's house.

On the way back Calvin told me more about himself. He told me about his family, most of whom, he said, lived in Chicago. At one point he said, "I got one sister teachin' school, and I got a brother who's a foreman in the [steel] mills. My dad's retired now and he and my mother lives up in Detroit. They doin' al'right. Then I got one brother who's a policeman and a sister goin' to Loop College." By this time we were just passing Jelly's. Some of the fellows were standing outside watching the traffic go by. As we passed he said, "I'm the only black sheep in my family. I'm the onliest one who a even now come up to a joint like that there. I'm the black sheep. Everybody else is gone and made somethin' outa theyselves, or else they tryin' to." After saying this, Calvin laughed and shook his head as we blew the horn and waved at the men standing on the corner. They waved back.

Shortly, we arrived at Calvin's apartment and he invited me in for a drink. I accepted the invitation and parked the car. As we walked up the stairs his dogs began barking loudly.

"Shaddup! Shaddup!" shouted Calvin, as he began to unlock the steel stretcher that covered his door. "I guess Mae ain't made it yet," he said. Then, as we started to enter, he said, "Al'right! Al'right now! Shut up! Eli, you better wait here till I get the muzzles on 'em."

Calvin fetched the dog muzzles and leashes and finally tied the dogs up, took their muzzles off, and put food out for them to eat. Then Calvin offered me a drink of vodka, which I accepted. I sat down on the couch and he sat in an overstuffed chair in front of me. At this very point he began telling me about his home and the *rules* of his *apartment*—words he emphasized. In a very matter-of-fact voice Calvin said, "Now Eli, I don't 'low no bad language in my apartment. I'm the only one to use bad language in my house. I don't even 'low Mae to cuss in here. I don't 'low no cussin' and no fightin'. You can fight and cuss all you want 'long as you do it out there, outside that door in them streets. When peoples come to my apartment they got to act decent. Ain't gon' be no humbuggin' [fighting] up in here, less'n I'm doin' it myself. When you come over you can relax, 'cause it ain't gon' be no mess. Not in my house. I pay the rent here. I bought all this here furniture you see 'round here."

These "rules of the apartment" that Calvin pronounced for me represent values and standards that regulars appear to strive for and meet. But most regulars don't seem as sensitive about them as Calvin was. By informing me through his invocations that he was upholding the rules he believed decent and regular people upheld, Calvin expressed his own approach to being regular. After he had established his rules, assuring me that I was in "regular"—as distinct from "hoodlum"—company, we relaxed and lounged around. We discussed numerous issues, including the police, local politics, Mayor Daley, Jelly's.

After more than two hours of drinking vodka—Calvin's drink—and talking about various issues, I told him I should be getting home. He expressed regret that I had not been able to meet his "wife" and said I should come by again soon so Mae could cook us a meal. We then parted company.

When I saw Calvin again, about a week later, there was some difference in our relationship. Standing outside by the light post, Calvin saw me inside the doorway of Jelly's. He called my name and walked into the liquor-store room, greeting me as though we were old friends.

Patting me on the shoulder, he said, "What's been happenin', Eli?"
"Nothin' much," I replied.

Others who were standing around, including Herman, Sleepy, T. J.,
and a few others, greeted Calvin. Spider, a marginal, asked Calvin if
he had seen one of Spider's woman friends. Calvin said he hadn't.
Then the members of this small group just stood around while the
liquor-store room buzzed with conversation and laughter.

Calvin pulled me aside and said, "Let's get somethin'. What you
drinkin'?" he asked, since I had no drink in my hand.

"I could go for a tall Bud," I said, reaching for my money.

"No, this is on me. I got it," said Calvin. He walked over to the
counter and asked Jelly for a half-pint of vodka for himself and a
tall Budweiser for me. He returned and handed me the beer. For the
next hour we stood around inside the liquor-store room. Customers
entered and left, punctuating the noise levels, since the group members lowered their voices whenever someone came through the door
and promptly raised them when the person left or was judged familiar enough. After a time Calvin announced he had to "split" and
left the liquor store, bidding the others good night. He untied his dog
and went off down the street.

Later that evening Herman and I discussed Calvin. Herman reminded me that I should watch "cats like Calvin, 'cause he tryin' to
cut into you. See, Eli. Cats like Calvin look al'right on the outside.
He got li'l regular in him. But see, cats like him can be cold-blooded
at times. See, 'cause the thing that mess him up is them hoodlum
buddies of his. They sho'nuff mess him up. 'Cause he might could be
regular if he didn't fuck around with them jitterbugs all the time. He
with them hoodlums all the time, everytime you see him, damn near
anyway. They into him. See, 'cause he grew up with them studs. And
he bear watchin' just like they do. Terry, Oscar, Knaky. All them
studs bear watchin'. If you let him cut into you, first thing you know,
his li'l hoodlum buddies be hittin' on you for this and that. You can
see that gangster in 'em as soon as they open they mouth. All they
gon' talk about is what the county jail look like and all that ol' type
o' shit. Don't nobody decent be wantin' to hear that kinda talk, not

comin' from Calvin and his buddies. When the deal comes down, don't none o' 'em mean nobody no good, don't even now mean themselves no good. Got to watch 'em."

Calvin's identity within the extended primary group depends in part on the identities of those "others" he associates with. Like others of the extended primary group, his "associates" include all "types of people"—regulars, wineheads, and hoodlums—in some way or another. What gives Calvin his own status in the group is what he does with these various people. It is the interpretation of the *quality* of these associations that helps determine what others conceive him to be. Moreover, it is this that indicates to others of the group *how* he is approachable and what interests he may be used to further. For regulars, his observed association with hoodlums, including the various liberties they take with him, defines him and "lowers" him in their estimation, making him approachable and useful as a scapegoat. Using Calvin as an example of what they are not, for instance, regulars often "talk about" him to identify and uphold the standards they claim to have.

The kind of liberty-taking I refer to was exemplified by Oscar's asking Calvin to hold his pistol and by Calvin's consent. This kind of social transaction not only helps define Calvin for the general group but also prevents him from gaining full acceptance among the regulars.

Some situations arise wherein people normally thought of as hoodlums are given an opportunity to present themselves as distinct from the hoodlum group. In these situations—which might be characterized as "openings"—a person who wants to distinguish himself from the hoodlums behaves in clearly nonhoodlum ways in the presence of others who may then be used to help establish a new, if provisional, identity. To take advantage of such "openings" or opportunities, hoodlums may attempt to "associate" with certain others who can help them "look good." This point is illustrated in the following conversation—a kind of association really—that Herman and I had with Cochise, an occasional "dope dealer" whom group members commonly regard as a hoodlum.

Herman and I were standing beside a tree in the park not far from Jelly's when Cochise approached, greeted us, and sought an opportunity to enter our conversation about hoodlums. With his hair greased back, dressed in light green gabardine pants and a red long-sleeved shirt, Cochise stood around listening to Herman and me.

"If the wrong type o' nigger come up here now, I'm gone. I just left. I mean they ain't gon' run me out the park, but I'll go to that bench. And if they get too loud on that bench, I'll go to the next one," Herman stated.

To which Cochise added, "I'mo tell you what gon' happen one day. A nigger gon' be sittin' right here, doing what these niggers do, gamblin' and shit, and the wrong motherfucker like li'l Tom, see he might be instigatin' that shit, no tellin', you understand [referring to the hoodlums]?"

"He was gamblin'. He was one o' them gamblin' over here yesterday," Herman replied.

"Yeah, talkin' loud! He a dirty li'l ornery motherfucker. Look here. He'll send some nigger over here on you while you gamblin', you understand? [Identifying with hoodlum conduct himself.] Hell, yeah, he'll stick yo' motherfuckin' ass up. They lucky they ain't been stuck up out here yet. Old niggers [regulars] out here tryin' to blend in with them shit. When they go to gamblin', this is what I do. I get the fuck on out [attempting to distinguish himself from the hoodlums]," said Cochise.

"You catch guys, any motherfucker who fucks with this here shit [dope], some heavy motherfuckin' shit—they cold-blooded, man. Motherfuckers fuckin' with that hoss [heroin]," commented Herman.

"Looka here. These motherfuckers who ain't got a barrel to piss in. They'll come over here and say, 'Al'right, motherfucker, this is a stickup. All you motherfuckers!' They may just have one pistol, 'Al'right, got to have it. All you motherfuckers, lay flat down.' They did us like that last summer. Looka here, we were sittin' over there, right where them bricks at. And man, the nigger walked up. Now dig this. Now this is the freakiest stickup I ever saw, ha-ha-ha. I had to laugh at the nigger boy. You understand, 'cause I use to sell the nigger spoons of dope, when I was dealing dope. [Here Cochise criticizes the stickup, implying his expertise.] Now dig this. The nigger walked over, his name is Harris, named William Harris, see. I know. Dig this. He said, 'Now let me read this verse before I stick up anyone. Thou shalt not kill, Lord, let me pray. . . .' So I ain't payin' him no attention. I'm high. The motherfucker walked to the curb right there, boy. The motherfucker come back. Had a .38! One o' them slide hammer, you understand. Ain't got no cock trigger. It one o' them slide hammer. He say, 'Al'right, give it up, I got to have it!' Now it's six of us out there. Two standin' up and four sittin' down. This motherfucker say, 'Give it up,' you understand. So his partner say, 'Get the money!' So he took the first two dudes' money that was standin' up. And this boy, ha-ha. This gon' gas you. Dig this. So he got to Sonny Ferguson. You know Ferguson, don't you?" questioned Cochise.

"Yeah, I know Big Sonny Ferguson," replied Herman.

"Looka here. He say, 'Ah, leave him alone.' So then he got to Smitty. You know ol' dark-faced Smitty. He say, 'I don't like you no way, Smitty. Get his money.' So I knowed the nigger, even knowed where he lived at—really. So he got to me. I say, 'What about me, nigger?' He said, 'Aw, g'wan.' Then he got to Knaky and say, 'Don't move, Knaky.' You understand? They took three people. Out of six people, they took three people's money. And then these niggers just skated [left quickly]. I just laughed at 'em," proclaimed Cochise.

"Yeah, they don't be bullshittin'. And if they had resisted, they woulda blowed one o' them niggers away from here," said Herman.

"I'm tellin' you. He shot that nigger, Jones, over there on that corner. I swear. The nigger walked up. Now Jones and the nigger is tight, but the nigger on that dope. The nigger is cold-blooded. Just like if Smitty hada acted crazy, he woulda bust a cap on him [shot him] without a shadow of a doubt," stated Cochise.

"And these cats don't be thinkin' 'bout no penitent'ry. They be thinkin' 'bout what they doin' right now," declared Herman.

After deciding he had gotten enough of Cochise's "conversation," Herman said, "Come on, now, Eli. 'Member you promised to run me over to the West Side." Getting the hint that we were intending to leave without him, Cochise said, "Well, I guess I'll catch y'all later on." At that Herman and I got into my car and drove toward the West Side.

As we drove down Forty-seventh Street, Herman said, "Damn. That Cochise sho' want to be regular. Always tryin' to cut into me, now. The stud'll stand up there tryin' to talk about them hoodlums and jitterbugs, and he be the biggest li'l gangster in Chi. The boy give himself away as soon as he open that hoodlum mouth of his, always talkin' 'bout dealin' dope or somethin'. You know don't no decent person want to be 'round him, not for too long anyway." Herman then seemed satisfied that he had put the hoodlum back in his place. Although Herman had not been convinced by Cochise's stated distaste for hoodlum behavior, Cochise had tried, in front of Herman and myself, to come on as *not* part of the hoodlum crowd. By pointing out others, like Sonny Ferguson and Smitty, Cochise was attempting to distance himself from the crowd with which he usually associates closely. But he gave himself away as a hoodlum with his attempts to impress us with his inside knowledge of drug-dealing and stickups. This example shows the limits on a hoodlum's ability to make a self-consistent presentation of himself as a regular.

Reminding the Hoodlums of Who They Are

It often takes a specific issue to make the hoodlums see themselves as a crowd distinct from the regulars, for one of the most important facts about this part of the extended primary group is that men viewed and treated as hoodlums do not always see themselves this way. Most seem not to know they are hoodlums until they are reminded by someone else, either their fellow hoodlums or regulars who feel the need to exclude them. Until they are reminded, they often attempt through associations to pass themselves off as regulars. The term "hoodlum" is considered derogatory and consequently is used more often to describe someone else rather than oneself.

In the fall of 1972 Mike, a black Chicago policeman, began an effort to recruit new members for his social club from the men of the extended primary group at Jelly's. When Mike came around Jelly's to choose members for his club and, more important, systematically left out hoodlums, he made the category of hoodlum into something the hoodlums had to deal with. The hierarchy that exists, at least in the minds of regulars, became unusually explicit in the following sequence of events, which are themselves an example of ways group members point out hoodlums to each other and to themselves. Having patrolled Jelly's neighborhood for many years, Mike was very familiar with the area and the people of Jelly's. And the people of the neighborhood knew him well, both in and out of uniform. This was particularly true of the extended primary group, many of whom, especially the regulars, considered Mike an honorary member.

Around Jelly's Mike is the embodiment of "the law." Group members, particularly the regulars, tend to speak of him as "the law." When Mike comes around he "looks for trouble." On numerous occasions he has settled disputes and intervened in fights between group members. Also, he has been quick to arrest some group members he has been socially involved with at Jelly's. Six feet two, about 235 pounds, and very dark-skinned, Mike is a striking figure in his neat blue uniform. On the streets and inside Jelly's, Mike attempts to carry himself in a "professional" manner and demands respect for "the law."

Although Mike and the regulars seem to have an amiable relationship based on mutual respect and a certain commonality, some regulars merely defer to him and try to stay at a distance from him. They stop short of fully trusting what they view as his capricious and somewhat personal application of "the law." Some of them complain about Mike when he is not around, saying, "He sho' think he somethin', don't he," or "Mike gettin' too big for his britches." They claim he has arrested and policed some of them "when he feels like it." Yet in general the regulars, and others who like to see themselves as regulars, find it easier to act as regulars when he is around. Their own tough sides, which they sometimes feel constrained to exhibit so as to maintain a certain degree of respect and civility around Jelly's, can then be minimized.

When the circumstances are right, Mike is able to fit himself into the social order of Jelly's. His own safety may well depend on knowing what various group members are likely to do under certain conditions. Thus as "part of my job" Mike has come to know the hustlers, the fences, the pimps, the whores, the "would-be gangsters," the wineheads, and the regulars. He prides himself on this knowledge and is able to say who "works for a living" and who is "barely eatin'." For example, Mike knows that "Red Mack ain't no 'count and blow his li'l money on junk or wine soon as he get it good. Then he'll nod out for the rest o' the night." Mike knows that "Oscar think he a big-time gangster, but he just a jive-time li'l hustler." Mike knows that "Sleepy drink a lot and'll stay tore up for days," and that if you mess with him, "he'll fight anybody, and really can go." For him, as for the regulars, such people "bear watchin'."

If these are the people he must keep careful watch over, and who make him somewhat uneasy, the regulars are the ones he feels most at ease with. To him regulars are "out here," but are on his side against the others. For example, he knows that "studs like T. J. are decent. T. J. got him a good wife, some grown kids, all doin' al'right. He a try to go for bad, but he a run quicker 'n shit from a sho'nuff humbug [a fight]."

Regulars are the people of Jelly's who seem socially closest to Mike, for most of them appear to share with him belief in decency and wider social values, the most important of which is perhaps "a visible means of support." Whereas Mike and the regulars tend to invoke "the law," which they so much associate with the civility and morality of proper blacks of the far South Side, wineheads and hoodlums are not ordinarily concerned with these standards of propriety. Mike is often seen as a protector of the regulars, as the law "out here" that helps them leave a "humbug" peacefully, without having to show their tough sides, and to get by the hoodlums and others with their decency intact. At the same time, Mike seems to view many of the regulars as allies in his battle against "hoodlums" and "gangsters." In dealing with members of the group and others on the streets, Mike puts his knowledge to work, making his own role more manageable.[8] This knowledge was also useful to Mike when he went about recruiting new members for his social club.

One Friday evening in October, Mike arrived at Jelly's and, after a while, began "hittin' on" group members to join his club, the Gallant Gents of WMPP, a local black-oriented radio station. The club's activities included raffles, formal dances, social gatherings, and efforts to help others who were less fortunate. This was a voluntary organization that catered to black people of the white-collar occupations and the working class.

When the liquor-store room, as always on Fridays, was crowded with men who had just been paid, Mike appeared, off duty. He was dressed in a black sweater, black "dress pants," and black "low-quarter" service shoes. He also wore rose-tinted "shades" and smoked a large cigar. On his right pants leg was a bulge that group members knew was the "piece" Mike always carried.

When Mike appeared there was an abrupt silence. People stopped what they were doing and turned to watch him. Before he arrived, T. J. had been arguing with L. C. and Calvin over the value of seeing a particular black film being shown at a downtown theater. Their argument stopped. Red Mack was in the process of "hittin' on" Pope for some money for a "taste." Mack stopped, and both of them looked toward the door. Virtually all activity in the liquor-store room was in some degree affected. Mike acknowledged his own presence by "speaking" and greeting the others. He stopped at the counter and began a conversation with Jelly, attempting to catch up on "the news." As they began talking, the others, mostly regulars but a few wineheads, returned to what they had been doing before the intrusion, but with a studied awareness of Mike's presence. It was clear that Mike's being there affected the group's sense of social order. On duty or off, group members saw Mike for what he was—the police— and treated him accordingly, with a certain degree of distance.

After talking with Jelly for a few minutes Mike walked over to Pope, a regular, and "hit on" him to join the club. Standing a few feet away from Pope and Mike, Pee Wee, Red Mack, The Homey, and I watched while we talked among ourselves. Mr. Thompson,

who had been talking with Pope before leaving for the toilet, returned to find Pope now with Mike. Mike showed Pope a circular
describing the club and its activities.

To this I overheard Pope say, "Naw, Mike. I can't handle it." "Ol'
man" Thompson, who had been politely looking away from this exchange, which clearly did not involve him, soon eased off to join
our group. Mike and Pope talked for a while longer, then Mike left
the liquor store.

This was the beginning of Mike's attempt to recruit new members.
Within a few days a number of the other men had been approached
and asked to join the club. All the people he asked were considered
regulars. In Mike's mind they were "safe" and relatively trustworthy
members of the group. They were the people at Jelly's who would not
make Mike "look bad" in the eyes of "those big shots" he knew
"back at the club." Though regulars were usually acceptable to Mike,
wineheads and hoodlums generally were not. Such people not only
were unable to afford the dues of fifty dollars a year, they were just
not the "right kind of people." Mike chose to ask only those he felt
could "handle" the club and those the club could stand. These were
the regulars.

As it turned out, only three regulars joined Mike's club, though
many more were asked. Just to be asked by Mike was a sign of affirmation for some. T. J., Otis, and Herman were the regulars who
joined. As Herman told me one day to explain why he joined Mike's
club:

"Well, I gave him a play. I wanted to be involved. He only chose
us regulars, anyway. Regulars right down the line. Only workin'
men. That's all Mike wanted. He didn't give a damn if he knowed
you or not. If you wanted to join the club, 'C'mon in,' he said.
'We'll meet you. We'll be yo' friend. But we wanta know, do you
work?' Because a workin' man is gon' be respected. And if he
work regular, he *is* respected. All workin' people is damn near
regular. If you work, you a Mr. so and so. See, 'cause people know
you ain't in no trouble. You ain't doin' no wrong.' "

During the next few weeks, these men attempted to make a "big thing" of the club by making announcements whenever they were to attend a club meeting or function or were selling tickets for some club-related activity. Before a club function they would sometimes meet at Jelly's and stand around "clean" (dressed up) for an hour or two, collecting compliments and admiration from regular peers and receiving silence or disparaging looks and comments from hoodlums. The hoodlums and others would sometimes call the club "square" and label its members "square" for joining. Or they would call the club members "puppies," implying that Mike had coerced them to join by threatening to arrest them. Spider, a marginal person, gave me his view of why Otis, Herman, and T. J. had joined Mike's club:

> " 'Cause they was chumps. That's what they was. I coulda been in that shit, but Mike know I don't dig the motherfucker [club] from the get-go [beginning]. When he was trying to get up the club, know what he did? He brought his li'l sheet around and tried to get me to sign. I looked at the motherfucker [sheet], laughed, and walked away. I kept on steppin', walked on by. So he didn't say shit else to me. What the fuck I look like bein' a club member with them chumps. Besides that, Mike is a rotten cat. He done arrested every motherfucker 'round here. He ain't arrested me 'cause I don't fuck with him [associate with him]. Mike'll be with you one minute and arrest yo' ass two minutes later. Like, I done seen T. J. buy the mug a taste and drink it with him, and T. J. be afraid of the cat arrestin' him. One day T. J. had his ride parked right out in front of Jelly's. Later on Mike sittin' right across the street parked in his police car waitin' for T. J. to pull off. And I said to T. J., 'Man, why you wanta fuck with a mug like this?' T. J. said, 'Now, I tell you what you do. He ain't gon' fuck with you. Take my car and park it over on Indiana Avenue so I can get home.' And so I took his car and parked it over there on Indiana and walked on back and gave him his keys. So Mike had thought I took his car and gone somewhere. Now T. J. and Mike had been drinkin' together. T. J. buyin' all the tastes. But if T. J.

hada pulled off in front of Mike, he woulda arrested him before he reached the next corner. That's why I don't fuck with Mike. He's a rotten cat.

Though the social club never really became very important within the extended primary group, Mike's attempts at recruitment and their ramifications were revealing of the social order. They helped remind me and others of the relative places of hoodlums and regulars in the wider group.

Goin' for Bad

When they are not associating with other group members, but are among their own crowd, hoodlums tend to involve themselves in what regulars and others are quick to label as hoodlum conduct. Operationally, hoodlum conduct is conduct that known hoodlums engage in; they help to define it by engaging in it. Often its qualities are magnified and exaggerated by others of the group, especially by those who want to be regulars. Gambling in public, "street fighting," flashing one's weapons, hustling, and gathering with other hoodlums to "do what they do" are examples. A distinguishing feature of much hoodlum conduct is that it suggests an ability to "be tough" and to "get big money." These are important values expressed by those defined as hoodlums.

Regulars and others see hoodlum conduct as threatening, since it intimidates some of them. One reason regulars attempt to downgrade fighting ability, for example, is that many of them have seen better days physically and can no longer fight well. But even when they are physically able, regulars have a "decent" sense of themselves to protect, a sense that would be violated by the use of violence—except perhaps in dire circumstances. Closely connected with protecting their decency is the very real concern among regulars about maintaining their "clean slates" downtown, which they know will affect their ability to get and keep employment. For other reasons as well, as a rule regulars defer to hoodlums and shy away from any involvement when hoodlums begin to exhibit their toughness.

It is for the very same reasons that men who want to be viewed as "hoodlums" or "hoodlumlike" intentionally involve themselves in activities they know will mean "trouble" to regulars and will at the same time generate a sense of self-esteem. By being tough, they can get the regulars to defer to them, move away from them, or stay around and, by implication, support their hoodlum conduct as something worthwhile. In such circumstances "hoodlums" feel that it is all right "to go for bad" or to extol the virtues of "big money." When there is enough support, and enough other men to be used as a supportive audience, the tables may be turned and the situation redefined so that those who otherwise may enjoy "being regular" can have second thoughts. In such situations and company, regulars themselves may engage in conduct almost indistinguishable from that of hoodlums, except that it is carried out by people who are not known as hoodlums. This is one of the main incentives for regulars to move on when too many hoodlums appear. Status is precarious, and it is very easy to become "involved with the hoodlums."

Enough perceived involvement in such activities helps qualify group members for the status and identity of hoodlum. For men who have previously been defined as hoodlums, mere social conduct in the "rough" setting of Jelly's can be seen as an attempt to exemplify hoodlum standards and values, though these at times overlap, conflict with, or support other values of the general group. In such a context, people with successful hoodlum biographies and definitions may be measured for the determination of their social worth. Though one's past conduct and known personal biography may act as a handicap in a contest for "regular" status, the same biography can place the person very much in the running for "hoodlum" status. Hence the group members with undeniable "hoodlum" biographies and personal attributes are encouraged to express themselves as "hoodlums" or as nothing at all.

Whereas regulars take pride in their "visible means of support," many hoodlums seem to pride themselves on having an "invisible means of support," particularly when they are among their own. Hoodlums often disparage "hardworking men." Many are chronically unemployed, though a few, like Calvin, are engaged in a "visible

means" and can present a more regular side of themselves when circumstances warrant it. The hoodlums who are employed usually do
not brag about it around Jelly's. Though group members know who
is working and who is not, a hoodlum does not broadcast his job
because the kind of work he usually can get, when compared with
the "good jobs" of regulars, pays little, is "hard," and is considered
demeaning, especially by himself. Thus the hoodlum has little incentive even to be employed, let alone to brag about it.

Because of the average hoodlum's experience with the military
and with law enforcement agencies, he is likely to have a "record
downtown" or a "bad discharge." Such a record, which may involve
"time" in jail, makes it difficult for hoodlums to get "good jobs."
The hoodlum knows what is in store for him before he looks for a
job: a low-paying "shit job." For example, some hoodlums hire
themselves out to do day work. Many of them try not to let out this
information, since it is a very poor showing compared with regulars
whose stable jobs allow them to support their families. The hoodlums
seem to respect the "hardworking" regular, though they do not publicly express it. In the hoodlum's mind, given the nature of the status
arrangements at Jelly's, he has lost before he begins to try for a
"visible means of support."

One way out of what may appear to the hoodlum to be a losing
game is to play another game. In dealing with their situation, many
hoodlums play up their "invisible means of support." If they do have
jobs they tend not to emphasize them in the company of peers, or
they talk about them negatively, speaking freely about how much
they hate to work or hate their current jobs. Some threaten to quit,
though continuing to work for weeks or months. In presenting themselves as getting by "invisibly," they spend as much time as possible
around Jelly's. Some may take off from work a day or two each
week, boasting about not having to work every day or saying, "I'd
rather be out here with you studs any day, 'stead o' being in that ol'
factory."

Job or no job, one of the most important concerns among hoodlums is money. They talk about money much of the time they are
together. They discuss people they believe have money, both inside

and outside the extended primary group. Some talk about their own
ways of getting money. They boast about a close friend who "got big
money," sometimes individually comparing him with others they
know in the group, particularly the regulars. Some talk about this or
that person "who ain't got to work, but who still gettin' over big."
Now and then a person will tell the others about a relative "who got
big money," but this is kept to a minimum, since the persons listening also "bear watching" and some are known to be or suspected of
being thieves and robbers.

Sometimes stories are told about pimps and successful hustlers of
the community. There is talk about a "big-time gangster, who doin' it"
(making lots of "easy money"). Some men talk about the days when
they had means of making "big money," days when "I had a stable
of bitches" (prostitutes) or when "I worked and made enough money
to get a new car every year." And although some are known for their
"stickups" within and adjacent to Jelly's neighborhood, I have never
heard anyone openly brag about a "stickup" he had committed.

Group members, including some hoodlums themselves, take pre-
cautions against possible stickups by having others walk them home
or to their cars parked near Jelly's at nights. They are aware that
there are men in the group who will rob them, particularly if the
stickup man does not like them. This was indicated in the conversation Herman and I had with Cochise. It is also indicated in the
following incident reported to me by Mr. Thompson, a sixty-seven-
year-old regular.

"You got to watch out for these roughneck hoodlums up in here,
son. They some crazy assholes, now I ain't kiddin' you. Lemme
tell you 'bout what happened to Jones the other night. [Jones is a
fifty-year-old regular.] You know Jones don't you, son? Lemme
tell you. Last weekend, he went out with some of them hoodlums.
Went out with Genie Boy, Knaky, and some of the rest of 'em.
They tell me they stopped by the Baroque [a local night spot], and
all o' 'em went inside and left Jones and Li'l Tom in the car. You
know ol' dopehead Tom don't you? Well, anyway, Li'l Tom pull
a rod [gun] on m'boy Jones and say 'Give it up!' Jones gave it up.
Tom got 'bout ten dollars off him. Now Jones walkin' 'round here

shame. Now, he shouldn't been out there in the first place, out there tryin' to blend in with them hoodlums. And it's his own fault, shoulda knowd better. Them hoodlums' somethin' else."

Some hoodlums, as we saw in the case of Oscar, get money by "hustlin' " on the ghetto streets and in taverns and other establishments around the area. Though some hoodlums have legal occupations and may also be seen as "hardworking men," some of them do not feel they make enough money to live and support their families as they would like. To augment their incomes they develop what group members call a "hustle"—that is, an often illegal commercial transaction with peers or whoever happens along. A "hustler" appears always to be looking for ways to make money by selling something. Indeed, some hustlers are professional street fences who make much of their living selling "hot" merchandise.

However, for most hoodlums around Jelly's, hustling is only a side involvement, the main source of income coming from unemployment or welfare checks or full- or part-time jobs.[9] Some hustlers maintain peddler's licenses to show the police if they are stopped. Oscar, for example, who works full time at a local auto factory but hustles a great deal on the side, carries such a license. Almost every other day, or when his supplies run low, Oscar goes to a wholesale house "across town" that sells salable items to hustlers. There he buys "damaged" phonograph records, "Benrist" watches (imitation name-brand), socks, shirts, and other items that he might misrepresent as "hot" to unwary strangers as he makes his rounds to the various joints of the South Side and West Side.

But occasionally Oscar and other hustlers buy goods they know are stolen and attempt to sell them for a profit. Some are known to steal the goods themselves, telling others, "I stole this today, and I need a fix" or "I need some money, lemme hold a nickle [five dollars] for these shoes." Some hustlers are believed capable of stealing property from the homes of "friends" and acquaintances, one of the main reasons people around Jelly's are protective about their homes. Few will invite others to their homes unless they know them extremely well, and often they try to keep their addresses secret.

Some hoodlums bring stolen goods directly to Jelly's to sell in broad daylight. It is not strikingly unusual at Jelly's corner, for example, to see a person trying to sell a small color television set, a new coat, or a gold watch. Once, Li'l Tom, a person regarded as a hustler and a hoodlum, stole an automobile from a corner two or three blocks away, then brought the car to Jelly's to find a buyer. For more than an hour he stood around the alley trying to sell the car. Finally he found a man who gave him thirty dollars cash for the 1966 Buick. Later that night Li'l Tom and his hoodlum buddies drank up the money and laughed and joked about the "fool" Tom had found.

On another occasion Knaky struggled through Jelly's alley carrying a large portable television set, crying, "Who gon' lemme have thirty-five cent [dollars] for this here tube?" When no one seemed interested, he lowered his price to fifteen dollars, but finally settled for six dollars from someone unknown to the extended primary group. Among a number of group members that had gathered away from Knaky, Pope said, under his breath, "The boy probably just ripped somebody off. . . . His sister, auntie, or somebody. Maybe some woman he know just went to the store—no tellin'." The others bumped and hunched one another and chuckled in agreement. To all those witnessing such transactions, people who hustle most certainly bear watching.

More than almost anything else, the hoodlum likes to see himself as tough. Everyone in the extended primary group likes to see himself as being "as tough as the next guy." When challenged in certain circumstances, even regulars will exhibit toughness, and wineheads will do the same. But it seems to take greater challenges to provoke a regular into exhibiting his toughness, and wineheads, who seem to care relatively little about this, have to be greatly provoked before they do so. But hoodlums, particularly when among their own kind, are especially sensitive to anything that may be taken as a challenge. Depending on the audience and the "challenger," they are often ready to seize the opportunity to exhibit their own toughness.

Hoodlums exert a certain hegemony over toughness in the extended primary group. When toughness becomes an issue, any person rising to the occasion runs the risk of being perceived as hoodlumlike, since toughness is so characteristic of the men others call hoodlums. To be tough is to engage in hoodlum conduct and is one of the few ways a hoodlum can gain an affirmation of self. Regulars have more ways to be somebody, and the wineheads seem not to compete so actively in the whole game.

One way the hoodlums exhibit their toughness is through their peculiar orientation toward trouble: they seek out trouble and are ready to face it head-on. Whereas regulars like to talk about "decent" experiences, hoodlums readily talk about things that involve "trouble" and express their own toughness. For example, some hoodlums boast about having spent the night in "County" jail, excitedly telling stories about their own involvement as though no stigma were attached. They easily relate tales about their involvements in fights where they had "to beat the shit out o' " this or that person, attempting to collect status from others in the exchange for such stories.

Among the hoodlums, and the extended primary group more generally, there exists a status hierarchy based on toughness. This hierarchy, like the others in the general group, is precarious and action-oriented; men who care about it and participate in it must "test" and "try" this aspect of the social order time and time again to find out where they rank. The group members might fight one another to test their abilities and consequently defer to, and require others to defer to, those who stand superior. Group sanctions are applied to anyone who violates the shared sense of social order along this standard. These points are illustrated in the case of The Terry.

Terry: A Hoodlum Career

The Terry stands about five feet ten and weighs about 210 pounds. He is thirty-three years old, but his large, brown-skinned face looks much older. Like many of the hoodlum crowd, Terry grew up in Jelly's neighborhood. His father used to hang at Jelly's, but he died when Terry was sixteen. Older group members say young Terry once hit Jelly in the mouth for saying "things" about his dead father. After his father died some group members attempted to "raise" Terry, stepping in for his father as guardians and advisers on his personal problems. One of the most prominent in this effort was Herman, who knew Terry's father well and acted as a stepfather for Terry, advising him on "the jitterbugs and the chicks and life."

Throughout his younger life Terry was known as tough and bad. He was quick-tempered and was "always jumpin' on somebody." In those years he was considered a leader of one of the toughest local street gangs. When he was old enough, Terry quit high school and enlisted in the army paratroopers, following an established pattern in his crowd. The paratroopers, because of the organization's emphasis on toughness and "good money," holds a great attraction for former street-gang members like Terry. Unlike some of his buddies who "went through the 'troopers" and received "bad" discharges, Terry returned to the neighborhood with a "good" (in this case general—next to the best one can receive) discharge. And because this type of discharge is rare among hoodlums, Terry carries his discharge papers in his wallet and presents them whenever he has the slightest opportunity. Since he left the army, Terry has been sporadically employed and in and out of various kinds of "trouble" and jail. The group members see him and treat him as a hoodlum.

About four years ago, Terry was convicted of murdering a woman in the area but was released from prison after serving a small part of the sentence. Though Terry proclaims his innocence by saying to others, with a kind of smirk, "That wasn't my murder," group members believe he was guilty. For Terry, the formal accusation in a court of law, followed by conviction and imprisonment, carries a heavy stigma on the streets around Jelly's. He has found life as an "ex-con" difficult to manage in the extended primary group.[10]

Group members are reluctant to give him the deference and respect he used to take for granted. Though he used to have a reputation as a gangster and was known as tough, this reputation no longer follows him. Now he must absorb verbal assaults like "jailbird" and other taunts from men he used to push around and consider less tough than himself, including other hoodlums. On the streets around Jelly's, Terry's toughness and fighting ability are now questioned at times, whereas before they were assumed to be of the highest degree and were deferred to by most.

One reason for the change in Terry's social identity is the general degradation he went through by being formally accused and then convicted of the murder. But also important for the group's current estimation of Terry was his stay in prison or, as some say, "the pen" or "penitent'ry." For those around the streets, such a record has a mystical quality. Group members imagine all kinds of things going on in "the pen," from the homosexual rape of new inmates to the thorough "hoodlumizing" of the prisoner. All this changes people's orientation to the man. Now they watch him carefully, attributing any "hoodlum act" to his "jailbird" status. He is no longer what he was when he went to prison, but is something extraordinary. He especially bears watching.

Another reason for the change in the group's treatment of Terry is that he can no longer intimidate them as he used to, for he is on probation and must watch himself. He can no longer "jump on people" without risking the real possibility of re-imprisonment. Group members know this and treat Terry accordingly. Many who once deferred to his toughness are now quick to challenge him. If before they viewed and treated Terry as "bad" (tough), they now talk about him as "trying to go for bad" (trying to *pass* for bad), and as not meeting group standards of toughness. Terry often finds himself in the position of having to "campaign" for the deference and regard he once took for granted. This is illustrated by an encounter between Terry and Dicky, a person he used to push around.

For a few days, Terry had been engaging in what group members call "campaigning." The term refers to an activity and situation in which a person, usually but not always a hoodlum, carries himself in a manner that lets others know he is looking for a fight or "carrying a chip on his shoulder." This practice is engaged in by anyone uncertain of where he stands in toughness or fighting ability. When a "campaigning" person enters the group, he radiates a general and unfocused hostility that is usually kept under control by his inability to find a suitable object. When he does find an object, he may make use of the person and the situation to express and demonstrate his superior toughness and fighting ability. Initially, the social act of focusing one's hostility usually consists of baiting and taunting someone. Group members call this "wolfing" or "selling wolf tickets." As the "campaign" advances, the campaigning person becomes more and more direct with the object of his hostility. If he responds to the campaign, his gestures and words tell the campaigner that he is indeed in the market to see a "wolf show." Once this happens, the campaigning person must "perform" by rising to and withstanding the countercampaign. If the campaigning person, because of lack of courage or an inability to beat the "suitable" person, is unable to follow through, group members say his "wolf tickets" were "no good" or that the show itself was no good.

One Friday afternoon in August, Terry, Red Mack, T. J., Dicky, and a number of other members of the extended primary group were gathered in the park near Jelly's, as they normally are on warm summer afternoons. Terry had been "wolfing" since about noon and now had begun to focus on Dicky, a young regular who is well liked by many in the group. It was clear to all present that Terry was trying to "sell wolf tickets" to Dicky. Terry initiated the "deal" by continually "signifying" about Dicky in front of the others, including wineheads, regulars, and hoodlums. Once he called Dicky a "pussy," a derogatory term within the group and on the streets generally. In the past Terry had been able to get away with such talk to Dicky's face. Dicky had been in such situations with Terry before but would never "buy" Terry's wolf tickets. But this time was different. Dicky bought Terry's wolf tickets by responding with his own barbs and counterchallenges.

"A'right, Mr. Motherfucker! I'm buying yo' wolf tickets! Now show me somethin', since you so big and bad," said Dicky, standing directly in front of Terry's face. In a second Dicky pushed Terry. Then the two men went to blows. They tussled on the ground while the others looked on, laughing, talking, grunting, and moving out of the way. Most of the men who were watching the fight cheered Dicky on.

"Get him, Dicky! Get him, Dicky!" came one shout.

"Kill the son' bitch," came another shout from the audience.

"Hey!" "Hey!" "Hey!" "Uh-oh!" came other shouts from the audience.

It appeared that most of the men sided with Dicky, to Terry's apparent demoralization.

Before the fight stopped, Dicky, who was about Terry's size, had picked Terry up and thrown him crashing to the grass. Terry then sat on the ground, holding his head in his hands, looking sad. Some of the men pointed at Terry and laughed, while others just shook their heads and walked away. Dicky stood around, his shirt torn and one shoe off. He found his shoe and went home, sensing that the other group members were even more on his side than before the fight.

As Terry sat on the ground hurting and holding his swelling head, Red Mack, one of his followers, drunk as usual, staggered over and said, "I told you, Terry. You don't be fuckin' wit' no Dicky. You don't want no part of Dicky. You must be crazy, man," pointing his finger at Terry.

The "wolf tickets" Terry sold Dicky had turned out to be "no good." Both Terry and Dicky continued to come to Jelly's without further incident, except for the silent stares they exchanged. Group members continued to talk about the incident for weeks, thus helping to solidify the social reordering they had all participated in.[11]

The hierarchy of toughness is a social order that even Terry defends and attempts to protect, as long as he is included in some way. He appears to believe in its justice, exchanging his belief for the friendship he can acquire by fitting himself in with what others are now inclined to expect of him. In attempting to gain "friends," Terry now knows that he must be something other than tough—or at least that he cannot be tough with highly regarded members of the group. He now senses, after numerous "tests" and tribulations, that he can gain "friends" and social regard in the extended primary group by enacting roles that are socially acceptable for a person like himself—that is, the kind of person he has become. This means he must enact roles that somehow support the recognized, prevailing arrangements of social relationships within the group.

After his fight with Dicky, Terry was reluctant to fight anyone else in the extended primary group. But he would quickly challenge "outsiders" he sensed as threatening the group. He was prepared to "take up for" those "in the family," including people he was not particularly close to, as is indicated in the following incidents involving "the family" and a stranger to the group. Several men were sitting around Jelly's one afternoon talking about service experiences, a subject that lets men depict themselves as having interesting and manly adventures. Herman talked about Japan, and the men listened intently.

"I mean goddamn, I knew I was home. Guess what. When I got off the train, I got off in a place called Gilkehooke. That's about two hours outside of Yokohama, the suburbs," announced Herman. Herman said this in his usual authoritative voice, trying to convince the men that he knew what he was talking about. At this point a stranger, Cooley, saw his chance to enter the conversation and to "match" the level of the talk or even to outdo Herman.

"I was airborne," commented Cooley, flatly.

To deal with this intrusion, Terry, a known authority on army paratroopers, quickly responded to put the outsider back in his place.

"You a lyin' motherfucker. What's a canopy, nigger? What's a canopy, if you a paratrooper? I mean what is a goddamn canopy?" demanded Terry.

"Then's when yo' lines all mixed up," answered Cooley.

Terry, without allowing the outsider to finish, began answering his own question. "The canopy is the hole in the top of the goddamn chute. You a lyin' son of a bitch."

"I know what a canopy is," replied Cooley.

"The hole in the middle of the chute. That's the canopy, right! Now, don't tell me in a goddamn lie you a paratrooper, nigger. I got four motherfuckin' years in that goddamn shit. Don't be lyin'. If you tellin' the truth, let the truth go. You was in the marine corps, or you was a motherfuckin' ah, ah, mortar man, understand? You was artillery; let it go. But don't tell me. . . . How many jumps you have?" asked Terry.

"Ninety-seven jumps," Cooley replied.

"You a lyin' son' bitch. I'm a master jumper, and I only got thirty-two," challenged Terry.

At this point some of the men began to laugh, as Dicky chimed in. "I got ten, ha-ha. That's a hell of a lot of jumps, man."

"Aw, man, I don't want to hear that goddamn shit," said Terry.

"Ah, uh, uh, I wasn't in the service. I was a paratrooper. I jumped out in Thailand. I knew how to fold 'em up," Cooley said.

"How long you stay in the service?" asked Terry.

"I wasn't in the service. I was a paratrooper, trainer-jumper for a private company, over there in Switzerland," Cooley replied.

"You a lyin' motherfucker. You ain't got no hundred and somethin' jumps, goddamn, in no three motherfuckin' years," accused Terry.

"I was a trainer," Cooley said.

"I got a reef. What is a reefer on your star on? Now, what is a reefer on your star on?" Terry asked. "It's on yo' motherfuckin' wings, nigger. Your goddamn wings. A reef on yo' goddamn star. You wasn't no goddamn paratrooper. Can't be no trooper."

"But I know what a streamer is, know what a line is. I used to fold 'em up, make 'em, fold 'em," explained Cooley.

"Wasn't no goddamn government job, nigger. You was a goddamn, ah, ah, what's his name. You was a goddamn, ah, ah, you was a goddamn shoot 'em up, hang 'em up, and dry 'em out, re-fold the motherfuckers. And in [Fort] Benning, they fold they own goddamn chutes," Terry declared.

"You don't never trust nobody to be fuckin' with your own goddamn chute, man. That's like your own motherfuckin' rifle," Cooley said.

"You don't be talkin' that shit to me. Now if you want to be talkin' that shit, go talk to them monkies over there. [As Terry pointed to a bench in the park.] If you jumped, goddamn, you jumped. If you a paratrooper, you a paratrooper. Don't tell me you fucked around and you jumped, goddamn it, and you ain't, nigger! said Terry.

"Nah. I didn't say I was no army paratrooper. I said I used to jump for this company," answered Cooley.

"Aw, you ain't jumped for shit!" stated Terry.

"Yes I did," Cooley said.

Taking sides with Terry against the outsider, Dicky said, "What's the longest fall from an airplane?"

"He ain't never been in the paratroopers," said Terry.

At this point, Herman attempted to defuse the situation. "Tough niggers, man. Hey, they bring out the truth. They don't be lyin' to each other out here. Motherfucker, you suck pussy, you a garbage motherfucker, whatever you is. This is the truth. This is the truth!" Herman said.

Dicky agreed with Herman, "There it is" (like "right on").

"Now, Cochise came up here, not too long ago, told them niggers, 'Get up off some o' that liquor, and smoke some o' that good shit." (Cochise is a former "pusher".)

Attempting to redeem himself, Cooley said to Terry, "Hey, you jump out o' one of the C-47s, man?"

"130s, 140s, 123s, helicopters, H-11s," replied Terry.

Cooley said, "I jumped from one of the big jets."

"You a lyin' motherfucker, you ain't jumped from no jet. 'Cause a jet got to slow up there to a hundred miles an hour. And when you come out, goddamn, yo' chute bursts. Can't jump out that motherfucker!" Terry answered.

"Right, 'cause it go too high," said Cooley.

"An a man can't jump out 'cause that jet stream, you know, you a kill yourself," Dicky stated.

"A'right, how a jet shoot you out?" Terry asked.

"B-52 . . ." stated Cooley.

"Do it shoot you straight out or down?" persisted Terry.

". . . right before bomber," replied Cooley.

"Well, do it shoot you straight out or down?" asked Terry again.

"Uh, it shoot you straight out!" said Cooley.

"You a lyin' son of a bitch. It shoot you straight goddamn down like the goddamn helicopter, you motherfucker!" Terry screamed.

After a short pause, Cooley said, "I don't know, I wasn't in no service when they . . ."

"I come out in '61. And I had jumped out of everything they had." (At this point Red Mack, a winehead, walks over.) Hey, MacDonald! Here come one [a paratrooper] right here. Ask him. Hey MacDonald! MacDonald!"

"What?" said Mack.

"Come on white folks," said Herman (referring to Mack's very light complexion, while alerting Mack that he was on).

Pointing to the outsider, Terry said, "He don't know what a canopy is, gon' tell me he's a paratrooper."

Now it was Mack's turn to interrogate the outsider, again to put him in his place, constructing the place and reminding Cooley of who he was. "You know what a apex is? You know what a apex is?" asked Mack.

"Apex? I, uh, never did go through that shit," replied Cooley.

Terry now began to laugh, as Mack "proved" him right.

"Aw, you ain't nothing," Mack stated in agreement with others about the status of the outsider.

Herman added (again trying to defuse the situation and protect the outsider), "Aw, man. Don't strain yourself, man. Them cats really jumped. I mean all these cats. They really do that shit."

Terry laughed again, heartily, apparently happy that "his side" was winning.

Herman said, "They tell me this the way they go to the door [of a plane]. Herman begins to do the "paratrooper shuffle" as the others join in. "Hey, they [paratroopers, since he was not one] tell me this the way you go to the door. 'Shuffle left, shuffle right.' All the type o' shit."

Herman's rendition was enough to get Terry to perform the *real* "paratrooper shuffle." Terry rose from the bench and demonstrated his ability to do the shuffle. The others watched urging him on, as they laughed and joked at what could have developed into a tense situation. But in a few minutes the interrogation started up again, as the men thought up new tests for the outsider.

"Hey, what's a slip, what's a slip?" asked Mack.

"Well, uh, when you coming down . . . ," answered Cooley.

"You ain't no goddamn trooper! It's when you come out, and yo' parachute don't open," Terry stated.

"Then you slip to the left, and you slip to the right," Mack said.

"How many jumps you have, Mack. About twenty-six?" Dicky asked.

"Nah, I ain't had but twenty-three," Mack replied.

"I encouraged him [Mack] to go to school [jump school]," Terry said.

Grimes, a hoodlum who had been watching the show, entered with, "If you get one motherfuckin' jump, I mean two mother-fuckin' jumps a year, then you a bitch!"

"I'm a master jumper. That man ain't had no hundred and ten jumps. A hundred and somethin' jumps my motherfuckin' ass. Look here, if he had a hundred and ten jumps, his mammy had a hundred and ten jumps," Terry proclaimed.

"Can't jump out no jet with a motherfuckin' parachute," Herman said.

Then Mack began to interrogate the outsider again.

"Hey, what's a air pocket, what's the air pocket, what's the air pocket?" Mack asked. "What's the air pocket?" But before letting the man answer, Mack said, "You a lyin' ass! You a lyin' ass! You a lyin' ass! What's a PLF, what's a PLF, what's a PLF?"

"What is a PLF?" Terry said to the outsider.

"What is a PLF?" Mack asks (this in following Terry, with the same voice intonation).

"A PLF, nigger? You don't know what the fuck a PLF was! That's when the monkey hit the motherfuckin' ground, you motherfucker, you," Terry said.

"Parachute Landing Fall, baby. Oooh, ha-ha, baby," says Mack, congratulating himself for his show of knowledge. "What's a popsicle? What's a popsicle?"

"That's when yo' line get tangle up and you dead before you even hit the ground. But I wasn't no army jumper. 101st Airborne, Screaming Eagles," Cooley said.

"Talk about the 101st. We ran you motherfuckers all across Nam. Fuck you motherfuckers. Chickenshit son of a bitches!" snapped Terry.

"I was with the Airborne Rangers. Damn right!" Cooley said. Here the outsider contradicts himself, getting in as the situation allows him an opening.

"You was in the troopers?" asked Mack.

"Yeah!" answered Cooley.

"I'm gon' ask one question," Mack said.

"What?" Cooley replies.

"You was in the troopers?" Mack asked.

"Uh-huh," Cooley said.

"Then what's a **PLF**?" Mack asked.

"That's where you land, fall," answered Cooley.

"What drop zone did you drop in?" Mack asked.

"I was in uh, uh, Benning," Cooley stated.

"You had to have some United States training," Mack said.

"Yea, but I went to Benning and then to Germany," Cooley explained.

"Well, where'd you have your basic airborne training at?" asked Mack.

"Fort Benning," replied Cooley.

"How many drop zones you got at Benning?" questioned Mack.

"Four," Cooley answered.

In the foregoing situation the group, led by Terry, ganged up on Cooley, the outsider. To distinguish themselves from him, they joined ranks and opposed him verbally, and through this process created a "victim." By taking—or creating—such an opportunity, all who are able to "get in on" the put-down of the outsider simultaneously make claim to their own belongingness. Terry, the principal instigator of the outsider's degradation, seems to have a special personal need to find and create such scapegoats. These days his scapegoats tend to be from outside the extended primary group. This is supported in the following episode.

On another evening, a stranger from "over on the West Side" approached Jelly's corner and walked into the liquor-store room with Red Mack. Mack and the man appeared to be together and thus did not attract much attention. They stood around inside the room until Jelly put Mack out, as he does when Mack is out of his favor. The stranger followed Mack outside. Shortly afterward there was some commotion on the sidewalk near the alley. The outsider was wildly swinging his large belt and buckle at men gathered on the corner. Paul, a regular who apparently had done nothing to provoke the attack, was caught unawares. Dicky, the regular who had fought with Terry a few months before, was in the way of the buckle and attempted to move away. As he tried desperately to dodge, Paul's arm and shoulder were caught by the outsider's belt, and the buckle ripped his brown suede jacket. The others present, most of whom were regulars, appeared dumbfounded by the pandemonium. Though the group's attention was focused on the outsider and the trouble he was making, no one took any action to counter the violence.

Suddenly The Terry appeared, after having sized up the situation from across the street. While the group members looked on, Terry ripped off his own belt and scampered across the street in pursuit of the outsider. With an enraged look, Terry adroitly looped his white vinyl belt around the outsider's throat and began pulling it tight, clearly attempting to choke him, but the belt snapped under the pressure. The outsider then moved away from Terry and the others, holding his sore neck. Terry pursued the man, who then picked up a jagged brick and raised it to throw at Terry.

"Look out, Terry! He got a brick," shouted Mack.

"Look out!" shouted others of the small group, including Dicky, who a few months earlier had been fighting with Terry.

Terry just stood the man off and watched him carefully. By now the group of spectators was growing. Regulars, wineheads, and hoodlums observed the show.

Clearly aware of his performance, Terry glanced over at his friends. Then he looked on the ground for a weapon but saw nothing he could use. Pointing his finger at the man, who was not twenty feet away, he said in a deadly serious voice, "Now, if you miss, I'm gon' kill you!"

The outsider looked at Terry and then over at the rest of us. After a few long seconds he slowly lowered the brick and threw it to the ground. He broke into a wide nervous grin, as if to claim he had been playing all along. The tension subsided. Then The Terry walked over to the stranger and, taking his hand, said "You almost got yo' ass killed. Now you better carry yo' ass back where you belong 'fo somethin' happen to you sho'nuff." Before releasing his hand Terry said, for the benefit of both the man and the group members looking on, "You don't be fuckin wit' members of the family, you dig?" Then he placed the man's hand on his own heart in a grand gesture and said "Love." With that, the stranger left quickly.

Afterward, the group members simply shook their heads and resumed their talk, spicing it with references to the incident. They tried
to make sense of the outsider and his motives. Wondering aloud about
the outsider, T. J. said, "I thought the cat was with you, Mack."
"Naw, now see, I don't even know the man," disclaimed Mack.

By now Terry had moved back across the street, rejoining the
man he was with before the incident. Paul, the person who was attacked, Dicky, Knaky, and others stood around on the sidewalk.
Mack and T. J. came up to them also. As the men talked, it was
clear that Terry had violated no one's expectations of him, and that
he had played the kind of role others were satisfied with. Certainly
no one was outraged at Terry's performance. In Terry's words, the
"family was under attack." In these circumstances Terry could feel
unconstrained in displaying and demonstrating his "toughness" and
"fighting ability." At the same time, Terry readily identified himself
as a member of the "family," while distancing himself from the role
that many readily put him in—as persona non grata. It is through
such opportunities and actions that Terry is now able to include himself in the "family" and take up the status of "somebody."

A few days after this incident I was able to talk with Terry about
his role in it and about his more general role in the group—how he
viewed himself in relationship to the others. On that particular day
a good number of us were gathered in small groups spread out over
a section of the park near Jelly's. It was hot, much like the day when
Terry attacked the outsider. Some men sat on the ground around the
trunks of trees to get the benefit of the shade. Others stood around,
their hands dug into their pockets, looking around the park and at
the passing traffic in the street and on the sidewalks. Dogs romped
through the park, occasionally distracting the men from their involvements with one another, their talk and play. Herman, Blue, and I
stood by a tree, looking down at Mr. Thompson and getting ready
to share a bottle of Old Forester. An atmosphere of gaiety prevailed.

Suddenly, Pee Wee broke into the group with, "Ha-ha! Did y'all
see that? Ha-ha. Did y'all see that?"
"What?" I said.

"Huh?" said Herman.

Our group focused its attention on Pee Wee, prompting him to tell us more.

"Smut and Kelly! [two large dogs] They ran over him! They ran over Knaky!" said Pee Wee, pointing to Knaky and the other hoodlums who were shooting dice about twenty yards away. "Knaky was laying in the grass fucked up [high]," laughed Pee Wee. "Am I lying?" he continued, prompting us to look over and see for ourselves.

"Them two big motherfuckers?" inquired Herman, referring to the two big dogs.

"They ran over Knaky's chest 'bout twenty times. Knaky say 'fuck this' and got up," laughed Pee Wee. "Didn't he, Terry?" (Terry had been with the hoodlums but was now joining our group.)

"Ha-ha, Ha-ha," laughed Terry, shaking his head in agreement. "They ran across his chest and scared the shit out of him. Ha-ha."

"Then they ran on through the crap game. Niggers over there shootin' dice? Oscar and the rest of them. Them dogs didn't give a shit. They just ran through and kicked all them dice over," continued Pee Wee. Everyone laughed at the way Pee Wee told this story, which could be partly verified by our looking over and seeing the last of it. Shortly, people broke off this talk and moved away from Terry. But I stayed and talked with him.

"Eli, wonder how he felt with all them feets on his chest?" said Terry.

I laughed. He then asked me for a drink of my whiskey. I gave him the cup, and as he drank he said, "I know just how he felt. How would you feel like. Laying out on the ground, Eli. Yo' eyes closed, you nice and high after smokin' some good herb [marijuana] and then all them dog feets hittin' you in yo' chest. You wake up and say, 'Hey!' Ha-ha. Looka here, you wanta kill the nigger the dog belong to. Fuck this shit. Ha-ha," said Terry.

I talked and laughed with Terry for a while, then asked him about the incident with the outsider a few days before. "Have you seen the cat you ran out the neighborhood the other day?" I asked.

"Naw, I ain't seen the motherfucker. I bet' not see him too soon. Broke my belt on his neck. That belt cost me seven dollars," said Terry.

"Seven dollars?" I said.

"And it broke. I was standin' across the street and I seen the dude lickin' [hitting] Paul and Paul kept tryin' to duck. So I came out to stop the dude and the belt broke, you dig?" said Terry.

"Yeah," I said.

"I was mad," said Terry.

"You were definitely out to stop him," I said.

"I was out to kill him. Break his neck," said Terry.

"If it'd been a leather belt, you mighta broken his neck," I said.

"That's what I meant to do. I don't be bullshittin'. I'm for real. Paul. Paul cannot fight. Paul is like a kid out here. He not a pussy, though. He just can't fight. So when I seen what was happenin,' I just ran across the street, took my belt and caught him 'round the neck. Meant to break his neck. And the belt broke. I look at the motherfucker [the belt] for ten seconds and say, 'ain't that a bitch.' I said 'C'mon nigger, fuck that. Get on me.' Then the motherfucker picked up a brick and shit. Was gon' throw it. Told him, 'You miss, I'm on yo' ass any damn way!' You dig? 'If you miss, you dead. I'm gon' kill you.' Now this is why they call me dirty Terry. 'Cause I will kill, I been known to kill. I went to Viet Nam and killed. Went to Lebanon, in June '58. Went there and killed. I got a wound right here [points to shoulder] and still bother me. And I killed every motherfucker that wasn't quick enough. And my partners out here, man. I like to sit around here and get high, listen to music, stand, be smooth. But if the shit break out, it just break out. Looka here. Ain't no coolness about it. Just c'mon. I'm gon' fight for my partners. But you know what though, Eli. Niggers out here hate me. They hate me. I know they hate me. But they respect me 'cause I will fight. I fought the other night and I caught a nigger from the back, 'cause he talk too much. . . ."

At that moment Herman, who had been listening to the latter part of this conversation, moved over closer to Terry and me, causing Terry to say, "Now Herman taught me every goddamn thing. That's why I quit being slick. I used to be the slickest young nigger in the neighborhood. 'Fore you come along, Eli, I would change clothes three times a day, and be makin' four hundred dollars a month, plus a little crookin' on the side. Hey, Herman! Tell him what I was makin'. Man, me and my wife . . ."

"You used to make big money, Terry," said Herman.

"And plus I used to gamble," said Terry. "Used to shoot pool, all that shit."

Then Herman said, putting Terry in his place as a hoodlum, "But see, Terry. You ain't cut out to be out here in the streets and gamblin' and shit. You know what you cut out to be?"

"What?" asked Terry.

"A motherfuckin' workin' man. And when you were workin' . . . If you'd go straighten yo'self up and work, you'd be one o' the greatest niggers in the neighborhood. But you wants to be out here, gamblin', hustlin', and thinkin' you slick. Tryin' to get the fast money. But you ain't cut out . . . God didn't make you like that. God made you the kind of man that could work. Use yo' motherfuckin' muscles and take care of yourself and yo' wife and kids."

"Yeah," said Terry, "To use my mind."

"Look how well you was doing, Terry. You had big Buicks. You had a plush apartment. And yo' wife and little daughter was taken care of," said Herman.

"Marie Antoinette Davis," says Terry, murmuring his daughter's name and reminiscing about the past.

"See, this the kinda man you was. 'Spose'n you hada stayed on that track. You woulda been a *Mr.* Davis," preached Herman.

"I'm still a Mr. Davis! I don't give a fuck what you say. Just like you, Herman. I'm Mr. Davis," declared Terry, recoiling at Herman's remarks.

Herman said, "You still Mr. Davis to me. I'm just tryin' to say, 'stead o' wishing for somethin', you coulda had it. If you hada put yo' muscles to it and work for it and don't fuck up . . ."

"I coulda bought me a new Cadillac every year. Every year," declared Terry.

"Yo' daddy bought him a new car every year," said Herman.

"Every year! He bought one, a Dodge," said Terry. "I just didn't want the motherfuckin' car, understand? I coulda been better than T. J., man. I was makin' twenty-six thousand dollars a year. Before any of 'em [regulars] was makin' money, I was makin' all the money," continued Terry.

"Aw, you had big money, man, shit," said Herman.

"Big money! I was makin' money 'fore *you* niggers [regulars] even thought about money," proclaimed Terry.

Although Terry likes to see himself as a person who has had the choice of having "big money," he now lacks the motivation and the means for getting it. He has been fired from numerous laboring jobs and now does not seem concerned about finding a job. He lives on his welfare check and the money he can beg from others. Some believe he "sticks up" people in the neighborhood. When he has money, he usually spends it quickly on his "friends" and himself. And his friends talk among themselves about Terry and when "he gon' get his money again," so they can get some of it. This kind of spending may be viewed as just another effort by Terry to "buy" back a "place" in the group. Evidence supporting this view is presented in the following story.

One Thursday afternoon in July, a number of the group members, including Herman and me (regulars), Oscar (hoodlum), Knaky (hoodlum), and Clay (hoodlum) were sitting in the park, laughing and talking and joking with one another. Herman was discussing a woman a number of the fellows had been wanting to "get next to."

"In public, she a kiss ya, talk that shit, kiss ya, but when you get her alone, she'll say, 'Get on way from here, boy. What the fuck wrong with you?' " said Herman.

"She might say, 'My husband home, and he don't like that,' " said Knaky.

"Aw, she a say any motherfuckin' thing to get you off her ass. Yeah, but she got somebody she givin' up that pussy to, huh," said Herman.

The others then chimed in with "Uh-huh."

"I saw ol' Bobby ease off with her," said Knaky.

"Yeah, she probably like her pussy sucked. Let them young niggers eat her up," said Herman.

Then Oscar said, looking up at the sky, "It ain't gon' rain . . . I used to think Terry was eatin' it!" (putting Terry down).

"He get his check today?" asked Knaky.

"Gimme a drink, Herman," asked Clay.

"I don't know, but I heard that the post lady was callin' him," said Herman.

"I got the news, and if he ain't been 'round here, somethin' wrong," said Knaky.

"Hey, I got the news! I got the news! Hey, hey. Guess what. Guess what I heard. I got the last report! I got the last report, Knaky," said Herman.

"What was it?" asked Knaky.

"A cat got in me and Eli's car and says a . . . Naw, I mean we got in his car, and he says a Terry got his check. I say 'how you know?' I say 'They don't get no check till the third of the month.' He say, 'He musta got it,' he say, 'anytime the post lady be callin' . . .

"What's the date?" asked Oscar.

"Today's the sixteenth," I said.

"Well, he got the cake," said Knaky.

"He got the cake, but he ain't got it on him," said Oscar.

"Pope. We got in Pope's car, and Pope brought that to me and Eli, way over there on Indiana. I say what the fuck I care 'bout Terry gettin' a check. He ain't gon' gimme nuthin'. He don't owe me shit," said Herman.

"He don't owe me nuthin'," said Oscar, not wanting to appear that he was excited by the prospect of getting some of Terry's money—that is, until it was declared all right to do so.

"Herman, but like I'm tryin' to say. The nigger that's wit' the nigger [Terry] when he get his money, Jack. You with him all day long," volunteered Oscar.

"All day long?" I asked.

"All day long," answered Oscar. " 'Cause whatever he buy him, he buy you too."

"Is that right?" I inquired.

"Who, Terry?" asked Knaky.

"Yeah, Terry," said Oscar.

"Oh, yeah," said Knaky, verifying Oscar's statement.

"That's why that check ain't gon' last but a couple days," said Herman.

"It ain't gon' last that long," said Oscar.

"If he go buy a jacket, he'll buy you one," said Herman.

"No shit?" I said.

"If you wit' him," said Knaky.

"If you wit' him," chimed in the others, agreeing with Knaky.

"Anything he buy him, he a buy you. If he get a haircut, he a get you a haircut. He get a shave, he a get you a shave. If he a get a pair a shoes, he a get you a pair shoes," said Knaky.

"Yeah," chimed in the others again in verification of Knaky.

"No shit?" I said again.

"Yeah!" said the others in chorus.

"That's the way Terry is," said Herman. "That's why he get so goddamn mad when niggers . . ."

". . . don't turn him on," finished Knaky.

"I be tryin' to tell him that to get his check once a month and be broke the next day—that ain't no hip," and by so saying distinguishing himself from "people like Terry."

Just at this instant, Herman threw his empty vodka bottle into a trash can about twenty feet away. This action interrupted the discussion of Terry.

"Ain't that a bitch, and I missed," said Oscar, referring to Herman's successful shot at the can. "And I missed."

"I bet you five dollars you won't do it again," said Knaky.

"Aw, I ain't bettin' no five dollars, nigger! I sit there and aimed, Goddamn, long enough!" shouted Herman.

"I wish I could find him now, man. I know where he at. If he got his money, I know where he at," said Oscar, switching the subject back to Terry.

"Him and Underwear together," said Knaky.

"They down at the Indiana show. Spider with him. They down at the Indiana show," asserted Oscar.

"Naw, they at the Palace," countered Knaky.

"Uh-uh. They 'round the Indiana show. 'Cause Terry . . . I heard him this morning talkin' 'bout . . . ," said Oscar.

". . . Going to the show," said Knaky, completing Oscar's sentence.

For more than three hours we sat and stood around the park bench, talking and laughing and having fun with one another. When the rain began we continued to stand around, enduring the light drizzle under the trees in favor of sociability. Most important about this social experience was the way it illustrated Terry's place within the group, even in his absence, and showed how Terry is now required to negotiate his way around the group. To be somebody, he renders certain favors, seemingly in exchange for being a person who counts. Terry's current identity is very different from the "way it used to be." Now, for example, he is not allowed to push around significant group members, as was indicated when the group would not sanction his fight with Dicky. If he is to demonstrate his toughness and fighting ability, he must focus on objects that significant group members care little about. He must direct his own actions in ways that do not threaten, or appear not to threaten, the concept of social order that significant others want to perpetuate. In these ways the group works to create the Terry it wants; its members require a set of behaviors "out of him" that allows them the sense that they are being the kinds of people they want to be.

For Terry, the way to "be somebody" is to attempt to behave "in line" with the directions of the others—in ways that are collectively sanctioned by the group. By their actions, group members remind him of what is sanctioned and what is not. Taking their cues, however subtle, he attempts to act in accordance with his perceptions of what the others most appreciate in him. They reward Terry's displays of toughness and fighting ability with deference and attention—but on the condition that these exhibitions are directed toward the "right" objects. Group members, particularly the hoodlum crowd, allow him to act as though he has "big money," socializing with him, even running with him—but only as long as he spends his money on them. Most don't bother to reciprocate, for they are well aware that Terry is short of help and support in "being somebody." This shortage intensifies his desire to get big money and to be regarded as tough. Without help in the form of "runnin' buddies," Terry feels himself to be less than he wants to be. The nature of the associations he is able to make on the basis of toughness and big money and the activities related to them qualify Terry for the label of hoodlum.

Though this process may not occur in exactly the same way for all the men who come to be known as hoodlums, something broadly like it does go on. But though those who get labeled as hoodlums tend to exhibit values of toughness and big money, they sometimes choose to display what they perceive as conduct becoming for "decent" people. One of the major differences between the men defined as hoodlums and the men who successfully define themselves as regulars stems from differences in ability to manage their "public relations." To manage his public relations a person must behave in ways that credit or discredit certain aspects of his "known" personal biography. Such attempts may further a claim to "being regular," or claims to "regularity" may be socially negated and the person encouraged to settle for "being a hoodlum" and to involve himself more completely in the conduct expected of his kind. This has become the group-sanctioned way for him to "be somebody" within the extended primary group.

Social Order and Sociability

Men come to Jelly's to socialize and "to see what's happenin'." The members of the extended primary group exhibit status attributes during such social interaction, drawing upon whatever supports they can use to gain esteem and identity among peers. Their personal characteristics and resources for social regard help put the men "in the running" to be "somebody" in the group at Jelly's, somewhat independently of how these characteristics and resources are regarded in the wider society.[1] It is here at Jelly's, among peers from similar backgrounds, that a member of the extended primary group feels he has a chance to be "somebody," and the men care how other group members see them. Jelly's affords them a chance to be known and to know others intimately during sociability, and this is the primary reason many of them regularly come to Jelly's.

By their long-term involvements at Jelly's, the men make a social investment in the extended primary group and in the particular social order they create. Each group member gains a sense of place in this social order, however precarious and open to negotiation it may be, that emerges through social interaction. A person's place within the group is always situationally sensitive and needs public demonstration from time to time. Indeed, what each man's conception of place at Jelly's *is* is shaped situationally by what liberties other group members allow him and take with him. Others' conceptions of the man's place depend in part on what group members have seen him demonstrate in the past, what they "know" him to be capable of, and what all this might mean for their own sense of who they are. In this socially competitive and precarious context, each man's sense of place is affected by what these others can allow him while still maintaining their presuppositions of "the order" and their places within it. The character of this negotiation affects their collective judgments. The social estimation of the person is communicated to him and others by the way others treat him or attempt to treat him. His reactions to this treatment help define his place within the social order of Jelly's.

Accordingly, a place in the group requires continued association among the men who make a habit of Jelly's. It depends in large measure on some long-term and intimate involvement with a group whose members' social identities depend on one another. Thus status, as achieved in the hierarchies at Jelly's, is not transferable to just any street corner. Street-corner groups do not typically allow a stranger an automatic sense of place, a comfortable feeling of fitting in. With all its different kinds of people, each one having some sense of his own place in the group, Jelly's serves as a source of personal identity.

Group members, regardless of rank, feel that others care for them; they belong to the corner group at Jelly's. This caring is expressed in many different circumstances, most often when a crisis arises in which one person seems to be suffering more than others and more than is expected of his role in the group. The person's predicament can arise from extreme poverty, death, injury, illness, or general trouble in one's life. The extended primary group offers supportive social ties for its own. For example, when Herman's wife, Butterroll, went to the hospital for two weeks, many people around Jelly's talked about her health, expressing their concern for her and also for Herman himself. Within the group, it is well known that Herman cannot cook and will not do "women's work." While Butterroll was in the hospital, he would show up at his regular times on most days, and when he didn't the others at Jelly's wondered and worried about him. As time passed Herman began to come unshaven and unkempt, looking more and more like a winehead. Even the wineheads were worried about Herman's becoming a winehead, or acting like one. More and more, the group members talked about Herman's condition, describing to others his "winehead-lookin' self."

As it became increasingly clear that Herman was not eating properly, group members began coming to his aid. T. J., for instance, began going home with Herman to "fix him somethin' to eat," and the wives of some of the regulars began sending him dinners. Group members who had jobs in restaurants began bringing extra "grub" for Herman. Throughout Butterroll's illness, people were almost as concerned for Herman's well-being as for Butterroll's.

Another expression of the group's caring for its members is the case of Uncle Cleo, a retired regular about sixty-seven years old, who held everyone's respect and affection until he died of a heart attack. He came around to Jelly's regularly, and when asked, he would say, "I live up in here. All these here people you see are my chillun'." Cleo lived alone in a kitchenette apartment not far from the corner. It was known that he had a heart ailment and high blood pressure, and various group members, including wineheads, hoodlums, and regulars, took it upon themselves to look out for him. When he had not been seen for two days or more, Jelly or one of the other men would either go and "see 'bout Cleo" or send someone else to do so. Late at night when Cleo was about to leave Jelly's, someone was almost always ready to "walk him home." Even those viewed as hoodlums would walk with him, protecting him from others on the streets.

Many evenings Cleo would come to Jelly's and sit around on the radiator looking out the window, gazing at the traffic. Then, for no apparent reason, he would begin to cry almost uncontrollably. "I don't want to die. I don't want to leave y'all," he would cry. And those within earshot, winehead, regular, or hoodlum, would try to comfort him. He would cry for a few minutes, then "straighten up" and begin to talk with the person helping him. This happened on one occasion when Oscar, a hoodlum, was standing not far from Cleo.

About ten people sat and stood around in the liquor-store room. Jelly served up Budweisers to Knaky and Bemo. Mr. Thompson walked around Herman and T. J., who were "clowning" and "play fighting." A woman with a five-year-old child entered. The playing stopped and the noise level dropped, but rose again after the woman and child left. I watched the Cubs and Dodgers game on the TV set on top of the soda-pop cooler. Oscar and Spider stood by the cigarette machine and talked. Cleo was sitting on the long radiator carrying on a conversation with Jelly, who moved back and forth to his seat behind the counter to wait on people. When Jelly would leave, Cleo would continue his talk, for the benefit of all who could hear him. Suddenly he burst into tears. Everyone turned their attention to him. He cried uncontrollably. Oscar moved close to Cleo and put his arm around the old man's shoulder.

"Hey, man. It's a'right. It gon' be a'right. Just take it slow and easy. You hurtin' anywhere? What's the matter, Cleo?" said Oscar, trying to comfort him. Sam moved closer, too, but did not attempt to do anything except look on.

"I'm a'right now," said Cleo after a few minutes. Oscar took his white silk handkerchief and wiped the old man's eyes. Soon things were normal again.

The attitude of caring is also expressed when group members die, become ill or otherwise incapacitated. When a regular becomes ill enough to be "off work", group members associated with any of the crowds—winehead, hoodlum, or regular—will sometimes come to his aid. They contribute out of moral obligation, but also with the hope that their offering will be reciprocated when they are in need. Albert, a regular, became ill and was off work for an extended period. Herman began a collection for him and was able to raise twenty dollars. Because Albert was well liked by the group, almost everyone gave what he could, including wineheads (if they had any money), hoodlums, and regulars.

During my three years of fieldwork, eight members of the extended primary group died, and several others were wounded through various acts of violence or became seriously ill. Willie, a hustler, was shot and killed a few blocks from Jelly's on the street in front of his tenement. Freddie, a regular, died of stab wounds he received in a fight late one night in Jelly's alley. Tooney, a young hoodlum, was found dead early one Friday morning in Jelly's alley with his own machete in his chest. Jimmy Lee, a twenty-nine-year-old winehead, was found dead in his bed by his aunt, after months of complaining about stomach pains. Maurice, a young hoodlum, drowned late one summer night when he broke into a closed swimming area. Melvin was shot and killed when "he jumped on a man in a tavern over on the West Side." Uncle Cleo died of a heart attack while cooking in his kitchenette apartment; some blamed the fire department for not coming to his aid promptly enough. And Bobby was "knocked in the head when he ran into some o' them jitterbugs up on Thirty-fifth" and died a few days later.

When death occurs, members of the extended primary group usually acknowledge this by becoming more intimate and supportive of each other. They interrupt things as usual. As people arrive, others echo the recurrent question, "You hear 'bout Bobby?" This question and its tone always expresses as much as it asks; it communicates that something awful has happened to Bobby or, more likely, that he is dead. The immediate reaction is usually one of shock and concerned talk about the person. Sometimes, when a man is not very interested in the dead person, the reaction may be a matter-of-fact shrug of the shoulders and a lack of surprise.

When Bobby—a young winehead with a history of jail and chronic unemployment—died, Herman tried to collect money for flowers. He approached those arriving at the corner in the following manner. As Oscar arrived, Herman said, "Hey, Oscar. You hear 'bout Bobby?" "Naw, what?" said Oscar, with a look of shock on his face. "Bobby dead, man. He dead," said Herman. After a few seconds' pause, Oscar said with a shrug, "Well, he all the way gone now. All the way gone." Oscar stood still, shaking his head from side to side and looking down. "Yeah, no mo' pain," said Herman, pausing and looking very serious. "Lemme have a dollar for Bobby." At that, with no further questions, Oscar reached into his pocket and handed Herman a dollar bill.

As others arrived, they were summarily informed about Bobby by whoever they happened to see first, and later by Herman, who was taking up a collection. With this news, the general attitude was solemn, but certain group members took the opportunity to express their dislike for Bobby. When Herman asked them for money, they would say, "I ain't got no money for him. I didn't dig him before, and I don't dig him now." Or they would simply not acknowledge Herman's information or would move away. A few days later there was a wake for Bobby, which some of the group members attended. The wives of certain regulars close to Bobby "fixed a dish" and took it to the wake. During this period people talked about Bobby and his relationship to the group, remembering him and reminding one another of his group membership. Certain group members closed ranks in claiming Bobby as a full partner in the group, conveniently forgetting his past failings and the treatment they had accorded him. At the same time others would speak up and say openly that "He wasn't worth a shit."

Regardless, each time a death occurs, people take time to pause and ponder the person and the group itself. It is important for them to make sense of the person's death, as they attempt to figure out who and what was to blame. In this endeavor, some men will talk about the person's "bad" habits and may seek to blame him for his own end rather than blaming the precarious street conditions. If they can find out what he did wrong, then they can hope to know better what situations to avoid. In the search for clues, they talk among themselves and scan the local newspapers, which are usually of little or no help. If they are lucky enough to find something about the dead man, it is usually brief and sketchy. In reading the newspapers in vain, group members are reminded that their friend's death is not considered newsworthy and that, by implication, the wider society places low value on people like themselves. This is indicated in the following note:

The day after Bobby's death, T. J., Jelly, Knaky, Red Mack, Otis, and I stood and sat around the liquor store scanning the newspapers for information about Bobby's death. T. J., Jelly, and Knaky each stood with a section of the paper, leaning on Jelly's counter. I looked over Jelly's shoulder at the day's obituaries. Jelly shook his head, "Nothin' here." At that point, Knaky and T. J. finished their sections, the last of the paper. "Nothin'," said T. J. Knaky then shook his head and said, "Nigger ain't shit. Get his ass killed out here and don't even now make the paper. Nigger gon' be a nigger all his life." The others just looked at Knaky and said nothing. There was a long silence.

Group members know intuitively that killing a black man is a less serious crime than killing a white man. They also know that the crime will not be thoroughly investigated, and that if a suspect is found he may well get off. This lore of the streets states also that those who commit such crimes are seldom brought to justice and serves as justification for many who carry small handguns for protection and threaten to resort to violence quickly if they need to. Such indifference, as the men interpret it, helps affirm the extended primary group's sense of position and its own values in relation to the wider society.[2]

Another instance of group support occurred when Ollie—a regular and the group intellectual—was cut by an outsider in front of Jelly's. The assailant was said to be "from Detroit and just passing through," but some of the hoodlums within the group "knew" the man. Ollie and the man had an argument. The man took out a switchblade and "went to work" on Ollie, cutting him on the arms and the neck. Luckily Pee Wee, a former medic in the paratroopers, was present. He quickly tore off his own shirt and applied a tourniquet to Ollie's arm, very probably saving his life. People say the assailant fled to Detroit; he was never heard from again. The hoodlums especially vowed to "get" the man, which seems to be their rightful role—toughness and the physical defense of the group. Some of the regulars also, but now safely, vowed to get the man if they ever saw him again. For a very long time group members talked about "what happened" to Ollie. After a few days in the hospital, Ollie was expected to recover fully. All the group members closed ranks and expressed joy over this. Jelly himself and Herman began a collection for flowers. Wineheads, regulars, and hoodlums visited Ollie in the hospital. Distinctions, at least for the moment, appeared to be blurred.

That people should "take up" for each other physically at Jelly's, appears to be a rule of many relationships, particularly among wine-

heads and hoodlums, but also among most regulars. Many expect
this of friends and hold "false friends" accountable to standards of
loyalty. This principle was illustrated during a conversation at Jelly's
one Wednesday evening.

Otis, a regular who usually preaches nonviolence and decency to
the hoodlums, arrived at Jelly's complaining about having been attacked on the street the night before by a known assailant "up on
Thirty-fifth." As he told his story, some of the group, which included wineheads, regulars, and hoodlums, broke in with affirmations of allegiance and offers to go out and get the "son of a bitch."
"What'd the stud do?" inquired Red Mack, a winehead.
"The cat swung on me, caught me on my jaw, dirty motherfucker," said Otis.
"We ought to go and get the son' bitch," proclaimed Knaky, a
hoodlum.
"Yeah. We need to go out and get that son of a bitch," chimed
in T. J., a regular, in a manner that is very uncharacteristic for
him. It looked as though he was trying to "get in on" being tough.
Others chimed in with T. J., affirming his sense of himself as capable of going out and "getting somebody," but Oscar and Calvin,
who were standing within earshot, smiled and laughed at T. J.'s
"tough" posture.
Otis, who knows T. J.'s capabilities, said "Don't y'all worry
'bout nothin', 'cause I know y'all with me. But I'll take care of
'um. I ain't gon' off the mug [kill], but he gon' wish he was dead
when I get through with him."

In this case the group members, including wineheads, hoodlums, and
regulars, sympathized with Otis and made declarations of allegiance
to him against the man who attacked him. Sometimes such a display
appears to be a ritual. At other times, when not "cooled out," it can
result in real retaliation. This, of course, depends upon the situation
and the immediate context. In this instance Otis dismissed the men
from their "taking up" obligations, particularly T. J., and attempted
to reassert a measure of self-esteem by declaring that he would "take
up" for himself. Actually, the incident was soon forgotten, and he
never took revenge on his assailant. The point is that in this sequence

of interaction, which followed a not-uncommon pattern, members of the extended primary group from several different crowds acted together to express their solidarity. Instances of caring and "taking up" like those described above give group members opportunities to express their emergent sense of communion with others in the extended primary group. They also provide what might be called "openings" in the social order through which people can get close to each other by focusing their attention on some common object. When the focus of action is a person, it is an object the group itself has created and pointed out. During such times, distinctions between group members appear not to be so important. The men can easily close ranks and orient to an equality in a group that is otherwise stratified into particular crowd identities.

In normal times, when a member of the group or the group as a whole is not threatened, the men are concerned with pointing up distinctions among themselves. Identity and rank in the extended primary group depend continually on what others think of one, and it is evident from the talk and action at Jelly's that group members not only care for each other in certain situations, but also care very much what others think about them.

The lengths to which a group member will go to manage and "maintain," his identity within the group is illustrated strongly in the following incident that occurred one afternoon in the park near Jelly's between a regular, T. J., and a known hoodlum named Stick.

One Saturday afternoon in July about thirteen men, most of them young hoodlum types, were sitting and standing around a park bench watching or participating in a crap game. Knaky, Oscar, Stump, Clay, and others surrounded them. The men were drinking whiskey, wine, and beer. As someone would finish one "taste," others would "be tryin' to get up" money for another. Some men sat on the back of the bench with their feet on the seat. Others sat on the proper seat, and still others stood around or sat on the ground. They watched the crap game and talked to one another, taking breaks from the action to look out for the police. It was now T. J. against Stick. T. J. is a fifty-five-year-old, employed regular who often boasts to others that he earns $17,000 a year at the electric company. Stick is a tall, thin man of twenty-three. At the time, Stick was unemployed and said by others to be "barely eatin'." Most group members consider Stick a hoodlum and feel he "bears watchin'."

By three o'clock, T. J. had won about five dollars from Stick, who was beginning to show signs of strain, swearing at the dice and stamping his foot. Stick seldom has much money. T. J., on the other hand, always has some money, and appeared to be enjoying his winning streak. He was demonstrating his ability not only to bet along with the crowd of hoodlums, but also to "beat one of 'em" in a crap game.

T. J. threw the dice and hit his point, which was four, winning the game. But after T. J. retrieved the dice, Stick began to argue.

"Hey, man! Them dice didn't hit no four! They hit five, man. C'mon back!"

"Uh-uh, Stick. They hit four. My money. Tell him, somebody. Tell this man!"

"Naw, man. C'mon T. J. My money. You ain't hit yo' point. You a motherfuckin' lying ass! That's what you is, a lying ass," said Stick. The others present, mostly hoodlums, watched the men and laughed at the show. T. J. became outraged and felt insulted by "this young gangster."

"Who you s'posed to be, chump? Who you think you talkin' to?" said T. J.

The others continued to look on, still laughing and awaiting the outcome. This crowd of hoodlums always seems ready to watch a good fight.

"I'm talkin' to you T. J. You a lyin' ass. You ain't hit no point. Them dice hit five," said Stick, again.

At this T. J. became outraged, for the young gangster had gotten out of his place—and had done so in front of others. It was wrong for a young "gangster" to be calling a proper regular "a lyin' ass" to his face—and in public. To deal with this situation T. J. slapped the younger man across the face. After slapping Stick, T. J. ran across the park. The younger man, at first appeared dumbfounded, then became very angry and began chasing T. J. across the park. Catching T. J. about thirty yards away from the crap game, Stick pulled out his rusty razor knife and began slashing at him. Incoherent with anger, Stick agonizingly cut at T. J.'s face. While he did this Stick was crying real tears, as though he were doing something he didn't really want to do—but still he cut T. J.'s face again and again, crying all the while.

Finally, Herman and Goat, a close friend of Stick's, pulled Stick away from T. J. and held him back. Then Stick, with fire in his eyes, looked down at T. J., who was now on his back on the ground, writhing in pain and holding his bleeding face. Stick looked around at his audience, apparently searching for approval of his actions. Pointing at T. J. he said, "This motherfucker stole me! He stole me!" He started to walk away, somewhat confused, but quickly turned back to T. J. and said, "I got to rob him." With that, Stick reached for T. J.'s wallet and jerked out all the money and papers he could find. He was desperate to get even with T. J. Then, as though all this was not enough, he threw the wallet on the ground and angrily mashed it into the dirt with his foot, his eyes still watering. Next he picked up the wallet and threatened to set it afire, but Herman and some of the others stopped him. Goat, Stick's friend, urged him to leave before the police arrived. Shortly, the two men left running, as the others dispersed, while some waited for the ambulance that took T. J. to the hospital.

The foregoing incident illustrates the importance of a sense of place or identity within the extended primary group to both T. J. and Stick. It is clear that there are circumstances where group members show great concern for how they may be regarded by others. T. J., as many of the group members agree, had "no business bein' over there tryin' to blend in with them hoodlums." A number of the men expressed this sentiment in trying to explain the incident. Many group members felt T. J. was "out of place," for most are used to seeing him as a regular, hanging and associating with other regulars, not with the hoodlums.[3] They see him as a "decent" man with a "good" job. He is a family man and sometimes brags about his "grown daughter and kids doing good in school." Thus, to many, the role T. J. was "tryin' to go for" among the hoodlums seemed inconsistent with his generally accepted status and identity within the extended primary group. As Oscar, a man commonly thought of as a hoodlum, told me,

> "Now T. J. s'posed to be a respectable cat. Got him a wife and some kids and shit. The man takin' care of plenty business at home, even now go to church. What he look like wallowin' and wrestlin' 'round wit' Stick? He ought to be 'shame of himself. What you think he'd feel like if one of his daughters or somebody off his job was to come up here and see him shootin' craps? Down on his knees out here? I bet he'd straighten up then."

Yet, at the same time, among the hoodlums, where toughness and big money are primary values, T. J. seemed pressured into enacting the part or script of hoodlum to maintain a sense of self-esteem. When hoodlums, or men who want to claim the values hoodlums uphold, want to put a person like T. J. in his place, they disparagingly refer to him as "tryin' to go for bad," thus reminding him and others that he has not yet met their standards of toughness. Through such invocations they not only remind the person involved and other group members of who is who, but also distinguish themselves as worthwhile when toughness is the issue by guarding access to this identity.

When the young man Stick "talked back" to T. J., T. J. interpreted his conduct as disrespectful and nondeferential to a person who wanted to be seen as tough, at least for the moment. But at the same time, T. J. wanted his regularity respected. For T. J., not only should a young man defer to an older man by not "talking back," but a young person certainly should not call an elder "a lyin' ass." But there was more than this. T. J. felt personally slighted and insulted. The extreme breach of his sense of the proprieties of the social order was simply too much to stand—especially in public. To deal with this breach, T. J. attempted to put "the li'l gangster" back in his place by slapping him. Through this action, or reaction, it seemed that T. J. was attempting in some measure to meet the standards of toughness he presumed the others present cared about upholding.

This concern accounts in part for his uncontrolled reaction to what he considered an offense by Stick.

But by the standards of the extended primary group, T. J.'s posture reminded most people present that he was the one out of place. First, he slapped another man in public and then ran away—a cardinal sin among hoodlums and others of the streets. As one hoodlum told me shortly after this incident,

> "You don't be slappin' some stud in the face out here wit' yo' hand, man. Not less'n you got somethin' to back up yo' play. Then the worse thing you can do is to run off, 'cause then the cat you hit sho'nuff got to get even. He can't show his face if he don't do somethin' to you. That shit T. J. pulled was some sho'nuff weak-ass shit. Boy, that T. J."

This account also points to some of the reasons for Stick's actions. The crowd Stick spends most of his time with considers toughness a primary virtue. In the extended primary group, conduct that corresponds to a code of "being tough" helps qualify men as hoodlums "in good standing." People like Stick are known to look for any opportunity to exhibit their own abilities at "being somebody" by meeting the standards of hoodlums. They tend to avoid or defer to people who might show them up as failing to meet the standards of toughness and of having big money. But T. J. was viewed as someone few of the group present would have deferred to on toughness. He was a regular in good standing, after all. Thus, for Stick not to have responded to T. J.'s slap with an exhibition of toughness would have shown him up as not able to meet the standards of his close friends. They dub people who claim to meet their standards of toughness but blatantly fail with the derogatory terms "puppy" and "pussy." Regulars will also use these terms when they wish to distinguish themselves from men they regard as failing to be tough in situations that require it.

Stick was operating according to this principle of status in his encounter with T. J. In the public setting, he was under a psychological burden to perform for his peers—and for himself. In fact, he worked to meet the standards of the hoodlum crowd and to realize his own social identity by creating a "victim" in T. J.

Actions like these, recurring on the streets and inside Jelly's, illustrate the precariousness of the social order itself. The volatility of relationships indicated in this story suggests that identity and place are not simply achieved once and for all, but are subject to changing situational factors and emergent definitions. Identity and place call for public demonstration from time to time, in front of significant others who by their presence claim rights of censorship.

Although the incident between Stick and T. J. became more than play when T. J.'s face was slashed, it nonetheless began in the context of a game. The two men were shooting craps as many of the men, particularly hoodlums, do from time to time. The competitive aspect of crap shooting is characteristic of much playful behavior at Jelly's. In competitive play, often expressed through joking encounters, and through games like craps, group members are able to act out certain status arrangements within the group. In this way some men try and test one another and the social order. Such competitive testing of statuses and identities is necessary if the men are to begin to trust their sense of the general status arrangements.

There are degrees of play that signify degrees of close feeling within the extended primary group. For example, only very close friends are allowed to joke publicly about having sexual relations with another man's wife. Without a close bond, such words may be cause for physical fighting. But when used by the right person and in the right circumstances, they may be a sign of being close.

The play some men are able to engage in is not an effortless and mindless activity; it is important for the designation of social rank. Because the social stakes are high, play is complex and usually very selective; group members will not play with just anyone, but usually only with tried and tested friends. It is a liberty that is not to be taken lightly without the risk of conflict. Relationships must be nurtured, demonstrated, and renewed from time to time through interaction, for some people may not always remember or want to continue to acknowledge how much in the way of social liberties they have pre-

viously granted to certain others. Group members must often be reminded and kept up to date.

This was indicated to me one afternoon when Herman engaged
Bucky, another regular in the group.

It was a Thursday afternoon in April, and about twelve men had
gathered in front of Jelly's. Cars passed. Women and children
walked and ran by. Members of the group went in and out of
the liquor store. Some eased into the alley to get a hit of the liquor
they had bought. Herman and Dirty Jed, a regular, stood together
trying to get up enough for a taste. I offered sixty cents on the
bottle, which Jed quickly accepted. Jed then left us to buy the
taste. While we were waiting, Bucky arrived.

"Hey, motherfucker," Herman greeted him in a loud voice, then
went on to tell him, "I'm gettin' ready to go get me some o' Edna's
[Bucky's wife] good pussy."

Bucky, with no apparent sense of outrage or embarrassment,
calmly said, "I just left Butterroll in yo' bed, and she told me
she'd have my supper ready afterwhile."

Herman then grabbed Bucky affectionately and said, "Aw, you
dirty motherfucker, you."

The two men stood there laughing and talking for a while, as
the others, now apparently satisfied, turned or looked away.[4]

Herman and Bucky consider themselves the best of friends, and they
keep others, as well as themselves, aware of this by the verbal liberties they frequently take with each other. Herman and Bucky are
usually aware of the meaning of their playful interaction, as are those
looking on. Their bantering signifies that they are "tight," since few
others could say what Herman said to Bucky and vice versa without
offense. Playing in this verbally abusive manner is one form of association that is fairly common around Jelly's. It is one way group
members mark out and display their sense of rank and degrees of
status during social interaction.

When a person demonstrates closeness in this way he works to
define himself, letting others know "what kind of stud" he is. Such
associations, patterned over time, also indicate what crowd one is

with at Jelly's. Hoodlums usually play with their own kind. Wine-heads play with other wineheads. And regulars, or those who would like to be regulars, play with other regulars.

To be sure, there are times when members of different crowds will attempt to play with one another. When a person does this, as was illustrated in the fight between T. J. and Stick, he is usually sensed to be "out of place." Unless he exhibits the proper deference, for others and the situation, he may be considered to be trespassing. In a situation group members define as play, associations and interactions may be accomplished through emergent, if initially pretended or "play," violation of the boundaries of a man's most important social possession—his place. In this context, if the person is called on his "pushy" behavior, he can always say, "Oh, I was just playing."

Another form of play prevalent around Jelly's involves mock "physical abuse," the play-acting of physical violence toward others. This type of play is also important for the designation of rank. Certain group members will feint or punch lightly at others, grab at others, or wrestle another person to the ground. Their behavior is understood as "play" and does not mean all that it might in differently defined circumstances. It is not unusual to see two men "punch each other out" for a few minutes, looking as though they were seriously involved during the whole encounter. When such a play contest is going on, it may be hard for a passerby to tell that the men are "just playing." The participants themselves may not know for sure until the activity is over. At times, for example, one person will take out his knife and "go after" another, putting the dull side of the blade against the other man's skin or clothing. The person "attacked" usually stands still and tolerates the game for fear of accidentally being cut "for real." Such unpredictable physical play has plenty of chance to go amiss. For instance, even the slight appearance of the "attacker" getting the best of the "victim" may be just enough to violate the delicate boundary between play abuse and real fighting.

As with verbal play, like the joking between Herman and Bucky over their wives, there are only certain people with whom any given man will play physically—usually tested friends. For example, two regulars who had not seen each other for a long while stood in line to be waited on by Jelly. John said, "Hey, Otis. Where you been, man?!" "John, that you? Why I oughta bust yo' stomach open— again!" With this, Otis reared back as if he intended to strike a blow at John's stomach. John, as if in anticipation, moved back to dodge the blow, then came to a stationary position and smiled. Otis smiled. After this acknowledgment of each other's presence, the men exchanged other niceties and carried on.

But even when the men are good friends, they cannot always be sure of the outcome of playful interaction, as is shown by the following incident.

On a Friday evening at about six o'clock, approximately twenty-five men were gathered in Jelly's liquor-store room, to celebrate payday with friends. At this time the wineheads, hoodlums, and regulars gather at Jelly's. The liquor store, though, was dominated by regulars, and the room buzzed with conversation. People joked about their home life, about their jobs, about their wives, about their children; they talked about their good times and bad times. As on other evenings, the conversations and the social interaction were punctuated by customers and others entering and leaving. The noise levels rose and fell as Jelly's front door opened and closed. Now and then the public phone rang, and the closest man would answer and call for the person the caller wanted. T. J. and Herman were laughing and playing with each other—both were somewhat high. A number of small groups prevailed, as people moved from group to group to avoid certain others they did not want to be bothered with. Suddenly the sound of a loud slap penetrated the general noise. In their general joking around, T. J. had playfully slapped at Herman, but his hand had accidentally landed hard and loud on Herman's face. Though T. J. had not meant to slap Herman, those who looked on did not all readily understand that. A hush fell over the room as others waited to see what Herman would do.

Herman held his face and looked at T. J. with a serious expression. He said, "T. J., if you ever do that again, I swear I'll kill you. If you ever do that again." T. J. just stood and looked at the floor as Herman continued to threaten and tongue-lash him, apparently trying to get even. T. J. simply remained silent, apparently admitting he was in the wrong. Soon the men turned back to what they had been doing and the noise level rose, but it never reached the level it was before T. J.'s slap. After a while, Herman eased off for home.

As is shown in the foregoing incident, the liberties one may take with others are not always clearly spelled out but must be negotiated during social interaction between the participants, with an eye to the audience. In this case, the audience remained silent, allowing the men to work it out between themselves. Herman did not show up at Jelly's the next day, Saturday, but he did come on Sunday. T. J. was there, and he and Herman soon were laughing and playing with one another as though the incident had never occurred. They both seemed willing now to treat T. J.'s slap as part of play.

As has been illustrated, group members don't always know the full limits of their playful interaction, for these limits often depend on the situation. Indeed, many learn these limits through a kind of exploratory sociability that brings certain reactions from others that work to clarify the nature of status arrangements in the group. This is shown in the following story:

One warm Tuesday evening in May, Pee Wee, Dicky, Bill, Sleepy, and I stood around in Jelly's open doorway and faced the street, laughing and talking and generally having a good time. Leroy, a person known as a hoodlum, approached us and singled out Pee Wee.

"Hey, man," said Leroy. With that greeting Leroy lightly punched Pee Wee on the jaw and smiled as he walked away. The punch surprised us, for we were not aware that the two were so close.

Pee Wee himself looked somewhat stunned. He said, "Who that fool think he is, hittin' on people and shit." The others nodded in agreement. Soon the subject of our conversation changed. We talked about a new job Pee Wee's cousin had applied for, discussing his chances for getting it. Then Sleepy spoke of his encounter with the police a few nights before.

After about fifteen minutes Pee Wee said, "I got to set that nigger straight. Who the fuck he think he is?"

"Who? Leroy?" asked Sleepy.
"Yeah," said Pee Wee.
"Aw, that motherfucker. Forget him," urged Dicky.
"Naw, man," countered Pee Wee, "I got to set his ass straight."

With this comment Pee Wee socially registered his complaint about Leroy's definition of him and of their relationship. Such play, both verbal and physical, may seem at first to be a make-believe acting out of more important behavior, perhaps even a mockery of the "real" state of affairs and social arrangements. But the form this association takes—who one plays with and what the specific play comes to mean for others—works to remind the groups of who each participant "thinks he is" and how he conceives of his place. The ability to play smoothly with others at Jelly's is contingent on many factors. One of the most important considerations is the nature of the audience and how it changes with the evolving circumstances of play.

As has been shown, playful sociability can have serious consequences for the social order of the extended primary group. In jockeying for social regard and deference, whom one can play with and in what way, and how others react to the play, helps indicate one's place within the group. By a succession of actions and responses of others, including liberties taken, apologies, compliments, orders and commands, instructions, favors asked and rendered, and other acts involving the deference of one of the parties involved, the person and his audience are reminded of who he is, and he comes to sense what others might allow him to be in certain circumstances. Play sociability may be viewed as a dynamic and processual element in the development of rank and identity, for it is through this play that the parameters of social identity may be created and indicated. Moreover, through playful sociability the parameters can be stretched and delimited to fit one's conception of oneself. All this play, including its competitive character, lends a certain precariousness to one's sense of social rank within the extended primary group.

The volatility of sociable situations in and around Jelly's presents ever-present the possibility of serious and sometimes violent consequences of taking sociability for granted.[5] Sometimes people become violent very quickly, with almost no warning, and this threat helps keep people discreet in their relations with others they are unsure of. But such volatile consequences, as has been indicated, are most likely to arise when people are playing, when the situation is somewhat undefined and subject to varying interpretations, and when there is a ready audience conferring differences in social rank according to the apparent outcome of competitive play.[6] These points are illustrated in the following incident.

One Saturday evening in July, Herman, Terry, and I sat around on the ground in the park near Jelly's. Others, including wineheads, regulars, and hoodlums, sat in other areas nearby. As we talked, Terry began "messing" with me and engaging in what men commonly refer to as "selling wolf tickets." This had been going on for at least two weeks.

Rising to the challenge, I said, "Okay, Terry. Let's go over here on the grass and have this out."

Herman looked surprised and puzzled but said, "A'right now, Terry. You know Eli a pretty strong stud. You know that, don't you? You know that."

"I know that," answered Terry, as he got up and walked toward me.

Since Terry had been "messing" with me for some time in ways that at some point were bound to lead to trouble, I decided to settle his "in for me" then and there. Thus I urged him on. Herman attempted to dissuade us from the match, which Terry and others knew could easily turn into violent fighting. Apparently unmindful of such risks, we found a soft, grassy spot.

"Okay, now. Lie down on your belly, Terry. We gon' arm wrestle," I said.

"Aw, a'right," agreed Terry, assuming a prone position. We then locked our arms and began to match our strength. The contest drew others. Suddenly Terry and I had an audience, which was really more than we had originally bargained for. Just by their presence the newcomers infused what started out as "play" with a more serious import. Sides could now be taken. The situation was redefined. Slowly I put Terry's arm to the ground.

Herman laughed, "See, I told you to don't be fuckin' wit' Eli!"

Terry looked dumbfounded. The others began to laugh and point at Terry.

Then I said, "Okay, Terry. Let's try it with our left arms? A'right?"

"Okay," said Terry, seeing this offer as an opportunity to save face and redeem himself. The others still looked on, expecting, some even hoping, that I would beat Terry again. But this time I let Terry put my arm to the ground.

As we lay on the ground I said, "Damn, Terry. You stronger than I thought you were!"

"You a pretty strong stud, yourself," said Terry, acknowledging his earlier defeat. The others were now silent, as they slowly dispersed and resumed their earlier positions. But a few stayed with the three of us for a while, drinking scotch and water and exchanging stories. After a while Herman and I left.

In discussing this incident later, Herman told me that he had been communicating to Terry that "if the play had gotten out of hand, I was with you. He knew that." I then told Herman I had let Terry beat me the second time to allow him to save face in front of the hoodlums and others, but also to keep him from "having to get even" and carrying a grudge toward me in the future. To that Herman said, "Now that was a pretty down thing you did, Eli. A pretty down thing. But I always did know you was a down stud. Always did know that." The foregoing incident and Herman's response to it points up not only the volatility but also the intricacy of certain social relationships in the extended primary group. The incident also underscores the valued ability to know one's place and to enact that place in the interest of avoiding trouble and maintaining the social order.

Group members refer to knowing one's place in a situation and having the related ability to avoid trouble as being "down." When Herman referred to me as a "down stud," this was a compliment on my demonstrating understanding of my place as an outsider who did not want future trouble by acting in accord with the boundaries of my particular place in the minds of Herman and Terry and the others. When the hoodlum principle of status—toughness—emerged as an issue through arm wrestling in front of group members, I conducted myself as a person who had a limited stake in presenting a tough identity—especially in competition with a known tough person like Terry. That I let Terry beat me at least once exhibited my sense of "who I was" or what my place was, relative to Terry's, in the extended primary group. In Herman's words, my actions, which effectively "cooled Terry out," demonstrated that I knew "what time it was." That is, I exhibited behavior proper in those circumstances. And my actions furthered one of my own goals, being able to continue to come around Jelly's without trouble from Terry. Indeed, from that point on, Terry accorded me a certain deference, if not respect.

"Down" is an important word group members use to compliment others for their situationally effective, generally valued ability to avoid trouble within and outside the extended primary group. Group members use the adjective to refer both to personalities and to specific actions that seem to avoid trouble in a threatening situation, especially to describe the actions of group members who enact their places so as to complement or support the posture other group members want to enact. It refers mainly to what people feel to be wise conduct in confronting trouble. Usually a "down" person, acting "down" in a troublesome situation, outsmarts the person causing trouble. In these ways the term may be viewed as encompassing both objective and reputational aspects of social identity and place within the extended primary group.

Group members often use the term just to compliment behavior in a particular situation and do not necessarily mean that the person in question is always "down." Most people, in fact, are not wise enough to avoid trouble in all situations, and the word is sometimes used to recognize just one "down" act.

The evaluation of people's behavior depends on the nature of the audience—how many regulars are present, how many hoodlums, how many wineheads—and how strongly each of them is interested in and associated with the status attributes of a given crowd. Evaluation depends on the causes or felt needs that actors in a situation may want to promote or put down. Labeling specific acts "down" can be an effort to sanction certain kinds of behavior, as when Herman approvingly labeled my handling of Terry as "down."

While complimenting me, Herman was also showing me that he understood what "down" behavior was. This use of "down" as a compliment for acts on the street was illustrated on another occasion.

One Sunday afternoon in October about twelve group members, mostly hoodlums, with some wineheads and regulars, were standing around in the park near Jelly's. Some were shooting dice, and others looked on or socialized or stood or sat around watching the cars and people go by. Apparently from nowhere, two white policemen appeared, which surprised and shocked many of the men. Some froze, others looked around nervously.

Calmly, one policeman said, "Damn, y'all. It's a nice day for gambling. I gamble myself. I like to gamble, man, but when I do it, I don't do it in no public park. I go up to my place, my room somewhere." As the policeman spoke, the men listened intently. His partner looked around as he continued, "Now, me and my partner gon' take us a li'l walk, and we'll be back in 'bout a half hour." Then the policemen walked away. The men relaxed, but they did not resume the crap game. In minutes, at the mere suggestion of the policeman, many of those who had been shooting craps moved their game elsewhere, though some remained in the park.

Later I heard Stump, a young winehead who had been present, refer to the policeman's actions as "down." Among a group of men who had been part of the gambling crowd, he said, "That was a down white cop over here while ago. He coulda run us all in if he wanted to, but he was al'right."

"Yeah, he was smooth," offered Knaky.

"He knew what time it was. He was down," Clay commented.

Here the men were referring to and agreeing on the policeman's demonstration of his understanding of the situation. In his effort to do his job of maintaining the "peace," he was sparing the hoodlums any unnecessary trouble and also saving himself from any trouble from a group of "ghetto gamblin' men." He did so with a minimum of harm to himself or to the hoodlums. The policeman's deference seemed to be given in exchange for the group's expected deference to him—by ending the public violation of the law against shooting craps. The policeman was accomplishing his goal through "maneuverin'," to cause as little trouble and disruption of the social order as possible in doing "what he got to do."[7] When group members know that socially deft actions are designed to avoid trouble, they sometimes compliment the actor or the act as "down."

Another example of the use of "down" in describing action is illustrated in the following note.

> On a hot Tuesday afternoon in July, early in my career at Jelly's, I approached the park carrying a portable radio tuned to a local "soul" station. From a distance I could see a group of about ten men gathered around a bench. As I approached I began to see more clearly who the men were. Most were hoodlums, some of whom I knew, but most of whom I did not. Spider, who hangs with regulars, wineheads, and hoodlums, was there. I knew him better than I knew anyone else.
>
> As I approached the bench, one man I did not know commanded, "Hey! Bring that music over here!" I ignored his command, but I looked at him. He looked at me, waiting for my next move, "C'mon! Right now!" the man continued. Despite the commands I continued walking at my own pace. This was a role I felt I had to play in order not to encourage further attempted liberties. When I finally reached the bench I found that Spider was the only person I knew well. I knew that my radio, which could easily bring ten dollars from a street fence, had caught the eyes of certain hoodlums there. To most of them I was just a "strange" person and thus an eligible object for their collusion. By now I was close to the bench.
>
> I met Spider's eyes, and he greeted me, "Hey, Eli. What's to it? How you doin'?"
>
> "Hey, Spider. You got it," I said. As I moved toward Spider, I greeted the others. Some of them said hello. They watched me. Then, reaching out for some bond, I touched Spider's shoulder. Apparently aware of my uncertainty, Spider was unusually friendly to me. As we made contact, the tension seemed to dissipate and I felt more at ease.

Then, Spider reached into his back pocket and pulled out a half-full bottle of Canadian Club whiskey and said, "Here, Eli. Go 'n get you a hit." I reached for the bottle, opened it, and turned it up. To the others looking on, this was an exhibition of close feeling between Spider and me, for Spider is known to be "tight" about letting just anybody drink with him—without paying first. I had paid nothing, though I did later. We passed the bottle back and forth for the next few minutes. The others watched us and soon turned their attention elsewhere. Because of Spider's actions, I felt more at ease in the gathering. After a while others I knew, including some regulars and hoodlums, appeared and exchanged friendly greetings with me, thus including me even more. That evening Herman and I had a conversation about Spider and his place in the group.

"Now, you take ol' Spider. You can walk up to Spider. Spider ain't gon' come outa no bag with you, but with somethin' intelligent. He gon' be tryin' to tell you what's good for you. Tryin' to talk about somebody else or he gon' try to be very decent. He a say somethin' like, 'Herman was down here a li'l while earlier and I don't know . . . ' or anything that's cool. He ain't gon' come outa his ol' bag, 'Hey motherfucker, you.' But see that's all the bag he know to come outa with me. You know, we all regulars. But Spider ain't *too* regular. For the simple reason he's a rotten cat. And a regular stud ain't gon' really have no bad intentions toward another regular," said Herman.

"Spider and I were up here not too long ago. He was with the hoodlums. Spider was 'bout the regularest cat up there," I said.

"Yeah, man. Then I know *just* who you talkin' 'bout was up there: Cochise, Stump, Mo, Sims, Jay . . . gangsters and hoodlums," Herman said. "An' when you see them standin' up and talkin' to you like they regular, that means that they stone [complete] hoodlums."

"But Spider came up and made me known to the other cats. He said, 'Hey, Eli. How you doin'?' He let everybody know who I was," I said to Herman.

"Yeah, he was lettin' them monkeys know what time it was. Now, that's what I call a *down* way of maneuverin' from the head.

See, Spider is down when it comes to stuff like that. See, he lettin'
all these cats know—hey, that you one of us. One of Spider and
one of Herman. See, he introduced that quick. Lettin' all these
punks know you 100 percent regular. But that you too down to
'sociate with them. See, cause Spider be sittin' by hisself, and all
them monkeys go and try to be around him," Herman concluded.

Spider had seen the possibility for trouble because the hoodlums,
at that time, did not know me. Herman judged his act to be "down"
because Spider had demonstrated that he understood that the hoodlums he was standing with might not fully grasp the possible consequences of "messing" with me or stealing my radio. Spider knew that
they did not know who I was, that I "belonged," and he wanted to
protect me. By identifying me in terms of my being "one of them,"
Spider invoked the group and let them know that I had friends there.
Indeed, by being a known regular himself (among that tough bunch)
Spider was able to make clear that I was "tight" with Herman and
other men usually thought of as regulars, if not with other hoodlums.
Most important about Spider's remark, however, was that it implied
some association with or protection for me by other members of the
group at Jelly's. In effect, Spider included me in the extended primary group. By identifying me to the hoodlums, Spider warned them,
in a sense, that there could be trouble in the moral and social order
if they treated me with less care than they use with certain other
members of the extended primary group. Like other members of the
extended primary group, Spider is capable of engaging in "down"
acts from time to time. But he lacks the reputation some of the men
have for being "down" generally and consistently.

Basically, those who have established this reputation among the
men are people who are believed to be street-wise. Certain people
develop a demeanor of being very aware of interaction and make it
known to others. Those who exhibit this demeanor well enough to be
deferred to consistently have a certain number of "down" acts to their
credit. They are known to employ their knowledge of the possibilities
inherent in interaction so as to avoid trouble. At the same time, they
seem to manage their own identity to gain selected affiliations with
the three crowds. People become used to "down" behavior coming

from him; they expect it. Maintaining a place within the particular crowd one is most strongly associated with is not always easy given the demands placed on a person who tries to see himself and be seen as a wise person. However great the difficulties, such a person doesn't get involved in petty status battles. Being a hoodlum and being "down" may sometimes be conflicting identities. The person who manages to have some particularistic place within one of the crowds, and is seen by others as a "down stud," impresses them by knowing the rules of the social order at Jelly's well and by knowing his situationally sensitive place within that order.[8]

Protective about their images, people trying to be "down studs" tend to avoid very close associations with any one crowd. They tend to leave their identity fairly flexible, open to situational cues, and not tied to any one set of crowd-linked status attributes. To a certain extent they are loners, and they are close students of the social order, making note of who does what to whom under what circumstances. They are able, moreover, to put their knowledge of the streets into action that helps maintain order in a very immediate sense.

One of the most common statements others tend to make about "down" people is that "they've been through it all." For instance, they may have been former gang members, or they may have been to prison. They may have been heroin addicts. Often they have traveled and seen much more than others in the group, or at least they know how to make others think they have. From their diverse experiences, they have acquired an interactional survival strategy of sorts, which they use to handle others with minimal friction.

Basically, "down" people are very aware of what their action might mean for other identities in the setting. They seem to have an intellectual handle on the meaning of social interaction, but they also seem to have the wit and the astute sense of the meaning of others to handle them in the group deliberately. Accordingly "down" people are able to avoid trouble because of their knowledge of the possibilities created through certain kinds of interaction.

When a group member acts in accord with others' conceptions of his place, in ways that avoid trouble, the person and his conduct might be summed up in the word "down," for group members using

this word refer to a cognitively compatible range of personal attributes that usually corresponds roughly with what members of the
group sense they can afford to allow the person to be. They use the
concept when they *can* use it and still maintain a favorable concept
of themselves. What the group members sense about what they can
allow another to be is affected both by the person's reputation and
by their firsthand observations of his conduct that confirm that reputation. Thus, the way he can support aspects of his known biography
during sociability is a focus of social judgment. The degree to which
a person is "down" depends on how he manages himself in the presence of peers, who are in effect censors of his conduct. Group members use and generally understand the term "down" as a compliment
for those who wisely enact their places within the extended primary
group as wineheads, regulars, or hoodlums—who know who they
are. And the person making the compliment also makes a statement
about himself, defining himself as a person who "understands" what
it means to "be down," by finding or enlisting others who will agree
with him.

Implying a certain astuteness in handling others, the term has
achieved a kind of synonymy with what is believed to be "right" or
fitting behavior for members of the various crowds, statuses, and
places in the extended primary group. Meeting or failing to meet
group-imposed standards for this or that "type o' person," group
members are individually ranked along the principle of "down."[9]
Standards of evaluation are personal and form an integral part of
the whole person. In these ways "down" may be seen as a unifying
principle of status superimposed on whatever other crowd identity
one might have—be it winehead, hoodlum, or regular. It appears to
transcend any particular crowd's own principles of status, thus transforming the "places" within the particular status groups into a single
stratification system.

7 | Conclusion

The people who frequent Jelly's bar and liquor store have come to create their own local, informal social stratification system. People come to Jelly's to be sociable, but also to compete for social recognition and regard. For most Jelly's is their place to be somebody, for group members are important to one another. Status within this informal system is action-oriented and precarious, based in large measure upon what people think and say and do about other members of the group. A person's status depends upon what and who he can successfully claim to be, and this is made known through the deference and appreciation others show him.[1] Personal liberties given and taken provide a running commentary on the social order. In their quest for social recognition and appreciation, group members try to live up to their valued notions of themselves. They attempt to distinguish themselves by the means open to them, in large measure by pointing out others within the setting whom they judge as meeting or failing to meet certain standards of behavior upheld by the various subgroupings of wineheads, hoodlums, and regulars. Through the competitive quest for status and identity, subgroups emerge as the men attempt to take sides and identify with one or another "kind of person" against certain others. These processes, with their attendant status issues, lend a certain extended and hierarchical character to the group at Jelly's. By studying the nature of the issues that emerge during social interactions and that provoke certain men to defend, through words and actions, one or another ideal or conception of value, I arrived at an understanding of the interplay of social rules and standards of the extended primary group.

Group members move to associate with others in the group who will allow them to hold a certain view of themselves. In so doing, they help create the various core status groupings that make up what I call an extended primary group. The issue of status is sometimes settled through selective association. Wineheads, for example, tend to stand around on the corner with other wineheads. Hoodlums appear to seek out and hang with other hoodlums. And regulars tend to associate with others they view as like themselves. The issue of status is sometimes settled through arguments about who is allowed to talk about whom, in what ways, and in the presence of which others. Those who are found to be wrong usually defer. People at times stand around and debate a person's known biography—whether this or that person is really a "winehead" or a "hoodlum" or a "regular." Their judgments and the sides they take often express their own self-conceptions.

To be sure, there is a certain amount of mobility between the status groupings. Usually this mobility is related to the gain or loss of a job, or to some other major event in the person's life, and it is either sponsored or hampered by the collective efforts of others. It is not based on a simple decision to allow some person to join the status grouping or to prevent him from joining altogether. Nor is it the person's own decision alone. Within the extended primary group at Jelly's people's actions can be seen as separate but contributing parts of a collective process in the definition and construction of a social order and the places within that order. As I have argued in this book, the collective actions of the men sharing the space at Jelly's are important for the assigning of rank and identity within the group.[2] For example, when Tiger made his attempt for regular status, his success or failure was determined not only by his special awareness, motivations, and new job, but also by the felt interests of others in the setting, particularly those who make claim on regular status themselves. He could move out of the winehead status and associate with regulars only if they allowed him to do so. When Herman's wife was in the hospital and Herman began going around unkempt, keeping irregular hours, and behaving more like a winehead than a regular, group members worried about keeping him on the right track and out of the winehead group. Herman's friends were just not ready to allow him to fall into this residual grouping. And when Mike, the black policeman, was selecting members for his club, none of the hoodlums and wineheads were asked to join. Mike's actions here did as much as any of the hoodlums' own "hoodlum behavior" to mark them off as "not regular." Throughout my field notes, examples like these indicate that all members of the extended primary group at Jelly's contribute, through their collective actions, to maintaining the social hierarchy. Social order exists because people stay in their places, and they do so because other people help keep them there.

The members of the resulting status groupings are known in part by who and what they oppose. The various subgroups and individuals involve themselves in a certain degree of conflict as they vie for social regard and appreciation. But if group members care enough about one another to compete, they also care for one another intimately and protectively, particularly during times of trouble for the larger group. It is the competitive nature of intimate encounters that gives the group an extended and stratified character. With respect to the resulting hierarchy and ranks, especially to their situationally sensitive and precarious nature within the larger group, the extended primary group is distinct from the primary group as described by Cooley.[3]

Within the extended primary group at Jelly's, a "visible means of support" and "decency" appear to be the primary values, while "toughness," "gettin' big money," "gettin' some wine," and "havin' some fun" are residual values, or values group members adopt after the "props" supporting decency have for some reason been judged unviable, unavailable, or unattainable. When the opportunity to realize primary values of the group is denied to certain group members, the residual values become more prominent in helping them sustain a particular valued identity. The wider society is implicated at this point. For when one compares hoodlums with regulars in relationship to the wider society, one of the important differences is in their orientations toward work, or a "visible means of support." Regulars tend to have jobs, and hoodlums and wineheads tend not to. On the street corner, this makes for profound differences in styles of life and self-presentations. Regulars brag at the least opportunity, presenting themselves as "decent" and as having "an outlook on life." And the wineheads and hoodlums who continue to hang around generally defer, for they are compelled to compare themselves with the regulars on such issues, which are supported and grounded in the wider stratification system.

One implication of these differences is that employment, especially in a meaningful occupation, is a very important and effective means of social and personal survival. When jobs are not available, living up to rules of conduct based on the values of "decency" becomes difficult, and those rules based on the residual values become a more viable alternative for maintaining self-esteem. When what might be called "decent" avenues for regard have been exhausted, a person may find it easier to "be somebody" as a hoodlum or a winehead.[4] When a man cannot find a job, the tendency not to work and to "lay around the streets all day," which at first may constitute only an occasional outing, quickly becomes a substitute activity in which he invests himself. Then it often becomes increasingly difficult to break this habit as he gains social reinforcement for it.

Some writers have attempted to explain "low-class" values as weak imitations or approximations of the wider society's values. Rodman, for example, has suggested that low-income people are unable to meet the larger society's standards of social conduct and therefore must stretch their own values to adjust to their particular life circumstances.[5] Although there may be a certain amount of truth to this view, and it is supported by my own analysis, I believe it does not go far enough in appreciating the lives of the people involved and the internal coherence and integrity of their local stratification systems. The people I studied at Jelly's appear not so much to "stretch" a given set of values to meet some general standard as to create their own particular standards of social conduct along variant lines open to them. For example, at Jelly's certain people are esteemed among their immediate peers for being "good" hoodlums. And there are certain wineheads who, even if they had the means to leave the setting, would not be content without socializing with their drinking buddies.

The nature of the principles and standards of conduct invoked in and emerging from social interaction seems to depend in large part upon what resources the people at Jelly's have available for giving and commanding social regard among peers. I have thus argued that members of the extended primary group work to construct standards of conduct they can meet and demonstrate during social interaction in company they care to impress. The emerging values seem primarily to involve a social process, open to negotiation, of settling for what they have to work with in demanding deference and social regard.

At Jelly's group members engage in a good amount of bantering, joking, teasing, and general playing. Often, when people present themselves, members of their audiences expect them to be lying when they talk about themselves and their activities.[6] Anticipating this, people usually present more than enough evidence to back up their accounts, lest they be "blown away" or "shot down." Thus it is not uncommon for people who want to be believed to present rumpled old check stubs as proof of employment or to show pictures of their close relatives when family loyalties become an issue. Once when Herman was preparing to take a short bus trip for his two-week vacation, he went to Jelly's with his bags packed "to show the cats I was sho'nuff going." Among hoodlums, a hoodlum might come up and announce that he has just spent the night in jail, showing no compunction about stigma and expecting approval and interest. And a winehead might impress his drinking buddies, or even other group members, by winking at them and producing "the iron" (money) he has begged off passersby and the other members of the extended primary group. Jelly's is a place to be somebody, a situation of negotiated statuses where people matter to one another; they keep up with one another. Among their own crowds, group members can act as equals; but when confronted by different kinds of people they can all be reminded of shortcomings according to some principle recognized in the extended primary group. Group members can be somebody as long as they keep their rightful places, which reflect their own group-sanctioned ranking on one or another status issue.

In the men's words, "Cats hang with studs they can handle." They appear to exploit those means that are open to them for "being somebody." For a certain person this might mean "cutting into" or hanging around with a particular crowd of people who are unable or unwilling to remind him of what he lacks in resources for commanding deference—who compliment him, thus attracting him to them. Hence, the status attributes a person attempts to uphold are usually a function of the values of his closest peers. And his closest allies in the stratification system are determined in part by their joint control over various attributes that become resources for gaining status and regard.

A "visible means of support" is considered almost essential for meeting the value of decency. Those who from time to time are defined by certain members of the group as unqualified to make claims to decency may find some other group to associate with and settle for being something other than "decent." If a person settles for hanging with men others call hoodlums or wineheads, he finds himself categorized with them and defined as "doin' what they do," which may include anything from "tryin' to get some wine" to being able to talk only about the inside of the county jail.

At times people seem to be trying to live up to many prevailing values simultaneously as status issues rise and fall during social interaction. But the more a man positions himself to gain support for a particular crowd identity, the more "side bets" he accumulates. That is, he may find himself being supported or put down by people he had not anticipated this from when he first lobbied for the identity. Such side bets, supporting or denying what the person wants to be, can become crucial in determining one's commitment to a line of activity or a style of self-presentation.

Once this social identification has been made, the person may become increasingly constrained to carry himself in ways that significant others have come to appreciate in him; these others serve as censors of his conduct. It is this conditional appreciation, meted out as deference or psychological reward, that forms a basis for social control within the extended primary group. Not to engage in socially approved behavior—whether among wineheads, hoodlums, or regulars—creates the risk of trouble with one's peers; trouble in the form of embarrassment, ridicule, or misunderstanding, and thus a possible loss of standing within the group.[7]

Trouble occurs when certain group members appear to be getting out of place—when they appear not to be respecting agreed-on boundaries and the justice of the local stratification system. Then those who feel threatened may attempt to get even, or "set things right," usually through attempted ridicule or even outright conflict. It is in such circumstances that certain group members will try to "sound" on the transgressor, attempting to show some ridiculous disparity between who and what he is trying to go for and who and what they think they can prove he really is. If such strategies fail to keep certain people "straight," then more direct, possibly violent, means may be employed. The effectiveness of such games of personal attribution and their attendant threats of conflict in maintaining social control depends in large part on the nature of the audience—how it defines itself, and how this definition might be affected by the result of what becomes, through its participation, a status contest.

Most of the men want to avoid trouble outside the extended primary group as well, particularly with the formal agencies of social control. This is especially true of the regulars, who have a strong economic and social stake in living within the law. But regulars also show unusual respect for moral notions of decency. They have a broadly developed sense of what trouble is and are very sensitive to people and situations that might get them into trouble; these they try to avoid. Some even brag that they have managed to stay out of trouble, a claim that may be fully appreciated when one considers the backgrounds of others in the milieu of Jelly's. Hoodlums of the group, many of whom have "long records downtown," will brag about their involvements with trouble; they have learned to seek it out and meet it head-on as a means toward self-affirmation.

Connected with the process of social control and the concern with trouble is the concept of "down." Group members use this adjective for both individuals and acts. It is a positive word, referring to valued attributes within the social order of the extended primary group and to social actions of group members that are seen as having been based on worldly wisdom and good judgment. There are down wineheads, down regulars, and down hoodlums. There are also down outsiders. "Down" thus appears to transcend any particular crowd's own principles of status, transforming the "places" within the particular status groups into a single stratification system. The "down" person is wise to the social order. But most important, he understands his own place within that order; he knows who he is. He tries very hard to behave in accordance with his understanding in order to avoid trouble between himself and others within the setting.

The power of peer-group censorship appears to be a chief stratifying agent. Censoring acts include talk, silence, and focused movement toward and away from certain people. Group members therefore seek out others they feel will be unable or unwilling to remind them of their shortcomings. Others thus help provide the context in which identity and informal status are claimed. The censorship of significant others provides a basis for social control and stratification.

Claims to identity and informal status also depend on one's ability to manage his image by drawing distinctions between himself and others he does not want to be associated with.[8] People are identified here by the way they approach the rules of the group and by the ways they treat and are treated by others who have been identified in reference to group rules. People are known in part by what they allow others to get away with in their public interactions. Actions and interactions become matters of degree. A particular action coming from one person may be too much, while the same action by another person may be too little. And the proper degree may well be affected by who else is around and what one thinks these particular people consider appropriate.

By pointing to certain people as scapegoats who can be charged with rule infraction, certain group members are able to distinguish themselves both in their own judgments and in the judgment of peers. Such treatment of others within the group may become the basis for still further relationships and personal involvements within the extended primary group. By successfully singling out people who "fail," the person making the charges may be better able to cover his own shortcomings and to see himself as upholding certain standards of conduct.

Verbal communication is thus very important to assigning social identity. When group members talk about some person, some event, or some action, they simultaneously identify themselves in relation to the subject commented on. But also, group members identify people by the different ways they talk; as a regular, a winehead, or a hoodlum. Such talk gives others some sense of the "kind of person" the speaker is, and he can then be placed along some continuum of group standards that has become highlighted through such talk and the reactions to it. This is particularly true when great attention is being given to the places of others. One of the most effective means of making status claims is to gather with people one wants to identify with and to verbally oppose any others who would detract from one's desired identity. Thus, in taking sides against those one does not want to be associated with, one may seem closer to one's chosen group.[9]

But a person is not always acceptable to those he wants to identify with. These desired people may feel threatened by his advances and may simply move away from the interloper. By their actions, whispers, gestures, facial expressions, and conversational lulls, they remind the person of who he is in relation to them. If he misses the message in its more polite forms, he may be challenged verbally. Members of the extended primary group call these verbal attempts to stop unwanted advances "squaring off." They pull out the props sustaining the outsider's desired identity by pointing to any of his attributes the group can take as failing to meet their standards. These standards are created on the spot, for they emerge during interaction to measure the outsider in relation to the group. This is done to the outsider's face and in public. An interesting parallel can be made here between the uses of such talk within different class groupings in our society, especially for social control in interpersonal and group relations. Among middle-class people, for example, gossip or the threat of gossip may be used as a group device for maintaining social control. At Jelly's, social control is through the threat of direct talk "to your face."[10]

Also of particular interest has been the "on line" character of status and rank in everyday life among members of the extended primary group on the corner and inside Jelly's. A certain sociological benefit is derived from studying status processes among an extended group of black street-corner men like those who frequent Jelly's because they have been denied, both by the wider black society and by white society, the opportunity for full participation. It appears that the group members—especially the regulars—stress "decency" and "a visible means of support" because they want to be included in that wider society. Attention to their particular life problems in terms of status and identity can give us insights into the dynamics of social rank on a more general level; the way it is made and remade in the ordinary experiences of everyday life.

Some readers might attribute the precariousness and dynamism of status and identity I have described as ongoing at Jelly's to the structural position of black poor people in American society. But if one reaches this conclusion too quickly one has missed some of the important sociological lessons of this study.[11]

Through the processes I have described, people defer to one another, are deferred to, ally themselves with certain others, and help prop up the identities of valued members of their respective crowds. They gather with their own kind against other kinds of people, or groups of people, who may serve, at least for the moment, as scapegoats—or as examples of what they want to see themselves as distinct from. Group and individual identities are realized during social interaction. Those who can get in on drawing contrasts and distinctions through talk or specific actions can then define themselves as relatively worthwhile by emphatically pointing out that certain others are not. Social order can be seen as a matter of interaction occurring through negotiation and exchange. What people do to and with one another together is of crucial importance, for what they do collectively makes and is the social rank system.

Notes

Chapter One

1. For comparisons in the sociological literature, see Gerald D. Suttles, *The Social Order of the Slum* (Chicago: University of Chicago Press, 1968); Herbert Gans, *The Urban Villagers* (New York: Free Press, 1962); William F. Whyte, *Street Corner Society*, 2d ed. (Chicago: University of Chicago Press, 1955); Horace Cayton and St. Clair Drake, *Black Metropolis* (New York: Harper and Row, 1962); Elliot Liebow, *Tally's Corner* (Boston: Little, Brown, 1967); Ulf Hannerz, *Soulside* (New York: Columbia University Press, 1969); William Kornblum, *Blue Collar Community* (Chicago: University of Chicago Press, 1974); and James F. Short, Jr., and Fred L. Strodtbeck, *Group Process and Gang Delinquency* (Chicago: University of Chicago Press, 1965).

2. For comparative observations on informal drinking settings, see Sherri Cavan, *Liquor License* (Chicago: Aldine, 1966); E. E. LeMasters, *Blue Collar Aristocrats* (Madison: University of Wisconsin Press, 1975); James P. Spradley, *You Owe Yourself a Drunk: An Ethnography of Urban Nomads* (Boston: Little, Brown, 1970); James P. Spradley and Brenda J. Mann, *The Cocktail Waitress* (New York: Wiley, 1975); Samuel Wallace, *Skid Row as a Way of Life* (New York: Harper and Row, 1968).

3. For a classic account of this kind of social process, see Georg Simmel, "The Sociology of Sociability," trans. Everett C. Hughes, *American Journal of Sociology*, vol. 55, no. 3 (1949).

4. Critiques of this perspective may be found in Maurice Stein, *The Eclipse of Community* (Princeton: Princeton University Press, 1960), esp. pp. 13–46; John Madge, *The Origins of Scientific Sociology* (New York: Free Press, 1962); and David Matza, *Becoming Deviant* (Englewood Cliffs, N.J.: Prentice-Hall, 1969), esp. pp. 25–100.

5. Elliot Liebow used this term to suggest why the men he studied came together at Tally's Corner.

6. See Georg Simmel, "The Stranger," in *Georg Simmel on Individuality and Social Forms*, ed. Donald N. Levine (Chicago: University of Chicago Press, 1971).

7. For an imaginative and provocative theoretical discussion of microsocial aspects of status mobility, see Barney Glaser and Anselm Strauss, *Status Passage* (Chicago: Aldine, 1972).

8. For sociolinguistic analyses of this phenomenon, see William Labov, "Rules for Ritual Insults," in *Studies in Social Interaction*, ed. David Sudnow (New York: Free Press, 1972); Roger Abrahams, *Deep down in the Jungle* (Chicago: Aldine, 1970); and Lee Rainwater, *Behind Ghetto Walls* (Chicago: Aldine, 1970).

9. This lends an added dimension to the excellent conceptual presentation of this kind of general interactional process in Marvin B. Scott and Stanford M. Lyman, "Accounts," *American Sociological Review* 33 (February 1968): 46–62.

10. See Carol Stack, *All Our Kin* (New York: Harper and Row, 1974); and Liebow, *Tally's Corner*. Notably, Liebow uses the phrase "going for brothers" to describe a close relationship between men not related by blood. In my research experience, the men used the fictive kinship term "going for cousins." Although logically it might seem that "going for brothers" indicates a closer and more involved relationship than "going for cousins," this was not borne out by my data. The terms seem very similar in import. Such relationships as I observed moved from "low" to "high" involvement and intensity, yet the kinship term never changed.

11. See Erving Goffman, *The Presentation of Self in Everyday Life* (New York: Doubleday, 1959), for a general discussion of impression management.

12. For sociolinguistic interpretations, see Dell Hymes, "Ways of Speaking," *Exploration in the Ethnography of Speaking*, ed. Richard Bauman and Joel Sherzer (New York: Cambridge University Press, 1975).

13. See Erving Goffman, "On Face-Work," in his *Interaction Ritual: Essays on Face-to-Face Behavior* (Chicago: Aldine, 1967).

14. See Erving Goffman, "On the Nature of Deference and Demeanor," ibid.

Chapter Two   1. Lee Rainwater makes a similar observation in his "Crucible of Identity," in *The Negro American*, ed. Talcott Parsons and Kenneth B. Clark (Boston: Beacon Press, 1966).

2. Charles Horton Cooley, *Social Organization* (New York: Scribner's, 1909), p. 23.

3. George Herbert Mead, *Mind, Self, and Society* (Chicago: University of Chicago Press, 1934), esp. pp. 135–226.

4. See George A. Theodorson and Achilles G. Theodorson, *Modern Dictionary of Sociology* (New York: Crowell, 1969); A. Paul Hare, Edgar Borgatta, and Robert Bales, eds., *Small Groups* (New York: Knopf, 1950); Theodore M. Mills, *The Sociology of Small Groups* (Englewood Cliffs, N.J.: Prentice-Hall, 1967); George C. Homans, *The Human Group* (New York: Harcourt, Brace, and World, 1950); Edward A. Shils, "The Study of the Primary Group," in *The Policy Sciences*, ed. Daniel Lerner and Harold D. Lasswell (Stanford: Stanford University Press, 1951), pp. 41–69; Edgar F. Borgatta and Leonard S. Cottrell, "Directions for Research in Group Behavior," *American Journal of Sociology*, vol. 63 (1957): 42–48; Alan P. Bates and N. Babchuck, "The Primary Group: A Reappraisal," *Sociological Quarterly* 3 (July 1961): 181–91; and Gerald D. Suttles, *The Social Order of the Slum* (Chicago: University of Chicago Press, 1968), esp. pp. 175–94.

5. Donald N. Levine, ed., *Georg Simmel on Individuality and Social Forms* (Chicago: University of Chicago Press, 1971), p. 134.

6. Ibid., pp. 132–33.

7. For important comparisons in the social science literature, see Hylan Lewis, *Blackways of Kent* (Chapel Hill: University of North Carolina Press, 1955), pp. 232–38; Horace Cayton and St. Clair Drake, *Black Metropolis* (New York: Harper and Row, 1962); Elliot Liebow, *Tally's Corner* (Boston: Little, Brown, 1967); Ulf Hannerz, *Soulside* (New York: Columbia University Press, 1969); Lee Rainwater, *Behind Ghetto Walls* (Chicago: Aldine,

1970); Carol Stack, *All Our Kin* (New York: Harper and Row, 1974); and Peter J. Wilson, *Crab Antics: The Social Anthropology of English-Speaking Negro Societies of the Caribbean* (New Haven: Yale University Press, 1973). Andrew Billingsly, *Black Families in White America* (Englewood Cliffs, N.J.: Prentice-Hall, 1968).

8. For comparable theoretical statements along similar lines, see Robert K. Merton, "Social Structure and Anomie," in his *Social Theory and Social Structure* (New York: Free Press, 1957); Albert K. Cohen, *Delinquent Boys* (Glencoe, Ill.: Free Press, 1955); Richard A. Cloward and Lloyd E. Ohlin, *Delinquency and Opportunity* (New York: Free Press. 1960); David Matza, *Delinquency and Drift* (New York: John Wiley, 1964), pp. 51–59, 62–64; John I. Kitsuse and David C. Dietrick, "Delinquent Boys: A Critique," *American Sociological Review* 24 (April 1959): 213–15; and Howard S. Becker, "Notes on the Concept of Commitment," *American Journal of Sociology* 64 (July 1960): 32–40.

9. For an illustration of similar processes on a slightly more general scale, see Suttles, *Social Order of the Slum*, esp. pp. 195–220.

10. For a very fine conceptual statement, see Erving Goffman, "The Nature of Deference and Demeanor," *American Anthropologist* 58 (June 1956): 473–502.

Chapter Three   1. See Allison Davis, "The Motivation of the Underprivileged Worker," in *Industry and Society*, ed. William F. Whyte (New York: McGraw-Hill, 1946); Everett C. Hughes, *Men and Their Work* (New York: Free Press, 1958); William Kornblum, *Blue Collar Community* (Chicago: University of Chicago Press, 1974); James S. Coleman, *Resources for Social Change* (New York: Wiley, 1972); David Matza, "The Disreputable Poor," in *Social Structure and Mobility in Economic Development*, ed. Neil Smelser and S. M. Lipset (Chicago: Aldine, 1966); Elliot Liebow, *Tally's Corner* (Boston: Little, Brown,

1967); E. E. LeMasters, *Blue Collar Aristocrats* (Madison: University of Wisconsin Press, 1975); Lee Rainwater, *Behind Ghetto Walls* (Chicago: Aldine, 1970), esp. pp. 381–84.

2. For interesting sociological comparisons, see Horace Cayton and St. Clair Drake, *Black Metropolis* (New York: Harper and Row, 1962), esp. pp. 600–715; Hylan Lewis, *Blackways of Kent* (Chapel Hill: University of North Carolina Press, 1955), esp. pp. 232–48; Liebow, *Tally's Corner*; Rainwater, *Behind Ghetto Walls*, esp. pp. 362–97; Ulf Hannerz, *Soulside* (New York: Columbia University Press, 1969), esp. pp. 38–42.

3. For comparison with white working-class groups that express general social values for identity in "particularistic" settings, see Richard Sennett and Jonathan Cobb, *Hidden Injuries of Class* (New York: Random House, 1973), esp. pp. 53–118.

4. Herbert Gans reports similar definitions of work among Italians in Boston's West End. See Herbert Gans, *The Urban Villagers: Group and Class in the Life of Italian Americans* (New York: Free Press, 1962).

5. The dynamics of social exchange have, of course, been classically described by Marcel Mauss. See *The Gift* (New York: Norton, 1967). For important later statements, see Peter M. Blau, *Exchange and Power in Social Life* (New York: Wiley, 1964); and George C. Homans, *Social Behavior: Its Elementary Forms*, rev. ed. (New York: Harcourt Brace Jovanovich, 1974).

6. The regulars' repeated affirmations of "the law" sound at times like a ritualized litany. See Robert K. Merton, "Social Structure and Anomie," *American Sociological Review* 3, (October 1938):672–82.

7. For a comparative view on cultural orientations toward trouble, see Walter B. Miller, "Lower Class Culture as a Generating Milieu of Gang Delinquency," *Journal of Social Issues* 14, no. 3 (1958): 5–19.

8. See Herbert Hyman, "The Psychology of Status," *Archives of Psychology* 269 (June 1942):

6–15; and Tamotsu Shibutani, "Reference Groups as Perspectives," *American Journal of Sociology* 60 (May 1955):562; Robert K. Merton, "Continuities in the Theory of Reference Groups and Social Structure" in his *Social Theory and Social Structure* (New York: Free Press, 1957).

9. See Nels Anderson, *The Hobo* (Chicago: University of Chicago Press, 1923), p. 53.

10. For a fine discussion of the relationship between the self and embarrassment see Erving Goffman, "Embarrassment and Social Organization," in his *Interaction Ritual* (Chicago: Aldine, 1967), pp. 97–112; also see Howard S. Becker, "Notes on the Concept of Commitment," *American Journal of Sociology* 66 (July 1960): 32–40.

Chapter Four

1. For comparisons, see Earl Rubington, "Variations in Bottle Gang Controls," in *Deviance: The Interactionist Perspective*, 2d ed., ed. Earl Rubington and Martin S. Weinberg (New York: Macmillan, 1973); Howard M. Bahr, *Skid Row: An Introduction to Disaffiliation* (New York: Oxford University Press, 1973); James P. Spradley, *You Owe Yourself a Drunk: An Ethnography of Urban Nomads* (Boston: Little, Brown, 1970); Samuel Wallace, *Skid Row as a Way of Life* (New York: Harper and Row, 1968); Leonard Blumberg, Thomas Shipley, and Stephen Barsky, *Liquor and Poverty*. Center for Alcohol Studies monograph no. 13 (New Brunswick, N.J.: Rutgers University, 1977), esp. chap. 7.

2. This present-time orientation tends to be especially prominent among hoodlums and wineheads of the group, whereas the regulars appear to be more future-time oriented. Things in this environment, especially for people lacking stable financial resources, are "here today and gone tomorrow." This includes life itself. The concern with the present appears to be an adaptation to an uncertain life circumstance.

3. For a more comprehensive analysis of similar processes involved in the creation of rules and out-

siders, see Howard S. Becker, *Outsiders* (New York: Free Press, 1973).

Chapter Five
1. See Erving Goffman, *The Presentation of Self in Everyday Life.* New York: Doubleday, 1959.
2. For similar findings concerning neighborhood street-gang activity, see Gerald D. Suttles, *The Social Order of the Slum* (Chicago: University of Chicago Press, 1968).
3. Erving Goffman, "The Nature of Deference and Demeanor," in his *Interaction Ritual* (Chicago: Aldine, 1967).
4. These conceptions add perspective to the views presented by Miller. See Walter B. Miller, "Lower Class Culture as a Generating Milieu of Gang Delinquency," *Journal of Social Issues* 14, no. 3 (1958): 5–19. See also Richard A. Cloward and Lloyd E. Ohlin, *Delinquency and Opportunity* (New York: Free Press, 1960); Charles A. Valentine, *Culture and Poverty* (Chicago: University of Chicago Press, 1968); Albert Cohen, *Delinquent Boys* (Glencoe, Ill.: Free Press, 1955).
5. For a rare and very informative life history, see Henry Williamson, *Hustler!* ed. R. Lincoln Keiser (New York: Avon Books, 1965); for comparisons with the large-scale operator, see Carl B. Klockars, *The Professional Fence* (New York: Free Press, 1974), esp. pp. 69–101, 193.
6. See Marvin E. Wolfgang and Franco Ferracuti, *The Subculture of Violence* (London: Tavistock Publications, 1967); David Matza, *Delinquency and Drift* (New York: John Wiley, 1964); Albert J. Reiss, Jr., and A. Lewis Rhodes, "Status Deprivation and Delinquent Behavior," *Sociological Quarterly* 4 (Spring 1963): 135–49; James F. Short, Jr., and Fred Strodtbeck, *Group Process and Gang Delinquency* (Chicago: University of Chicago Press, 1965), esp. chaps. 5, 8, 9, and 10.
7. Jitterbugs are young gang members or those who look like them.
8. For a fine discussion of the "working personalities" of policemen, see Jerome H. Skolnick, *Justice*

without Trial (New York: Wiley, 1966), esp. pp. 42–62.

9. For cultural comparisons, see Erving Goffman, *Behavior in Public Places* (New York: Free Press, 1963), esp. chap. 4, "Some Rules about the Allocation of Involvement," pp. 43–79.

10. See Erving Goffman, *Stigma: Notes on the Management of Spoiled Identity* (Englewood Cliffs, N.J.: Prentice-Hall, 1963); idem, *Asylums* (New York: Doubleday, 1961).

11. This situation is reminiscent of the bowling and status incidents that William F. Whyte describes in *Street Corner Society*, 2d ed. (Chicago: University of Chicago Press, 1955), esp. pp. 14–48.

Chapter Six

1. By standards of the wider society, both black and white, members of Jelly's group may be viewed as deviant. For selected sociological literature, see Howard S. Becker, *Outsiders* (New York: Free Press, 1973); Jack D. Douglas, ed., *Deviance and Respectability* (New York: Basic Books, 1970); Robert K. Merton, "Social Structure and Anomie," in his *Social Theory and Social Structure* (New York: Free Press, 1957); Erving Goffman, *Stigma: Notes on the Management of Spoiled Identity* (Englewood Cliffs, N.J.: Prentice-Hall, 1963); and David Matza, *Becoming Deviant* (Englewood Cliffs, N.J.: Prentice-Hall, 1969).

2. For more material on this theme, see Marvin E. Wolfgang, "Real and Perceived Changes of Crime and Punishment," *Daedalus* 107, no. 1 (winter 1978): 143–57, esp. pp. 146–48.

3. See Erving Goffman's discussion, "The Insanity of Place," in his *Relations in Public* (New York: Basic Books, 1971).

4. See William Labov, "Rules for Ritual Insults," in *Studies in Social Interaction*, ed. David Sudnow (New York: Free Press, 1972).

5. For comparisons, see James F. Short, Jr., and Fred L. Strodtbeck, *Group Processes and Gang Delinquency* (Chicago: University of Chicago Press, 1965), esp. chap. 5.

6. For a fuller treatment of the dramaturgical analogy in the study of social interaction, see Erving Goffman, *The Presentation of Self in Everyday Life* (New York: Doubleday, 1959).

7. For a discussion of role conflict and the policeman, see William F. Whyte, *Street Corner Society*, 2d ed. (Chicago: University of Chicago Press, 1955), p. 138: "Law enforcement has a direct effect upon Cornerville people, whereas it only indirectly affects the "good people" of the city. Under these circumstances, the smoothest course for the officer is to conform to the social organization with which he is in direct contact and at the same time to try to give the impression to the outside world that he is enforcing the law. He must play an elaborate role of make-believe, and, in so doing, he serves as a buffer between divergent social organizations with their conflicting standards of conduct."

8. The "down" person is reminiscent of Goffman's concept of the strategic actor. See Erving Goffman, *Strategic Interaction* (Philadelphia: University of Pennsylvania Press, 1972).

9. From interviews with former and current members of black street gangs and with black ex-convicts from east coast urban centers, I have learned that such a person is often described as "an old head." The labels and meanings may vary between speech communities. See Dell Hymes, "Studying the Interaction of Language and Social Life," in his *Foundations in Sociolinguistics* (Philadelphia: University of Pennsylvania Press, 1974).

Chapter Seven

1. See Erving Goffman, "The Nature of Deference and Demeanor," in his *Interaction Ritual* (Chicago: Aldine, 1967); Erving Goffman, *Asylums* (New York: Doubleday, 1961).

2. For an excellent book on the social significance of space, see Edward T. Hall, *The Hidden Dimension* (New York: Doubleday, 1966).

3. See Charles Horton Cooley, *Social Organization* (New York: Scribner's, 1909), esp. p. 23.

4. See Robert K. Merton, "Social Structure and Anomie," in his *Social Theory and Social Structure* (New York: Free Press, 1957); Richard A. Cloward and Lloyd E. Ohlin, *Delinquency and Opportunity* (New York: Free Press, 1960).

5. See Hyman Rodman, "The Lower Class Value Stretch," *Social Forces* 42, no. 2 (December 1963): 205–15.

6. See Marvin Scott and Stanford Lyman, "Accounts," *American Sociological Review* 33 (February 1968), pp. 46–62.

7. See Howard S. Becker, "Notes on the Concept of Commitment," *American Journal of Sociology* 64 (1960) 32–40; and Orrin E. Klapp, *Heroes, Villains, and Fools* (Englewood Cliffs, N.J.: Prentice-Hall, 1962), esp. pp. 2–5.

8. See Erving Goffman, *The Presentation of Self in Everyday Life* (New York: Doubleday, 1959).

9. It may be that these types of status processes are interrelated sociolinguistically with "code switching" and the impressions such switches foster and maintain. See Dell Hymes, *Foundations in Sociolinguistics.* (Philadelphia: University of Pennsylvania Press, 1974), pp. 103–5.

10. See Samuel Heilman, *Synagogue Life* (Chicago: University of Chicago Press, 1976), esp. chap. 5. John Szwed, "Gossip, Drinking, and Social Control: Consensus and Communication in a Newfoundland Parish," *Ethnology* 3, no. 4 (October 1966): 435.

11. After reading these pages, for instance, my colleague, E. Digby Baltzell, noted that the subjects of his book *Philadelphia Gentlemen* (New York: Quadrangle Books, 1971), who presumably already "are somebody," have all sorts of mechanisms of deference: the intricacies of social interaction within upper-class club hierarchies are examples of social processes similar to those found at Jelly's bar, though perhaps more formal.

Bibliography

Abrahams, Roger. *Deep down in the Jungle.* Chicago: Aldine, 1970.

Anderson, Nels. *The Hobo.* Chicago: University of Chicago Press, 1923.

Bahr, Howard M. *Skid Row: An Introduction to Disaffiliation.* New York: Oxford University Press, 1973.

Bales, Robert F. *Interaction Process Analysis.* Cambridge: Addison-Wesley, 1950.

Baltzell, E. Digby. *Philadelphia Gentlemen.*

Becker, Howard S. "Art as Collective Action." *American Sociological Review* 39, no. 6 (December 1974): 767–76.

———. "Notes on the Concept of Commitment." *American Journal of Sociology* 66 (1960): 32–40.

———. *Outsiders.* New York: Free Press, 1973.

———. *Sociological Work.* Chicago: Aldine, 1970.

Bendix, Reinhard, and Lipset, Seymour M., eds. *Class, Status, and Power.* Rev. ed. New York: Free Press, 1966.

Billingsly, Andrew, *Black Families in White America.* Englewood Cliffs, N.J.: Prentice-Hall, 1968.

Blackwell, James E. *The Black Community.* New York: Dodd, Mead, 1975.

Blumberg, Leonard; Shipley, Thomas; and Barsky, Stephen. *Liquor and Poverty.* Center for Alcohol Studies monograph no. 13. New Brunswick, N.J.: Rutgers University, 1977. Esp. chap. 7.

Blumer, Herbert. *Symbolic Interactionism.* Englewood Cliffs, N.J.: Prentice-Hall, 1969.

Bonney, Norman. "Unwelcome Strangers." Ph.D. diss., University of Chicago, 1972.

Bott, Elizabeth. *Family and Social Network.* London: Tavistock, 1957.

Brown, Roger. *Social Psychology.* New York: Free Press, 1965.

Cavan, Sherri. *Liquor License.* Chicago: Aldine, 1966.

Cayton, Horace, and Drake, St. Clair. *Black Metropolis.* New York: Harper and Row, 1962.

Cicourel, Aaron V. *Cognitive Sociology.* New York: Free Press, 1974.

Clark, Kenneth, B. *Dark Ghetto.* New York: Harper and Row, 1965.

Cloward, Richard A., and Ohlin, Lloyd E. *Delinquency and Opportunity.* New York: Free Press, 1960.

Cohen, Albert K. *Delinquent Boys.* Glencoe, Ill.: Free Press, 1955.

Cooley, Charles Horton. *Social Organization.* New York: Scribner's, 1909.

Cressey, Donald R. *Other People's Money.* Belmont: Wadsworth, 1971.

Davis, Allison. "The Motivation of the Underprivileged Worker," in *Industry and Society*, ed. William F. Whyte. New York: McGraw-Hill, 1946.

Dollard, John. "The Dozens: The Dialect of Insult." *American Image* 1 (1939): 3–24.

Douglas, Jack D., ed. *Deviance and Respectability.* New York: Basic Books, 1970.

Erikson, Erik H. "The Concept of Identity in Race Relations." In *The Negro American*, ed. Talcott Parsons and Kenneth B. Clark. Boston: Beacon Press, 1966.

Evans-Pritchard, E. E. *The Nuer.* Oxford: Clarendon Press, 1940.

Finestone, Harold. "Cats, Kicks, and Color." *Social Problems* 10 (fall 1962).

Fortes, M., and Evans-Pritchard, E. E. *African Political Systems.* London: Oxford University Press, 1940.

Frazier, E. Franklin. *Black Bourgeoisie*. New York: Free Press, 1932.

———. *The Negro Family in Chicago*. Chicago: University of Chicago Press, 1939.

———. *The Negro Family in the United States*. Chicago: University of Chicago Press, 1942.

Gans, Herbert. *The Urban Villagers*. New York: Free Press, 1962.

Glaser, Barney, and Strauss, Anselm. *Status Passage*. Chicago: Aldine, 1972.

Goffman, Erving. *Asylums*. New York: Doubleday, 1961.

———. *Behavior in Public Places*. New York: Free Press, 1963.

———. *Interaction Ritual*: Essays on Face-to-Face Behavior. Chicago: Aldine, 1967.

———. *The Presentation of Self in Everyday Life*. New York: Doubleday, 1959.

———. *Relations in Public*. New York: Basic Books, 1971.

———. "Role Distance." In *Encounters*. Indianapolis: Bobbs-Merrill, 1961.

———. *Stigma: Notes on the Management of Spoiled Identity*. Englewood Cliffs, N.J.: Prentice-Hall, 1963.

———. *Strategic Interaction*. Philadelphia: University of Pennsylvania Press, 1972.

Gross, Neal; Mason, Ward S.; and McEachern, Alexander W. *Explorations in Role Analysis*. New York: Wiley, 1958.

Hall, Edward T. *The Hidden Dimension*. New York: Doubleday, 1966.

Hannerz, Ulf. *Soulside*. New York: Columbia University Press, 1969.

Hare, A. Paul; Borgatta, Edgar; and Bales, Robert, eds. *Small Groups*. New York: Knopf, 1950.

Heilman, Sam. *Synagogue Life.* Chicago: University of Chicago Press, 1976.

Homans, George C. *The Human Group.* New York: Harcourt and Brace, 1950.

————. *Social Behavior: Its Elementary Forms.* Rev. ed. New York: Harcourt Brace Jovanovich, 1974.

Hughes, Everett C. "Dilemmas and Contradictions of Status." *American Journal of Sociology* 50 (1945): 353–59.

————. *Men and Their Work.* New York: Free Press, 1958.

Hymes, Dell. *Foundations in Sociolinguistics.* Philadelphia: University of Pennsylvania Press, 1974.

Janowitz, Morris. *Political Conflict.* Chicago: Quadrangle Books, 1970.

Katz, Jack. "Deviance, Charisma and Rule-Defined Behavior." *Social Problems* 20 (winter 1972): 186–202.

Keil, Charles. *Urban Blues.* Chicago: University of Chicago Press, 1966.

Kitsuse, John I., and Dietrick, David C. "Delinquent Boys: A Critique." *American Sociological Review* 24 (April 1959): 213–15.

Klapp, Orrin E. *Heroes, Villains, and Fools.* Englewood Cliffs, N.J.: Prentice-Hall, 1962.

Klockars, Carl B. *The Professional Fence.* New York: Free Press, 1974.

Kornblum, William. *Blue Collar Community.* Chicago: University of Chicago Press, 1974.

Labov, William. "Rules for Ritual Insults." In *Studies in Social Interaction,* ed. David Sudnow. New York: Free Press, 1972.

Laumann, Edward O. *Prestige and Association in an Urban Community.* Indianapolis: Bobbs-Merrill, 1966.

Laumann, Edward O., et al. *The Logic of Social Hierarchies.* Chicago: Markham, 1970.

Leach, Edmund R. "Symbolic Representation of Time." In *Rethinking Anthropology.* London: Athone Press, 1968.

LeMasters, E. E. *Blue Collar Aristocrats.* Madison: University of Wisconsin Press, 1975.

Levine, Donald N., ed. *Georg Simmel on Individuality and Social Forms.* Chicago: University of Chicago Press, 1971.

Lewis, Hylan. *Blackways of Kent.* Chapel Hill: University of North Carolina Press, 1955.

Liebow, Elliot. *Tally's Corner.* Boston: Little, Brown, 1967.

Lindesmith, Alfred R. *Opiate Addiction.* Bloomington, Ind.: Principia Press, 1947.

Linton, Ralph. *The Study of Man.* New York: Appleton-Century, 1936.

McClosky, Herbert, and Dahlgren, Harold W. "Primary Group Influences on Party Loyalty." In *Social Organization and Behavior,* ed. Richard L. Simpson and Ida Harper Simpson. New York: John Wiley, 1964.

Matza, David. *Delinquency and Drift.* New York: John Wiley, 1964.

Mead, George Herbert. *Mind, Self, and Society.* Chicago: University of Chicago Press, 1934.

Merton, Robert K. *Social Theory and Social Structure.* New York: Free Press, 1957.

Miller, Walter B. "Lower Class Culture as a Generating Milieu of Gang Delinquency." *Journal of Social Issues* 14, no. 3 (1958): 5–19.

Mills, Theodore M. *The Sociology of Small Groups.* Englewood Cliffs, N.J.: Prentice-Hall, 1967.

Parsons, Talcott. "A Revised Analytical Approach to the Theory of Social Stratification."

In *Class, Status, and Power*, ed. Reinhard Bendix and Seymour M. Lipset. New York: Free Press, 1966.

―――. *The Social System*. New York: Free Press, 1950.

Parsons, Talcott, and Clark, Kenneth B. *The Negro American*. Boston: Beacon Press, 1966.

Pinkney, Alphonso. *Black Americans*. Englewood Cliffs, N.J.: Prentice-Hall, 1969.

Polsky, Ned. *Hustlers, Beats, and Others*. Chicago: Aldine, 1967.

Rainwater, Lee. *Behind Ghetto Walls*. Chicago: Aldine, 1970.

Reiss, Albert J., and Rhodes, A. Lewis. "Status Deprivation and Delinquent Behavior." *Sociological Quarterly* 4 (spring 1963): 135–49.

Rodman, Hyman. *Lower Class Families*. Oxford: Oxford University Press, 1971.

―――. "The Lower Class Value Stretch." *Social Forces* 42, no. 2 (December 1963): 205–15.

Rose, Arnold, ed. *Human Behavior and Social Processes*. Boston: Houghton Mifflin, 1962.

Rubington, Earl. "Variations in Bottle Gang Controls." In *Deviance: The Interactionist Perspective*, 2d ed., ed. Earl Rubington and Martin S. Weinberg. New York: Macmillan, 1973.

Schutz, Alfred. *The Phenomenology of the Social World*. Evanston: Northwestern University Press, 1967.

Shaw, Clifford R., and McKay, Henry D. *Juvenile Delinquency and Urban Areas*. Rev. ed. Chicago: University of Chicago Press, 1969.

Shils, Edward A. "Deference." In *The Logic of Social Hierarchies*, ed. Edward O. Laumann et al. Chicago: Markham, 1970.

―――. "Primary Groups in the American Army." In *Continuities in Social Research: Studies in the Scope and Method of "The Amer-*

ican Soldier," ed. Robert Merton and P. Lazarsfeld. Glencoe, Ill.: Free Press, 1950.

Shils, Edward A., and Janowitz, Morris. "Cohesion and Disintegration in the Wehrmacht in World War II." *Public Opinion Quarterly*, summer 1948.

Short, James F., Jr., and Strodtbeck, Fred, L. *Group Process and Gang Delinquency*. Chicago: University of Chicago Press, 1965.

Short, James F., Jr., et al. "Perceived Opportunities, Gang Membership and Delinquency." *American Sociological Review* 30 (1965): 56–67.

Simmel, Georg. "The Sociology of Sociability." Trans. Everett C. Hughes. *American Journal of Sociology* 55, no. 3 (1949): 254–61.

Spradley, James P. *You Owe Yourself a Drunk: An Ethnography of Urban Nomads*. Boston: Little, Brown, 1970.

Stack, Carol. *All Our Kin*. New York: Harper and Row, 1974.

Sutherland, Edwin H. *The Professional Thief*. Chicago: University of Chicago Press, 1937.

Sutherland, Edwin H., and Cressey, Donald. *Principles of Criminology*. New York: J. B. Lippincott, 1955.

Suttles, Gerald D. *The Social Construction of Communities*. Chicago: University of Chicago Press, 1972.

———. *The Social Order of the Slum*. Chicago: University of Chicago Press, 1968.

Szwed, John. "Gossip, Drinking, and Social Control: Consensus and Communication in a Newfoundland Parish." *Ethnology* 3, no. 4 (October 1966): 435.

Taeuber, Karl E., and Taeuber, Alma F. *Negroes in Cities*. Chicago: Aldine, 1965.

Theodorson, George A., and Theodorson, Achilles G. *Modern Dictionary of Sociology*. New York: Crowell, 1969.

Thrasher, Frederick. *The Gang*. Chicago: University of Chicago Press, 1927.

Turner, Ralph H. "Role Taking, Role Standpoint, and Reference Group Behavior." *American Journal of Sociology* 61: 316–28.

Valentine, Charles A. *Culture and Poverty*. Chicago: University of Chicago Press, 1968.

Wallace, Samuel. *Skid Row as a Way of Life*. New York: Harper and Row, 1968.

Warner, W. L. *Yankee City*. New Haven: Yale University Press, 1963.

Whyte, William F. *Street Corner Society*, 2d ed. Chicago: University of Chicago Press, 1955.

Williamson, Henry. *Hustler!* Ed. R. Lincoln Keiser. New York: Avon Books, 1965.

Wilson, Peter J. *Crab Antics: The Social Anthropology of English-Speaking Negro Societies of the Caribbean*. New Haven: Yale University Press, 1973.

Wilson, William. *Power, Racism, and Privilege*. New York: Macmillan, 1973.

Wirth, Louis. *The Ghetto*. Chicago: University of Chicago Press, 1928.

Wolfgang, Marvin E. *Crime and Race*. New York: Institute of Human Relations Press, 1970.

Wolfgang, Marvin E., and Ferracuti, Franco. *The Subculture of Violence*. London: Tavistock Publications, 1967.

Wolfgang, Marvin E.; Savitz, Leonard; and Johnston, Norman, eds. *The Sociology of Crime and Delinquency*. New York: Wiley, 1970.

Index

Anderson, Nels, 81

Bemo, 108–9, 118–19
Butterroll, 100–107

Carrying the stick,
   definition of, 31
Censorship, importance of
   in social control, 214
Christmas party, 17–19
Clarence, 8–10
Clay, 135–36
Closing, 40–49
Competition, 34, 36, 208–9.
   See also Status, as
   contrastive
Cooley, George Horton,
   33–34, 209
Crossing the track, 88

Death within the group,
   182–85
Decency, 55–56, 210
Distancing, 107–12, 125–
   26, 139–41, 143–46
"Down," 199–206, 213–14
Drug addiction, 130–31

Effortless sociability, 4, 23,
   192
Employment. *See* Visible
   means of support
Exchange relationships,
   64, 182
Extended primary group,
   definition of, 34–35

Fencing, 134, 156–57

"Goin' for bad," 152–53,
   172

"Goin' for cousins," 17–19,
   20–21, 135

Herman: first meeting, 12–
   14; brief biography, 22;
   and Butterroll, 100–107;
   and T. J., 195–96
Homosexuality, 86, 122
Hoodlums, 129–78; ages
   of, 129; Calvin, 139–41;
   Clay, 135–36; Cochise,
   144–46; distancing
   onself from, 139–41,
   143–46; dress of, 133;
   families of, 132; "goin'
   for bad," 152–53, 172;
   and jobs, 153–54; Oscar,
   131–35; Terry, 158–78;
   Tyrone, 130–31; values
   of, 129–30, 153–55,
   157–58; and violence,
   134–35, 187–92

Jelly's: gaining sponsorship
   at, 15–17; physical lay-
   out of, 4–5; as seen by
   South Side residents, 32;
   size of group at, 31
Jimmy Lee, 98–99
Jocko, 99, 121

Labeling, 45, 107–11, 112,
   146
Liberties, taking of, 136–37,
   143, 192–93, 196, 197

Marriage, 9, 69–70, 100–
   107. *See also* Butterroll;
   Women
Mead, George Herbert, 34
Methadone, 131

Mike's club, 147–52. *See also* Selective association
Mobility, within subgroup, 80–91, 100–107, 208

Nathaniel, 58–59

Oscar, 131–35

Pee Wee, 45–46, 59–60
Play, significance of for social order, 193–95, 197
Porter, Bill, 57–58

Rank, 52. *See also* Status
"Reading signs," 26
Red Mack, 122–27
Regulars, 55–91; ages of, 55; becoming, 67; criminal records of, 71–72; and crime, 72–75; and education, 62; family involvements of, 55, 58–59; and jobs, 60–63, 77; military discharges of, 70–71; political behavior of, 68–69, 70–71; racial attitudes of, 81–83
Roosevelt, 97–98

Scapegoats, 108–11, 112–15, 168, 214–15
Selective association, 34–35, 48–51, 75–79, 136–38, 142–46
Silence, rituals of, 50, 51
Simmel, Georg, 10, 35–36, 37
Sleepy, 46–47
Social disorganization, 4
Standards of conduct, 116–17, 210–11

Status: as contrastive, 53, 107, 112, 117, 138–39, 143, 209, 214; as negotiated, 177–78, 179–80, 208–9; as precarious, 52–53, 116–17, 125–26, 138, 158–62, 177, 212–13; transferability of, 35, 180
Subgroups, defined, 38–39

Teacher-student relationship, 22–23, 25, 27–28, 142–43
Terry, 158–78
Tiger, 80–91
T. J., 56–57, 187–92, 195–96
Tyrone, 130–31

Unemployment, general effects of, 210. *See also* Decency

Visible means of support, 63, 65, 87–89, 209
Visitors, 5, 7, 50–51, 163–70

"We feeling," 36–37, 180–82, 185–87
Wigfall-Porter debate, 81–83
Wineheads, 93–128; ages of, 93; as "social nobodies," 97; becoming, 100–107; Bemo, 108–9, 118–19; daily activities of, 93–95; deference from, 118–19, 121–22; distancing oneself from, 107–11, 112–13, 114–15;

jail, 124; Jimmy Lee,
98–99; and jobs, 95–96;
Jocko, 99, 121; Red
Mack, 122–27; Roose-
velt, 97–98; Spider, 94;
winehead stories, 108–15,
124–25

"Wolfing," 161–62, 198.
See also Status, as
negotiated
Women, 40, 100–107, 108.
See also Clarence